The School

The Schoolhome

Rethinking Schools for Changing Families

Jane Roland Martin

Harvard University Press

Cambridge, Massachusetts
London, England

#3401194

Copyright © 1992 by Jane Roland Martin
All rights reserved
Printed in the United States of America
Second printing, 1995

First Harvard University Press paperback edition, 1995

Library of Congress Cataloging-in-Publication Data

Martin, Jane Roland, 1929–
    The schoolhome / Jane Roland Martin.
        p.   cm.
    Includes bibliographical references (p.   ) and index.
    ISBN 0-674-79265-3 (cloth)
    ISBN 0-674-79266-1 (pbk.)
    1. Home and school—United States.   2. Education—United States—
Philosophy.   3. Montessori method of education.   4. Curriculum
planning—United States.   5. United States—Social conditions—1980—
I. Title.
LC225.3.M37   1992
370.19′0973—dc20   91-35659
                        CIP

To my LRSH/EI friends and our teachers

Contents

The Schoolhome

The View from the Bridge

In 1938 Virginia Woolf invited readers of *Three Guineas* to stand with her on the bridge "between the old world and the new" and watch the procession of men that moved from private home to public world each morning and back again each night. On those final days before the outbreak of World War II she said to women: "We have to ask ourselves here and now, do we wish to join the procession or don't we? On whose terms shall we join the procession? Above all, where is it leading us, the procession of educated men?"

Woolf was addressing her question to women who had a choice, not to those like my mother who were forced by economic necessity to cross the bridge connecting "the private house with the world of public life." In 1938 girls in Britain and the United States whose parents could not support them had long since gone out to work in factories, shops, offices, and schools. And while most, once married, managed to stay home each day to take care of house, husband, and children, many women could not afford this luxury. Because Woolf distrusted the civilization they would be entering, she asked on what terms the women who did not have to work outside the home should join the procession. Look at the men, she said. They have lost sight, speech, sense of proportion, humanity. The question for her was, How can women cross the bridge with the men and yet remain "civilized human beings"?

Today the view from the bridge has changed. Since 1960 millions of women have entered the procession and, right now, two out of every three new members of it are female. The great majority of these cannot afford to stay in their private houses full time, and of the ones who can, many ask why they, rather than their menfolk, should be expected to tend the needs of house and children.

It is time to take another look. Come stand with me on the bridge and watch the procession go by. See, women are no longer just traipsing along behind as Woolf said they were in the 1930s. They have entered the procession en masse. Some are even marching at the head looking as solemn as the men and almost as confident. But what is wrong with that woman at the very front? She looks distraught. Her child is sick and she is wondering how to sandwich a trip to the doctor between clients. What about that young couple close to tears? They are so dismayed by the unrelieved grimness of their preschooler's daycare center that they do not want to leave her there another moment, but they have not been able to find a better facility they can afford. And why are those women carrying infants on their backs and dragging toddlers beside them? Welfare workers have directed them to find jobs, but there is no place to put their youngsters.

Woolf worried that the possessiveness, jealousy, pugnacity, and greed she discerned on the other side of the bridge would contaminate women as they entered men's civilization. "Shall we not be just as possessive, just as jealous, just as pugnacious, just as positive as to the verdict of God, Nature, Law and Property as these gentlemen are now?" she mused. She did not ask how children would be affected by mothers' entry into the public world of work.

The *Boston Globe*, March 19, 1989:

Dear Beth:
   I have three kids, no husband, a busy job, and never enough time for anything! My kids do a lot of work, and I tell them how important they are to our family. However, the younger ones complain that I snap at everybody and never have fun with them alone anymore. How can I? I'm stretched to the limit keeping them fed, housed, and clean. Any ideas?
                                                    Stress City

Dear Beth:
My mom works, and she's always too busy for me. I know she's tired, but even after she rests, she never listens to me. It's like she doesn't care about me anymore. I want to live with my dad, but he can't take me. How do you find a foster home?

Sad and Lonely

Woolf may have thought that women of the future, like middle-class women in pre–World War II Britain, would have the choice of practicing the "unpaid-for professions" of wife and mother or entering paid ones like law, medicine, banking. She may not have expected women to be working both inside and outside the home, as 65 percent or more do today. If she did foresee this eventuality, she may have assumed that surrogate mothers in the form of nannies would continue to be as plentiful as they were in 1938. No one in Woolf's day could have known that the number of latchkey children would grow so dramatically. "I have been staying home by myself until my mom gets home since I was in kindergarten," twelve-year-old John David Gutierrez told the *Time* correspondent Melissa Ludtke in 1988. "I'm not really scared, because we have friends around here if anything happens." No one could have foreseen that little ones would increasingly have to sacrifice their childhood to become parents of their younger brothers and sisters. No one would have dreamed that a new category, the daycare child, would be created or that in the daytime homes would be empty nests.

Today women from all walks of life march across the bridge, and while the wealthy can afford the kind of private child care nannies used to provide, millions cannot even manage to pay the rates charged for daycare outside the home. To make matters worse, all too few of these facilities are places where young children can thrive. As for older children, after-school care is as dear a commodity as the proverbial honest man.

At century's end, society is more likely to ask how well or how badly women fare economically in comparison to men once the bridge is crossed than about their contamination by men's culture. We are also apt to hold women responsible for the plight of our nation's children. Society's analysts intimate that mothers should not be leaving the house each morning. Oblivious to the demands of necessity, they do not seem to realize that in an age when many homes are headed by only one parent, a mother, and most families need two salaries just to maintain a home, the question of whether women should join the procession is beside the point. These social critics make mothers feel guilty for doing what fathers have done since at least the nineteenth century. Blind to historical fact, they forget that it is not women's exodus from the private home each day that creates a vacuum in our children's lives. It is the exodus of *both* sexes. Had men not left the house when the Industrial Revolution removed work from the home—or had fathers not continued to leave the house each morning after their children were born—women's departure would not have the ramifications for children it does.

The question for us as we watch the procession of people move each morning from private house to public world is not, Who can we blame? We have to ask ourselves here and now, What are we as a nation, a culture, a society going to do about the children who are being left behind?

1

School and Home

It is radical conditions which have changed, and only an equally radical change in education suffices.

John Dewey, *The School and Society*, 1899

"I wasn't trained for this. I was trained to teach, not to deal with kids like this," said Chris Zajac, the teacher of the fifth-grade classroom in Holyoke, Massachusetts, that Tracy Kidder wrote about in *Among Schoolchildren*. Kids like what? Because neither Juanita's mother nor her father's new wife wanted her, she was living with an aunt and cousins and was spending every night in the bathroom crying. Pedro, whose four stepmothers had presented him with six brothers, lived with his grandmother and a transvestite uncle. A school counselor, sent to Blanca's house after the police called to say that the girl had not come home the night before, found two men there, neither of whom was related to the child. In class, Robert wrote letters to his absent father asking him where he lived, if he loved him, and when he, Robert, could see him. Glassy-eyed Jimmy seemed accustomed to staying up past midnight watching television. And Claude's mother, worried about her son, said to Chris: "I don't know what to do anymore. We do care . . . but I cannot quit my job."

"I put so much energy and so much emotion into those kids. Sometimes I think my job is being a professional mother," the high school English teacher Jessica Siegel told Samuel Freedman, the author of *Small Victories*, a first-hand report on the "real world" of New York City's Seward Park High School. Whose kids? Sammy Ryan lived at home only part time, and then simply to sleep. As a child he had spent several years with his grandfather, now dead, and also with a foster mother. Mary Tam lived in a group home where she had been placed by a social worker who thought it best to put some distance between her and her now divorced but still abusive foster parents. Lun Cheung, whose family had immigrated from Hong Kong, lived with three older brothers who bullied him into doing most of the housework while their mother sewed in a garment factory and their father spent months at a time in a psychiatric hospital.

It is a fact too seldom remembered that school and home are partners in the education of a nation's young. Like the housewife's labors that are at once counted on by her husband and discounted by him and his culture, home's continuing contributions to a child's development are both relied on by school and society and refused public recognition. This time-honored arrangement does not give credit where it is due, yet in periods of stability it has worked. Not perfectly, perhaps, but well enough because the hidden partner knows its role and is willing and able to carry it out.

The last decades of the twentieth century have been anything but a stable time, however, for "the" American home. As late as 1960 the norm of the two-parent household in which father goes out to work and mother stays home with the children accurately represented 70 percent of American families. But by 1986 only 7 percent of our families consisted of a male breadwinner, a female housewife, and dependent children. This shift in so short a period is itself remarkable, but the diversity exhibited by the remaining 90 percent of American families is positively astonishing. There are the two-parent families in which both adults go out to work and also the single-parent ones, 90 percent of them headed by women, that in 1986 were inhabited by one in four children. The picture in the two-parent families is complicated by the existence of blended families made up of stepparents and stepchildren—one in ten children today lives with a natural parent and a stepparent—of families with adopted children, of families with unmarried parents including same-sex couples. The single-parent families, in turn, differ from one another according to their economic well-being, the presence or absence of a father in the children's lives, and whether they are the result of divorce, desertion, death, or choice. And there is still more variability in that supposedly unchanging invention of nature, for an increasing number of couples are delaying childrearing or opting against it altogether, a growing proportion of the population is living alone, and a surprising number of adults, both unmarried and married, with children and without, are reentering the homes of their parents.

This is not the first time in United States history that home and family have changed form. In 1899 John Dewey told a Chicago audience that the Industrial Revolution had irrevocably transformed the American home by removing work from the household. He was thinking not of what is now called "housework" but of the production of such things as clothing, furniture, soap, candles, and cooking utensils that had been moved into factories. Remarking that it is useless to mourn the good old days as if the past could be brought back by exhortation, he called for a change in education as radical as the change in social conditions.

Dewey's philosophy has often been blamed for the failures of American education. Low reading scores and poor spelling, mathematical incapacity and scientific deficiency, ignorance of geography and a disregard of history, bad manners and delinquent behavior have all been laid at Dewey's door, and many also hold him responsible for the neglect of moral virtues, student cynicism about our political heritage, cultural illiteracy, and even poverty itself. Nevertheless, at the end of the twentieth century his insight that home's history has educational ramifications could scarcely be more apt.

The actual proposal Dewey made in Chicago does not address our own situation, however. The radical change in education he proposed was to put into the school the occupations of the earlier home. The critical factor in the second transformation of America's homes is the removal of parents, not work. Strangely, when he talked about the changes in the home wrought by the Industrial Revolution Dewey did not mention the exodus of people from the house each morning. Focusing on the uprooting of work, he did not seem to notice that when occupations left home, men and women followed suit. Had he been drawn to the plight of the very poor, as Maria Montessori was just a few years later, he might not have ignored this change in the household. As it was, he must have been assuming that mothers were staying home with their children and that the flight of fathers from the nest was therefore of little consequence.

With home and family having undergone radical transformation, it is downright foolhardy to overlook home's part in the educational enterprise. Now that both fathers and mothers are leaving home to go to work we have to ask anew, What radical change in school suffices?

Come stand with me on the bridge again. Do you see that piece of land jutting out into the river from the world of the private home? The men and women scurrying about over there are builders and architects, and the people they are consulting from time to time are teachers. Why are there so many children in the vicinity? A new kind of school is going to be constructed on this site, and youngsters of all ages, many of them dragging a parent along, have come here to make sure that their needs are met. Whose idea is this school and what is its name? I call it the Schoolhome and the idea is mine. I hope that by the time I have finished describing and presenting scenes from this new American institution you will agree with me that it is the kind of school our nation now needs. Let me begin by explaining how I arrived at my idea.

I

We Italians have elevated our word "casa" to the almost sacred significance of the English word "home."

Maria Montessori, *The Montessori Method*, 1912

When she spoke in 1907 at the opening of her second school in Rome, Maria Montessori also had home on her mind. She directed her audience's attention to the plight of the inhabitants of the district around the school. In the Quarter of San Lorenzo the underpaid and the unemployed mingled with recently released prisoners. The district had become the poor region of the city when a building boom followed by an economic panic left standing unfinished, unsafe, unsanitary apartment houses. Into these moved people, many of them families with children, who could afford nothing better; indeed, could afford not a whole apartment but merely a room or a corner therein. With twenty to thirty individuals huddled together in a space originally intended for three or four, disease and crime flourished. According to Montessori, the crowding was so bad and life in the apartments so miserable that it would have been more hygienic for people to take refuge in the streets had these not been scenes of brutality and bloodshed.

At the time of Montessori's address the Roman Association of Good Building, incorporated to acquire, remodel, and administer the "tenements," had bought fifty-eight houses, three of which had so far been transformed. Upon completion of these projects, however, the authorities found themselves facing an unexpected problem: the children under school age living in the new housing were running wild while their parents were at work. In Montessori's words, they were becoming "ignorant little vandals, defacing the walls and stairs." Deciding to establish a school in each building, the Association turned for help to Montessori, then a university lecturer on education as well as a physician and psychologist. Convinced that these children were neither being cared for properly nor learning what they should at home, she designed the Casa dei Bambini.

Reading *The Montessori Method* eighty years after Montessori delivered her Inaugural Lecture, I found myself wondering why "Casa dei Bambini" had been translated into English as "The Children's House" or "The House of Childhood." The more Montessori described her idea of school—the more she talked about the teacher's relationship to the children and the children's relationship to one another and also to their school environment—the more it sounded to me like a home, not just a house. Montessori's speech confirmed my hypothesis. On that opening day Montessori said, "We Italians have elevated our word 'casa' to the almost sacred significance of the English word 'home,' the enclosed temple of domestic affection, accessible only to dear ones." If any further confirmation was needed, it presented itself when I spied a book by Dorothy Canfield Fisher on the Montessori shelf in one of Harvard University's libraries. Fisher was one of many pilgrims who traveled to Italy to see Montessori's schools for themselves. In *A Montessori Mother*, published in 1912, she wrote: "The phrase Casa dei Bambini is being translated everywhere nowadays by English-speaking people as 'The House of Childhood,' whereas its real meaning, both linguistic and spiritual, is, 'The Children's Home.'" She added, "I feel like insisting upon this rendering, which gives us so much more idea of the character of the institution."

With my translation of "casa" verified, the question I still had to answer was whether the mistaken rendering of Casa dei Bambini really mattered. I soon discovered that the accounts Montessori gave of her schools and the published reports of visitors to Rome make sense only when "casa" is read as "home." But that is the least of it. The misreading of "casa" has effectively cut off generations of Americans from a new and intriguing vision of what school can and should be.

Read "casa" as "house" and your attention is drawn to the child-size furniture in the schools Montessori established, the exercises in dressing and washing, the self-education. Read "casa" as "home" and you perceive a moral and social dimension that transforms your understanding of Montessori's idea of school. Once I realized that she thought of school on the model of home, the elements of her system took on a different configuration. Where I had seen small individuals busily manipulating materials designed especially for learning, there now emerged a domestic scene with its own special form of social life and education.

Subtract home from Montessori's idea of school and we

have what sounds like a recipe for the open classrooms and integrated days that visitors to Britain's infant schools observed a generation ago. In the late 1960s and early 1970s journalists and educators from around the world traveled to England to see an experiment in education, just as in the early part of this century they had gone to Italy. In both instances, captivated by what they beheld, they returned to their own countries intent on introducing to their compatriots the new ideas. Perhaps few open education enthusiasts were aware of the similarities between the schools they inspected and Montessori's Casa dei Bambini.

Montessori's emphasis on children learning as opposed to teachers teaching, on the child's manipulation of concrete materials, on freedom and the absence of compulsion in the schoolroom were characteristic elements of open classrooms. Advocates of open education would doubtless have considered the "didactic" apparatus Montessori developed for learning too confining and would surely have thought that her conceptualization of the child's activities in school as "exercises" reflected an unfortunate rigidity. She, in turn, would probably have frowned upon the use of a given object in the children's environment for multiple educational purposes and would certainly have disapproved of what would have seemed to her the haphazard way in which concepts were learned and skills acquired in open classrooms. Still, the infant school teacher, like the Montessori "directress," was not supposed to take center stage. Nor was that teacher supposed to tell children the answer as opposed to helping them figure things out. Moreover, the distinction between work and play was as blurred in open classrooms as in the Casa dei Bambini and their location in time and place was as fluid.

The open education movement did not share Montessori's conception of school, however. Rejecting the features of traditional schools that had led critics to characterize them as prisons, open classroom advocates were determined to remove the barriers between school and world. Allowing children to cross the threshold into the out-of-doors, bringing materials from the "outside" world into the classroom, inviting members of the community into school to demonstrate their skills, they saw school more as a replica in miniature of the world than as a home. Indeed, the very presence in many open classrooms of a "family corner" where the children could lounge on rugs and slouch in easy chairs indicated that whatever the rest of school was seen as, it was not seen as home. Serving as a haven for those who wanted to withdraw temporarily from the hurly-burly of classroom life, a role analogous to the one so often attributed to home itself in society at large, this specially named area paradoxically reinforced a conception of school quite different from Montessori's own.

A homelike area does not transform a school or even a classroom into a home. And it was not the furniture that made the Casa dei Bambini a child's surrogate home. One dwells in a house. One feels safe, secure, loved, at ease—that is, "at home"—in a home, at least in the kind envisioned by Montessori.

Montessori was well aware that not all homes are safe and loving. Thus she did not dream of modeling her school on just any home. Maintaining that the Casa dei Bambini "is not simply a place where the children are kept, not just an *asylum*, but a true school for their education," she indicated that even in its homelikeness it was to be educative. Feeling certain that the "ignorant little vandals" were receiving neither the care nor the education they should at home, Montessori designed the school she had been asked to establish in the renovated tenement for the building's children as the kind of home to which the resident poor should aspire. Making it their school by giving them collective ownership, she modeled it on a version of home with which many of them were not even acquainted.

Montessori's description of what the literal home might one day become captures the spirit of that metaphorical home named school: "It may be said to embrace its inmates with the tender, consoling arms of a woman. It is the giver of moral life, of blessings; it cares for, it educates and feeds the little ones." Her idealized version of home is echoed by the image of a womb she invoked in the talks on education and peace she delivered in Europe in the 1930s.

Calling "the child" a "spiritual embryo," Montessori told European audiences that its promise will be fulfilled only if it is allowed to develop normally. Since its psychic life begins at birth, she said, the problem of peace becomes one of educating young children. Just as the physical embryo derives its nutriments from the womb, the spiritual embryo absorbs them from its surroundings. Put children in the wrong environment and their development will be abnormal and they will become the "deviated" adults we now know. Create the right environment for them and their characters will develop normally. The "second womb" is the way she pictured the young child's proper environment.

Montessori did not refer directly to the Casa dei Bambini in her lectures on peace, but, like a womb, it would provide a safe and secure, supportive and nurturant environment for children. Over and beyond this, the children in the Casa dei Bambini would have a double sense of belonging: they would feel that they belonged to this home and also that it belonged to them.

Commenting in *The Montessori Method* on the fact that the children worked so incessantly one might think they were repressed were it not "for their lack of timidity, for their bright eyes, for their happy, free, aspect, for the cordiality of their invitations to look at their work, for the way they take visitors about and explain matters to them," Montessori concluded: "These things make us feel that we are in the presence of the masters of the house." After insisting on the importance of the "real" translation of Casa dei Bambini, Fisher said of the Montessori school:

> It is, for instance, their very own home not only in the sense that it is a place arranged specially for their comfort and convenience, but furthermore a place for which they feel that steadying sense of responsibility which is one of the greatest moral advantages of a home over a boarding-house, a moral advantage of home life which children in ordinary circumstances are rarely allowed to share with their elders.

Deriving not from possessiveness but from attachment—to the school itself, to its physical embodiment, to the people in it—this feeling of responsibility explains the children's zeal in keeping the schoolrooms neat and clean, their joy in serving one another hot lunches, their pride in showing the school to visitors.

Having verified one implication of my reading of Montessori—that in her eyes the school building was treated as home—I checked out another. Did the inhabitants of school constitute a family? After referring to the children in a Casa dei Bambini as "these little citizens," Fisher corrected herself: "to call a Montessori school a 'little republic' and the children 'little citizens,' gives much too formal an idea of the free-and-easy, happily unforced and natural relations of the children with each other." In Rome the affectionate relationship between the directress and the children was palpable. Montessori noted the fervor with which the children "throw their arms around the teacher's knees, with which they pull her down to kiss her face." Fisher saw one teacher looking at her children "with shining eyes . . . I could have sworn, with mother's eyes!" The love that bound together the directress and the children of a Casa dei Bambini and also bound the children to one another served as both a precondition of the children's learning and an end point of their development. In her lectures on peace Montessori spoke of preventing adults from waging war by instilling in them in childhood "a love and respect for all living beings and all the things that human beings have built through the centuries." Long before those speeches to European audiences at a time when war was imminent, she had inserted family love into school.

Just as Montessori's model for school is an idealized version of home, an exemplary family serves as her model for the relationship in which those attending school stand to one another. That relationship constitutes a special kind of love. The love permeating the Casa dei Bambini was premised on the recognition and nurturance of individuality. Of the young child just beginning to be active she wrote, "We must *respect* religiously, reverently, these first intimations of individuality." She insisted that the teacher in a Casa dei Bambini be a scientist who would bring to her work "not only the capacity, but the desire, to observe natural phenomena." In this she sounds very like the Nobel Prize–winning biologist Barbara McClintock, who said seventy years later, "When I look at a cell, I get down in that cell and look around." The teacher, Montessori continued, "must become a passive, much more than an active, influence, and her passivity shall be composed of anxious scientific curiosity, and of absolute *respect* for the phenomenon which she wishes to observe. The teacher must understand and *feel* her position of *observer:* the *activity* must lie in the *phenomenon.*" Cherishing the uniqueness of each child as many decades later McClintock cherished each corn plant, Montessori saw both science and education as realms in which individuality would be valued and understood.

Overlook the elements of home and family in Montessori's educational system, as readers have consistently done, and the common opinion that individualization of instruction is its most significant feature seems warranted. Indeed, her own account of a school in Rome suggests as much:

> There are forty little beings—from three to seven years old, each one intent on his own work; one is going through one of the exercises for the senses, one is doing an arithmetical exercise; one is handling the letters, one is drawing, one is fastening and unfastening the pieces of cloth on one of our little wooden frames, still another is dusting. Some are seated at the tables, some on rugs on the floor. There are muffled sounds of objects lightly moved about, of children tiptoeing. Once in a while comes a cry of joy only partly repressed, "Teacher! Teacher!" an eager call, "Look! see what I've done." But as a rule, there is entire absorption in the work in hand.
>
> The teacher moves quietly about, goes to any child who calls her, supervising operations in such a way that anyone who needs her finds her at his elbow, and whoever does not need her is not reminded of her existence.

Given the amount of time the children spent working on their own, the conclusion many have reached that interpersonal relationships and social cooperation were not sufficiently emphasized appears credible too. I used to count myself in this group, but once I read "casa" as "home," the social nature of Montessori's idea of school became apparent. Instruction in a Casa dei Bambini was definitely individualized: during much of the day, at any given time the directress interacted with the children on a one-to-one basis, the children themselves pursued different activities, and each child proceeded at his or her own pace. However, all of this occurred within a context of domesticity. Like the individual members of the family of Montessori's imagination, even as the children were treated as individuals and their individuality was allowed to flourish, they felt connected to one another and concerned about one another's welfare.

Reports of the unselfish behavior of the children in Montessori's schools and of their genuine concern for their schoolmates abound. After remarking that quarrels in the classroom never arose over the possession of objects, Montessori wrote: "If one accomplishes something especially fine, his achievement is a source of admiration and joy to others: no heart suffers from another's wealth, but the triumph of one is a delight to all." Fisher gave a wonderful account of the smiling faces of several children who witnessed a little boy's long and ultimately successful struggle to tuck his napkin under his chin and of the way one then patted the napkin "as its proud wearer passed." An English educator described seeing a child "evidently much put out" because the teacher returned a composition to her indicating that it was not well done. Several of the children then "gathered round the girl, read the passages crossed out, found mistakes, and encouraged her to re-write. At last she unfolded her arms and took pen in hand. One of the children remained at her side until the work was started." The observer commented on this scene: "I had watched moral conduct in the making and it was all so simple, so natural, and so beautiful." Misread "casa" and observations like these have to be discredited. Yet the very events that cannot be understood—that indeed seem impossible—when "casa" is translated as "house" make perfect sense, are even to be expected, when the Casa dei Bambini is seen as home and the children in it are seen as bound together by domestic affection.

II

You should do for your children what their parents fail to do for them.

Johann Heinrich Pestalozzi, *Leonard and Gertrude*, 1781

As news was spreading of the "miracles" taking place in Montessori's schools in Rome—the three-year-olds serving soup tureens with aplomb, the four-year-olds learning to write in two months and to read in just a few more days, the small delinquents exhibiting remarkable powers of concentration and self-control—and as Montessori's name was beginning to be a household word in the United States, William James wrote an essay whose title entered our language. Once I saw the connection between Montessori's idea of the Casa dei Bambini and the concept of moral equivalency that James introduced into American thought at almost the same time, I was well on my way to answering the question of what to do about the children who are being left behind when both men and women cross the bridge each morning.

James's "The Moral Equivalent of War" was printed in 1910 in several popular magazines and was also widely distributed at the time in leaflet form. On hearing its title one naturally assumes that James was proposing peace as war's moral equivalent. In fact, his moral equivalent of war is a war against nature. He told readers that although war-making should be eliminated in modern society, the "martial virtues"—intrepidity, contempt of softness, surrender of private interest, obedience to command—should be preserved. Accordingly, the problem the "peace-party" faced was to detach these militaristic qualities from war but insure their continued existence. The solution he proposed was that the whole youthful population, by which he meant all young men, be conscripted into an army and sent out as railroad men and miners, tunnel-makers and fishermen to fight nature.

James was able to call his metaphorical war against nature an *equivalent* because he gave it the same function that he attributed to actual war—preserving the martial virtues and the benefits accruing to society from them. Had he embraced those martial virtues simply to win over the war-party, he could not have offered his substitute for war as a *moral* equivalent. But as it happens, he profoundly admired the "higher" aspects of militarism.

Just as James considered war to foster valuable character traits, Montessori considered home to have an educative function. Just as he insisted that if war were to stop inculcating the martial virtues some other institution would have to take on the task, she believed that insofar as home stopped teaching its lessons, school should step into the breach. Perceiving that for extended periods of time each day the private homes of children in the San Lorenzo Quarter were bereft of adults, Montessori created a radically changed school in which children would receive the affection and experience the intimacy and connection otherwise missing from much of their daily lives. They would also be the beneficiaries of that curriculum whose existence is seldom recognized in discussions of education.

Because home is the hidden partner in the education of our young, we tend to forget how much of who we are, how we act, and what we know was learned there when we were very young. Montessori knew that, as children spend less and less time at home in the company of their families, serious gaps in their learning will begin to emerge. She believed that among the small delinquents of the San Lorenzo Quarter these gaps already were in evidence. To her the remedy was to transplant into school the domestic atmosphere and curriculum she found missing from the children's private homes. Knowing how to wash and dress oneself, tell time, speak well and listen attentively, be gracious and generous to others, take care of younger children, work collaboratively, see a task through to completion: all this and more became the province of the Casa dei Bambini. Thus, by fulfilling some of the very same functions that home was expected to provide but in the case of the poor increasingly did not, the Casa dei Bambini constituted a *functional* equivalent of home. Serving functions that Montessori believed ought to be preserved for the sake of the children, their parents, and the larger society, it was also a *moral* equivalent.

That James, who had said in his earlier talks to teachers that "things that savor of danger or of blood" are the objects "natively interesting to childhood, to the exclusion of almost everything else," and who believed it to be inevitable that "most schoolroom work, till it has become habitual and automatic, is repulsive," would have approved of Montessori's moral equivalent of home is improbable. It is even less likely that she would have condoned his attitude toward nature. James's concept of a war on nature places the human race apart from the rest of the natural world and in an aggressive relationship to it. Montessori took attachment to the natural world as well as to other humans to be both the beginning and the end point of moral development.

Affirming in *The Montessori Method* that agriculture and animal culture "contain in themselves precious means of moral education," Montessori made them an integral part of the Casa dei Bambini curriculum. In what relation were the children to stand to the plants and animals in their care? In the same kind of relation as that of the observing teacher to the children themselves. They, like McClintock, would come to know individual plants and animals intimately and have absolute respect for them. Then out of their initial observations would grow "zealous care for the living creatures." A teacher in a Casa dei Bambini in Milan reported to Montessori that "when the children are tranquilly occupied in tasks, each at the work he prefers, one, two, or three, get up silently, and go out to cast a glance at the animals to see if they need care." Another wrote her a letter describing the day baby pigeons were hatched: "For the children it was a great festival. They felt themselves to some extent the parents of these little ones." Once Montessori herself found the children in Rome "seated on the ground, all in a circle, around a splendid red rose which had bloomed in the night; silent and calm, literally immersed in mute contemplation."

Montessori called the children who from the age of four sowed, hoed, watered, and examined the soil the "possessors of the earth." Yet in their ownership there was to be no trace of mastery or domination, no hint of a separation between possessor and possessed. Claiming that in the course of work with plants and animals "a sort of correspondence arises between the child's soul and the lives which are developed under his care," Montessori described the children's feeling for living creatures as "a form of love, and of union with the universe."

Saying in her lectures on peace that the child must be the point of departure for the personal reconstruction she deemed necessary and including girls as well as boys in this category, Montessori construed the problem of abolishing war as one of designing the right education for children. She specifically saw it as one of constructing suitable environments for them. When and only when there was a "harmonious interaction" between individual and environment, she said, would the child develop normally and love flourish. The kind of love Montessori had in mind was neither the romantic love of poetry and novels nor the self-sacrificing kind that Western culture attributes to mothers. Permanent and unconnected to either selfishness or a desire to possess, it was directed to all living creatures, to people, and to objects. This "higher form of love" was in her view a prerequisite for the "human harmony" and the "genuine community of mankind" that had to obtain if positive peace was to be achieved.

Although the "Montessori Method" is renowned for focusing on an individual child who works alone, albeit in a setting in which other children are doing the same, its creator clearly intended the Casa dei Bambini to replace what she termed the "isolation of the individual" with a sense of connection to both nature and society. Responding to those who asked what becomes of social life if the child does everything on his own, she explained the way social qualities in her schools derive from individual work:

> The child who concentrates is immensely happy; he ignores his neighbors or the visitors circulating about him. For the time being his spirit is like that of a hermit in the desert: a new consciousness has been born in him, that of his own individuality. When he comes out of his concentration, he seems to perceive the world anew as a boundless field for fresh discoveries. He also becomes aware of his classmates in whom he takes an affectionate interest. Love awakens in him for people and for things. He becomes friendly to everyone, ready to admire all that is beautiful. The spiritual process is plain: he detaches himself from the world in order to attain the power to unite himself with it.

This unity was to take effect outside as well as within the walls of the Casa dei Bambini and was to extend to the world of nature.

To be fair to James, his war on nature was merely a suggestion, just one possible moral substitute for war. If he were alive today he might withdraw his proposal and offer a different means for preserving what he called "absolute and permanent human goods." Montessori, however, would be telling us that the martial virtues of intrepidity, contempt of softness, obedience to command, and sacrifice of self are really capital vices.

Living in Italy well into the 1930s, she witnessed the military discipline that James so admired being transmitted from one generation to the next quite unconsciously by education. At a time when dictatorships were thriving—it was the very same time that Woolf was standing on the bridge—her aim was to transform education so that it would extinguish the very obedience to command James called a virtue. Protesting that "the obedience forced upon a child at home and in school, an obedience that does not recognize the rights of reason and justice, prepares the adult to resign himself to anything and everything," she charged this martial characteristic with opening the way to mindless idolatry and, ultimately, to slavery.

Montessori would have us replace obedience to command with individual self-determination. "No one can be free unless he is independent," she wrote in her chapter on discipline in *The Montessori Method*. After pointing to the dependency of masters on their servants, husbands on their wives, children on their mothers and teachers, she concluded: "We must make of the future generation, *powerful men*, and by that we mean men who are independent and free." She actually meant men *and* women, for in her Inaugural Address she had already said that the "new woman, like the butterfly come forth from the chrysalis, shall be liberated from all those attributes which once made her desirable to man only as the source of the material blessings of existence. She shall be, like man, an individual, a free human being, a social worker."

Montessori would also substitute for the martial virtue of surrender of private interest a desire to create a better collective life. These are not the same. Essentially negative, surrender of private interest involves the sacrifice of something one wants. Montessori's desire to create a better collective life consists in a positive concern for the general good. James and Montessori were both psychologists who had been trained as physicians, and the two of them seem to have started from the same dubious assumption: that human beings are at birth unconnected individuals. The difference between the two was that she viewed private interest as a defective character trait while he seemed to think it part of normal adult equipment. Provide the right education for children and selfishness will vanish in the course of normal development, Montessori claimed. But then, the *surrender* of private interest is no virtue. By the time a proper education enabled an individual to acquire a sufficiently developed will to surrender anything, the public spirit that characterized the "undeviated" adult should already have emerged.

In Montessori's philosophy the other two martial virtues—intrepidity and contempt of softness—meet the same fate. Reflective apologists for war take it religiously, said James, because it is human nature at its most dynamic. In their eyes war's horrors "are a cheap price to pay for rescue from the only alternative supposed, of a world of clerks and teachers, of co-education and zo-ophily, of 'consumer's leagues' and 'associated charities,' of industrialism unlimited, and feminism unabashed. No scorn, no hardness, no valor any more. Fie upon such a cattleyard of a planet!" No healthy minded person, he continued, can help partaking in the central essence of this feeling. For James, a world without risk and daring, without the possibility of violent death, without a supreme theater of human strenuousness, without heroism revolted the imagination.

Like the "unspeakable" Chautauqua that James visited one summer, the Casa dei Bambini contained as little peril to life and limb as possible. Indeed, he might have been discussing Montessori's moral equivalent of home when he said of Chautauqua, "there was no potentiality of death in sight anywhere, and no point of the compass visible from which danger might possibly appear." In the Casa dei Bambini, a place that barred competition and countenanced no violence, intrepidity disappeared and the only contempt that could possibly be encouraged would be of the hardiness James revered, not of the softness he condemned.

In a lecture to students James once said:

Sweat and effort, human nature strained to its uttermost and on the rack, yet getting through alive, and then turning its back on its success to pursue another more rare and arduous still—this is the sort of thing the presence of which inspires us, and the reality of which it seems to be the function of all the higher forms of literature and fine art to bring home to us and suggest. At Chautauqua there were no racks, even in the place's historical museum; and no sweat, except possibly the gentle moisture on the brow of some lecturer, or on the sides of some player in the ball-field.

Because the hardihood James extolled required the rack ·and Montessori would never have subjected children to pain, there was no place for it in the Casa dei Bambini. Without it there could be no place for James's contempt of softness.

III

Today the social and economic evolution calls the working-woman to take her place among wage-earners.

Maria Montessori, *The Montessori Method,* 1912

The fact that those small vandals in Rome were reading and writing at an early age gives the Casa dei Bambini a claim on our attention. But its kinship to the school under construction on the promontory derives mainly from its being a moral equivalent of home.

"We've got kids in the third grade using alcohol and marijuana," a drug-and-alcohol officer of the Seattle police department told Melissa Ludtke. Carlos Pimental, one of those Seward Park students Jessica Siegel mothered, started on drugs in the fifth grade. Within a year he was getting high three or four times a day. At age twelve, having witnessed a drug killing, he feared for his life. When he was twelve years old Lun Cheung joined a gang that ran protection and gambling and sold women and drugs. When he was in the tenth grade he was beaten up and his best friend was killed.

In June 1989 a teacher wrote the *Boston Globe:* "I used to wonder if my adolescent boys would remember my lessons once they left my classroom; now I wonder if they will live to remember them." At about that same time a Boston gang member was reminiscing:

When I was 12, I carried a .38 everywhere. I sold drugs in great balls. I was carryin' the gun just to be carryin' it. I wanted to be someone big. To me, a gun changes a person. It makes 'em brave. Sometimes I would go on the roof and shoot in the air. I felt like, let 'em come up on me. I'd be like Hercules. I even said, "Let a cop come. I'll get 'em."

Prophesying that women of all classes in the United States would one day be working outside their own homes, Fisher foresaw that the future significance of Montessori's work lay in the fact that most children would be in need of a home away from home. Little did she know how dire that need would become by the end of the century at whose beginning she was writing, or that so many people would be living under conditions that recall the district of Rome in which Montessori's original schools were located.

Telling her audience about the plight of the inhabitants of the San Lorenzo Quarter, Montessori said that children born there "do not 'first see the light of day'; they come into a world of gloom . . . Here, there can be no privacy, no modesty, no gentleness; here, there is often not even light, nor air, nor water!" Describing the Martinique, a once elegant hotel in New York City that in 1987 housed 438 homeless families, Jonathan Kozol wrote in 1988:

> It is difficult to do full justice to the sense of hopelessness one feels on entering the building. It is a haunting experience and leaves an imprint on one's memory that is not easily erased by time or cheerful company. Even the light seems dimmer here, the details harder to make out, the mere geography of twisting corridors and winding stairs and circular passageways a maze that I found indecipherable at first and still find difficult to figure out. After fifty or sixty nights within this building, I have tried but cannot make a floor plan of the place.
>
> Something of Dickens' halls of chancery comes to my mind whenever I am wandering those floors. It is the knowledge of sorrow, I suppose, and of unbroken dreariness that dulls the vision and impairs one's faculties of self-location and discernment. If it does this to a visitor, what does it do to those for whom this chancery is home?

Perhaps two million, possibly even three or four million people in the United States, the great majority of whom are families, are homeless. The average homeless family consists of a mother and three children. Living on the streets or in rat-ridden, roach-infested shelters, these children can scarcely be said to dwell in houses, let alone homes. "Home to me would be like this," a woman in the Martinique told Kozol:

> You have your dinner at the same time all together. You go out together—yeah, you go out to play bingo. Go to the ice cream, to the movies. Then you all go home together. You sit down in peace together. You read together. You say your prayers together. You go to sleep together and you don't have to be scared there'll be a fire. Here in this building, I don't sleep. What's on my mind? I'm thinking: there's so many people, trash piled around. What if there's a fire on my floor?

In the Martinique families of four or even five were living in single unheated rooms with no space for all to sit down and eat together, and in any case no chairs, no stove to cook on, often not even food to eat.

Kozol estimated that of the more than fourteen hundred school-age children who dwelt in the Martinique in 1985, over one-third did not usually get to school. Of those who did, many had to travel by bus or subway to outlying districts, and even the children attending schools nearby fell asleep at their desks and fell behind in their work. A young girl said to Kozol, "School is bad for me. I feel ashamed. They know we're not the same. My teachers do not treat us all the same. They know which children live in the hotel." Calling attention to the "dirty baby" stigma attached to children of the homeless, Kozol commented: "Whether so perceived or not, they will feel dirty. Many, because of overflowing sewage in their bathrooms, will be dirty and will bring the smell of destitution with them into class."

Whether they were attending school or not, children living in the Martinique at the time of Kozol's study received daily lessons in violence and futility. On one floor a small boy died after a beating by his father, on another girls sold crack. A twelve-year-old had just had a baby, and many thirteen-year-olds were pregnant. Outside the building children were accosted by drug addicts and pimps. A young boy on his way to school was arrested for jumping subway turnstyles when he had no tokens.

The picture of human misery Montessori painted in her speech in Rome in 1907 eerily resembles the situation of the homeless today in cities across the United States. But the homeless are by no means the only ones who stand to benefit from a concept of school as a moral equivalent of home. With mothers as well as fathers walking across the bridge each day that concept meets an increasingly pressing need of most Americans.

Elaborating on the claim that infants "are barely human and utterly unsocialized," the anthropologist Sherry Ortner has stated what every new parent knows: "Like animals they are unable to walk upright, they excrete without control, they do not speak. Even slightly older children are clearly not yet fully under the sway of culture. They do not yet understand social duties, responsibilities, and morals; their vocabulary and their range of learned skills are small." She makes the point starkly because children and parents alike tend to forget the unique contribution of the domestic "sphere" of society and of the women who inhabit it. Explaining that our culture—she says every culture—perceives the domestic context or realm as located close to nature and the processes that take place within it as therefore natural, she reminds us that it transforms newborns "from mere organisms into cultured humans, teaching them manners and the proper ways to behave in order to become full-fledged members of the culture."

Like the housewife's labors that are not considered real work, home's contributions to a child's development are not called "education." In keeping with an arrangement that has made home the silent partner of school, we use a special vocabulary to describe what happens there. The teaching mothers do at home is called "childrearing" or "bringing up," the resultant learning "socialization," "acculturation," or even "development." Denying through our choice of words both the seriousness of the teaching and the societal significance of the learning, we underestimate the educative powers of the domestic context and the importance of the curriculum of home for the lives of children and the continuation of society.

Why was Montessori so much more aware than contemporaries like Dewey of the extent to which the domestic context transforms creatures of nature into creatures of culture? The fact that she was a woman may have made her especially attuned to home's educative function, but I would say that her deeper insight had another source as well.

Before she established her schools in Rome Montessori worked with the mentally handicapped. Convinced that mental deficiency was chiefly a pedagogical problem, she traveled through Europe to study the methods then in use with "the deficients," conducted educational experiments with her students, and lectured to their teachers. It was in this period of her life that she discovered the writings of Jean-Marc-Gaspard Itard and Edouard Séguin. Itard is the physician who spent many years teaching Victor, the "Wild Boy" first spied in the woods of Aveyron in 1797, and who also developed instructional techniques to use with deaf youngsters. Séguin, his student, is the one who applied these methods to the education of retarded children. Montessori was so impressed with both men that she translated and copied by hand all their writings. "I chose to do this," she said in *The Montessori Method*, "in order that I might have the time to weigh the sense of each word and to read, in truth, the spirit of the author." She added, "the voice of Séguin seemed to be like the voice of a forerunner crying in the wilderness."

Just as Séguin extended his master's work to a new population of "deficient" children, Montessori extended the teaching methods developed by the two men—the individualized instruction, the use of specially constructed didactic apparatus, the emphasis on the development of the senses—to "normal" children. The legacy of Itard's reports about Victor to Montessori did not stop there. Like her, Dewey took seriously the advice the Swiss philosopher-educator Johann Heinrich Pestalozzi had given a century before that school should do for children what their parents were failing to do for them.

But Dewey seems to have had little appreciation of the domesticating function of home. Knowing Victor as she did, Montessori understood that office well. Referring to Itard's treatise on Victor's education she wrote that in his pages "we find vividly described the moral work which led the savage to civilisation." And she added: "I believe that there exists no document which offers so poignant and so eloquent a contrast between the life of nature and the life of society."

Going for many years without a home in the literal sense of the term, Victor had no exposure to the curriculum that inducts our young into human culture when Itard met him; not even to wearing clothes, eating food other than nuts and potatoes, responding to human speech, sleeping in a bed, knowing hot from cold, walking rather than running. He had to be taught the things that educators other than parents of the very young and teachers of differently abled children assume they know. Montessori understood, however, that Victor was different from other children not because he had to be domesticated and they did not, but because their domestication occurred so early, so gradually, and so imperceptibly as to appear natural. "In the education of little children Itard's educative drama is repeated," she said. She also must have asked herself just how wild the children of the tenement might become—or at least how wild *their* children might be— if she did not build into the schools she was creating the domestic curriculum, affections, and spirit she perceived to be lacking in their private homes.

If Montessori did not know, when she was invited to create schools for the poor, that the Industrial Revolution's removal of work from the private home was accompanied by the removal of workers, she soon realized it. "To-day the social and economic evolution calls the working-woman to take her place among wage-earners, and takes away from her by force those duties which would be most dear to her!" she said. "The mother must, in any event, leave her child, and often with the pain of knowing him to be abandoned."

I suspect that Montessori's familiarity with Victor gave her the insight Dewey lacked into the immense cultural significance of this profound change in home and into its implications for school. Her realization that school should serve as home's substitute when for one reason or another home does not perform its domesticating role well must surely have been due to Victor. Certainly her knowledge of just how little he knew of human culture when he came out of the woods and just how much Itard had to teach him has to have been a critical factor in the development of the Casa dei Bambini in Rome.

Shattering the illusion that what we call "second nature" is innate, Victor's case dramatically illustrates that what we adults learned at home as young children is far more basic than the school studies we call our basics. Years ago, one of the questions about education that I was asking in my capacity of educational philosopher was, What entitles us to call some studies rather than others "the basics"? My answer was that reading, writing, and arithmetic are considered essential—hence basic—components of education because of their roles in preparing young people for membership in the public world; specifically, for enabling them to be citizens in a democracy and economically self-sufficient individuals. In addition, we take the three Rs to be fundamental because of the part they play in initiating our young into history, literature, philosophy, the arts—"high" culture or Culture with a capital C. Study the partnership of school and home, however, and it becomes clear that these three goals—achieving economic viability, becoming a good citizen, and acquiring high culture—make sense only for people who have already learned the basic mores of society.

In calling the three Rs our basics, we assume that children have already acquired at least the rudiments of culture with a small c. Only if this learning is imperiled does it occur to us that it is the product of practice, patience, and directed effort. Only when we realize that children deprived of the curriculum the private home has been expected to teach may never acquire the skills, knowledge, attitudes, and values essential for full-fledged membership in human culture—or civilization, as Montessori preferred to call it—do we even begin to admit that our earliest learning is a critical part of our education.

Victor's case reveals that Itard and Séguin knew the educative function of domesticity. They went to great lengths to transform the living conditions of their pupils. What shape did their changes take? Attending like the best of mothers to hygiene, food, clothing, and contact with the outdoors, they injected into education outside the private home a strong dose of home's domestic component. They did more than create homelike environments for Victor and the other "deviants" in their care, however. Inventing techniques for teaching concepts and behavior that "normal" children were thought to acquire naturally as they matured, they cast in doubt the validity of any hard and fast distinction between the curriculum of school and that of home. Demonstrating that what can successfully be taught in school depends on what has or has not already been learned at home, their work with those who departed from the norm revealed the interdependence of the two kinds of curricula.

IV

This book of methods compiled by one person alone, must be followed by many others.

Maria Montessori, *The Montessori Method*, 1912

What radical change in school suffices given the transformations of the American home and family in recent decades? We cannot transplant into late-twentieth-century American soil the institution Montessori designed early in the century for Italian children. It would not take root. We cannot even graft onto our own schools the Casa dei Bambini's spirit of love. The two are incompatible. What we can do—what I will do here—is treat Montessori's idea of school the way she treated the pioneering efforts of Séguin and Itard. Just as she integrated elements of their work into her bold experiment in Rome but then molded them to her own ends until they were effectively transformed, I will incorporate aspects of her educational philosophy and practice into my own thought experiment, developing in the process a new concept of school appropriate to the here and now.

Not all aspects of the Casa dei Bambini are suited to my purpose by any means. Montessori put her schools in the buildings in which the children lived. Now that home and workplace are frequently situated miles apart, it may be advisable to establish at least some of our own moral equivalents of home on the other side of Woolf's bridge.

Location is not the only feature of the Casa dei Bambini that is out of date. The very name Montessori gave her school is obsolete. Quite simply, young children—bambini—are not now the only ones at risk when both fathers and mothers walk across the bridge.

Boston Globe, March 19, 1989
Dear Beth:
    I am a single mother with a 13-year-old son. He stays home by himself three days a week for a couple of hours after school. He's supposed to do his homework, but he mostly watches TV. How can I motivate him to work by himself? He says he needs help with it.
                                                                Worried

Try working out a program with your son. For instance, a half-hour of chores, a half-hour of reading, and a half-hour of TV. If he can call you with homework problems, let him. Otherwise, research the community for other parents, teachers, older kids, etc., who would be willing to answer his questions. Have you investigated after-school programs? What about Scouts, 4-H, or other activities that would keep him from being alone so much? Getting to know your neighbors could give your child the comfort of knowing there's someone to call on and might set up opportunities to swap off kids sometimes.

John David's greatest uncertainty involved drugs, Ludtke reported. He told her he sometimes thought about a group of older kids forcing drugs on him. "I might try to run where there is a bunch of people. But if I ran, they would just gang up and beat me up. They might carry knives, and they would stab me. They would probably leave the knife in and run off."

"I'm dreading when school closes," the grandmother of a thirteen-year-old boy, one of five ranging in age from eleven to sixteen arrested for the indecent assault and battery of a thirteen-year-old girl, told reporters. "Every time I look out there's a brand new group of kids out there. Kids love money. These kids who sell drugs are walking around looking nice with their sneakers and jackets. What's to stop other kids from looking at them and saying, 'I'm going to do the same thing?'" The mother of an eleven-year-old in the group locked up on the same charge said of her son: "He has no remorse about anything whatsoever. He thinks it's all a big game . . . I just let them put him some place where I know he's OK. Maybe now he'll learn; maybe it's too late. I don't know."

The ambiguity of the Italian word "casa" also detracts from Montessori's label. She may have meant "home," but nonetheless the word also means "house." We already have schoolhouses. Our challenge is to turn the schoolhouse into the Schoolhome: a moral equivalent of home for our young that will be as responsive to the needs and conditions of children and their parents at the end of the twentieth century as the Casa dei Bambini was in an earlier time.

Will the practical exercises of life Montessori devised for the children in Italy meet today's needs any better than the name she gave her school? It goes without saying that the Schoolhome must have a domestic curriculum. That some of the lessons she designed are dated and that ones she never dreamed of are now required is equally clear.

Washing yourself, brushing your teeth, taking care of your belongings, cleaning house, serving meals, tending to the needs of younger children are not yet outmoded activities.

Neither are the various forms of the three Cs of care, concern, and connection exhibited in the Casa dei Bambini, such as being civil to adults and hospitable to guests, entering into the joys and sorrows of your intimates, feeling a sense of oneness with them, and responding directly to their needs. But the children in Rome worked with small disks on a frame so that they could learn to fasten their buttons, a skill that in this age of Velcro may well be expendable. They also performed religious rites that are unacceptable in a nation that separates church and state.

Will the Schoolhome become one more vehicle for imposing "middle-class morality" on children? The line between basic socialization and middle-class veneer, between being a contributing member of a culture and acquiring the manners of a cultural elite, is not easily drawn. Yet many of the candidates for inclusion in the Schoolhome's domestic curriculum are matters of health, not etiquette. Some, like keeping the environment clean, relate to the health of the whole society. And as the moralizing dustman in George Bernard Shaw's *Pygmalion* knew, the middle class has no monopoly on the three Cs.

Transforming Alfred Doolittle's daughter Eliza, a Covent Garden flower girl, into a "lady" by teaching her superficial patterns of "proper" behavior, Henry Higgins was guilty of imposing middle-class morality on her. Eliza was poor, she was dirty, her clothes were ragged, but she was far more kind and considerate—a more civilized person—than he. In fact, Professor Higgins could teach her nothing about morality; only the manners and speech appropriate to another rank of society lay within his competency. A Schoolhome that did for today's children what he did for Miss Doolittle would be a travesty of a moral equivalent of home. On the other hand, to refrain from trying to create the genuine article lest a counterfeit be coined is to ignore the lesson contained in Victor's case.

Our young are not literally Victors. Born into human society, they have not only learned to walk upright and tell hot from cold. They have had the experience out of which morality—and also immorality—emerges. Growing up outside human culture, and very likely outside animal culture too, Victor was truly amoral. He had no concept of right and wrong, but more than this, he had matured without engaging in social interactions. Whereas young people today act well or badly, morally or immorally as the case may be, these labels cannot even be applied to Victor's behavior. Nevertheless, just as his very existence reveals human culture for what it is—a social construction—the enormous difficulty of the task of turning this creature of nature into a creature of culture demonstrates how vital it is to bring up our children from the beginning as contributing members of society. In a way it does Victor an injustice to invoke his ghost here, for the Wild Boy of Aveyron did no harm to others once he came under Itard's guidance. Yet if Victor fast became a gentle creature who in his splendid isolation posed no threat to society, his story discloses what could happen to a culture whose young people grew up unwilling or unable to live and work peaceably with others and to participate with them in the culture's continual renewal.

One secret of the Casa dei Bambini's success was that the practical exercises Montessori devised for the children were not decided upon in advance but were derived from her perception of what was missing in their private lives. The instructional methods of Montessori's schools were also the product of her continuing work with the children. Does this mean that instead of undertaking for ourselves the difficult task of discovering what pedagogical methods and materials work with which children, we can pattern the pedagogy of the Schoolhome on that of the Montessori schools that exist today?

"This book of methods compiled by one person alone, must be followed by many others," Montessori said in her conclusion to *The Montessori Method*. In a book published in 1982, Valerie Polakow Suransky described a Montessori school in the Midwest that differed dramatically from those portrayed in the reports of visitors to Montessori's Rome. *The Erosion of Childhood* contains a portrait of a school so rigid, so dedicated to a work ethic, so individualistic in emphasis that the prime value it seemed to be transmitting to those in attendance was possessiveness. I would not dream of condemning Montessori schools on the basis of one person's depiction of one. But Suransky's report underlines the danger of assuming that because an institution bears Montessori's name it will enact her domestic intention and display her experimental attitude. Her study is also a reminder that the spirit animating Montessori's system and the domestic curriculum constituting its heart can thrive in places quite different from the schools in Rome.

Take the federally funded, low-income daycare center Suransky visited whose stated aim "was to create an 'extended family' atmosphere that was both nurturant and secure for children." The Martin Luther King child care center sounds like a moral equivalent of home if there ever was one. Whereas the teachers at the Montessori center wanted Suransky to keep her distance from the children she was watching, here she found it impossible to maintain the observer role. The children, the teachers, and the grandmothers whose daily presence helped to blur the boundaries between this surrogate home and the children's private homes immediately welcomed her into their noisy, happy, warm, loving domestic world.

Luckily, a Schoolhome that adopts Montessori's experimental approach to pedagogy and exhibits her sensitivity to context will have a wide range of educational practice to consult. There are private Montessori schools, community nursery schools, and public kindergartens; 4-H clubs, summer creative arts programs, and winter after-school activities; neighborhood elementary and secondary schools and boarding schools for teenagers; Quaker colleges and institutes for schoolteachers.

We must take pains, however, lest the Schoolhome's experimental bent reduce it to an antiseptic laboratory whose inhabitants are ciphers on a computer printout. The success of the Casa dei Bambini depended on Montessori's managing to combine a scientific approach to education with the family affection and the three Cs of care, concern, and connection that were a part of the school's atmosphere and central to its curriculum. Her way of doing science is not, however, the dominant one today.

Typically, science views the uniqueness and complexity of individuals as problems to be overcome. Treating each child as a unique person, Montessori sought a kind of understanding that would honor the complexity of her "subject matter." Science also considers personal feelings and relationships to be impediments to objectivity. Montessori felt affection for the children she was studying and stood in an intimate relationship to them. Scientists today are trained to keep their distance but Montessori believed that if she was going to know enough about children to improve their education she would have to get down there with them and be part of the system. Scientists are told to bracket their emotions but Montessori's love for children was the force that moved her to develop the Casa dei Bambini in the first place and to want continually to improve it. In the search for uniformities they are taught to ignore whatever contributes to a thing's individuality. Montessori knew how inconsistent it is to try to nurture children's individuality and at the same time treat them as if they were identical. She also knew that the kind of information she needed could be gotten only from close observation of each child.

In the Casa dei Bambini individualized instruction prevailed. Because youngsters in the United States must learn to work and live with people from diverse backgrounds, the Schoolhome will have to try out new combinations of collaborative and individualized learning. But regardless of the type of instruction employed, teachers there will need to know their students as the complex people they are. Even to decide what kind of instruction is best suited to a particular child, one must have more information than grades and standardized test scores reveal. Besides, how can a girl or boy feel at home if she or he feels unknown? How can an atmosphere of love and trust develop if the children are not appreciated for themselves?

An experimental stance toward questions of school organization as well as curriculum and instruction is probably also the best policy. The Casa dei Bambini used "family" grouping—it put children of different ages in the same classroom—but local conditions today might favor different arrangements. Should children in the Schoolhome travel each day from one subject-matter specialist to the next as they do in our secondary schoolhouses, or should they stay put with a generalist for a year or more as they now do in most elementary ones? These and other formats need to be explored. Should there be standardized time periods marked by alarm bells, or will the schoolday be constructed more fluidly? To fulfill its function the Schoolhome will have to allow some children to arrive earlier and leave later than others. Will teachers need a similar degree of flexibility? To resolve issues like these in advance is to tie our own hands. Local conditions demand local solutions that are often best arrived at through trial and error.

An affectionate climate is, of course, a basic constituent of the Schoolhome. Although this will undoubtedly translate into daily practice differently in different circumstances, we can be sure of one thing. A school environment guided by domestic love cannot countenance violence, be it corporal punishment or teachers' sarcasm, the bullying of one child by others or the terrorization of an entire class, the use of hostile language about whole races or the denigration of one sex. Such a place cannot tolerate the destruction of the children's physical surroundings, either.

Another aspect of the Casa dei Bambini that cries out for preservation is the children's attachment to nature. In light of recent ecological developments, adjustments will obviously have to be made. At the least, the "zealous care" for plants and animals that Montessori instilled in her charges needs to be extended to oceans, rivers, the air, the ozone layer, the fields we plow, the landscapes we admire. But regardless of the details, while exemplifying and teaching the three Cs of care, concern, and connection, the Schoolhome will have to include the environment itself within their embrace.

One more ingredient of the Casa dei Bambini that I expect to see the Schoolhome mix into its brew is joy. In Montessori's schools the type of joy that many young children experience at home as a kind of by-product of intense concentration was a familiar feature of daily life. Here is Fisher's description of a child who, having worked on that button frame, then succeeded in fastening a button on his own shirt: "When the bone disk finally shone out, round and whole, on the far side of the buttonhole, the child drew a long breath and looked up at me with so ecstatic a face of triumph that I could have shouted, 'Hurrah!'"

The joy in the Casa dei Bambini was not only a function of individual effort. The game of silence in which all the children actively cooperated to attain an "absolute silence" in the classroom produced what seems to have been a near reverie state issuing eventually in an almost mystical joy. Said Fisher:

> Who of us, without seeing this in actual practice, would ever have dreamed that little children would care for such an exercise, would submit to it for an instant, much less throw themselves into it with all the ardor of little Yogis . . . their pleasure in it is inexpressible. The expression which comes over their little faces when, in the midst of busy play, they feel the first hush fall about them is something never to be forgotten.

In the Martin Luther King child care center the joy took a more boisterous turn. Suransky's notes on her first visit record: "Kids are very rough with each other, yet there is so much warmth and physical contact. Teachers are constantly hugging children, and the grandmothers shout instructions from their chairs in the front." On a later visit she wrote:

> Cedric arrived late today, wearing a new shirt. The staff and kids all clapped for him and made a great fuss. Teacher Pat brought out his breakfast. Teacher Joe began to tease him

saying, "Hey, man, that's my juice," grabbing it from him and putting it back. Teacher Joe then grabbed the toast from Cedric's hand. "That's my toast," Cedric squealed, and all laughed uproariously including Cedric.

V

What the best and wisest parent wants for his own child, that must the community want for all its children.

John Dewey, *The School and Society,* 1899

In an age when the lives of so many children besides Carlos Pimental, Lun Cheung, Mary Tam, and Sammy Ryan bring to mind Dickens's novels, what radical change in school suffices? The best answer I know is to turn the American schoolhouse into a moral equivalent of home in which love transforms mundane activities, the three Cs take their rightful place in the curriculum of all, and joy is a daily accompaniment of learning.

In May 1991 Anita Teeter, a curriculum specialist working with the Boston Public School System, wrote in a letter to the *Boston Globe:* "We need a new vision of education . . . We should be aiming to help children become caring adults, builders of communities, sharers of learning, lovers of the printed word, citizens of the world, nurturers of nature. This, of course, involves families and communities as well as schools, and it will require money." Money is needed to turn our schoolhouses into the Schoolhomes Teeter called for, but so is a refocusing of attention.

Teeter, a teacher in the Boston Schools for twenty-two years, described the havoc wrought by the misuse of standardized multiple-choice tests:

Thousands of dollars are spent on this scam. The tests are counter-productive in that teachers concentrate on teaching test-taking, not on thinking skills. Teachers have known this for years, but they are under horrible stress because it is believed that the test results reflect on their teaching abilities, and because their principals (also under stress to save their jobs and schools) tell them to do whatever needs to be done to improve test scores. Principals are told the same thing by their superiors. The teachers I work with as a curriculum specialist are desperate.

In a meeting at my university on the very day this letter was published a department head said, "We have too many people running through. The quality control isn't there." A program director countered, "What we're putting out now is people who are fully certified." Thinking of school as a special kind of production site—a factory that turns out workers for the nation's public and private sectors—government officials, business leaders, educational administrators focus on standards. As they see it, the products of our nation's classrooms, like the automobiles on a General Motors assembly line and the boxes of cereal in a Kellogg's plant, should be made according to specifications. When minimum requirements are not met, the obvious remedy is to tighten quality control. For colleges and universities this tightening is apt to take the form of raising entrance requirements. For America's public schools it translates into efforts to improve testing, to hold teachers accountable for student failures to measure up, and to standardize curriculum.

The new vision of education that the Schoolhome represents does not picture young children as raw material, teachers as workers who process their students before sending them on to the next station on the assembly line, or curriculum as the machinery that over the span of twelve or so years forges America's young into marketable products. It does not conceive of school as a marketplace and children as workers, entrepreneurs, and consumers either.

In 1973 George Richmond, then a teacher, developed the concept of the micro-society school: school as a capitalist society in which children do their academic work for money and try to get rich by providing services others want and need. At one school where Richmond tried out his ideas, Mannie collected the breakfast food that his schoolmates were wasting and hawked it at lunchtime for Micro-Economy dollars; a group of children made and sold Christmas cards; one grade tried unsuccessfully to put out and market a newspaper; every classroom had a savings bank and sundry other small businesses. Bringing into focus the enormous gap between the subjects children study in school and the work that they are expected to settle into after graduation, this capitalist vision of education directs attention away from performance on tests to what children actually do in school. It also stresses the virtues of hard work and initiative. But in mapping onto school the features of a marketplace and onto schoolchildren the economic relations and functions of a capitalist society, it necessarily ignores the three Cs. And in excluding the private home from the very concept of the macro-society that serves as school's model, it insures the neglect of all things domestic.

Instead of making entrepreneurial activity and money the primary values, the Schoolhome emphasizes domesticity and the three Cs. Rather than focusing on abstract norms, standardized tests, generalized rates of success, uniform outcomes, it sends attention in the opposite direction. Turning our gaze from the "big" economic picture to the local level, it brings into sharp relief individual classrooms. Once the quality of life in school commands the foreground, questions arise about the classroom climate, school routines and rituals, relationships between teachers and children and among the children themselves, the teachers' modes of teaching and the children's ways of learning. And with this refocusing of attention comes a reorienting of practice.

Is home an appropriate model or metaphor for school in a nation whose population, unlike that of Montessori's Italy, is so diverse? There is no doubt that those children in Rome were a relatively homogeneous bunch. The visitors to Montessori's schools may have come from all over the world but the schools' inhabitants did not. Yet they were not literally kin. The family-like bonds that existed between and among them and their teachers were creations of the Casa dei Bambini. In the United States today millions of children were born elsewhere. But rather than invalidating the idea of school as moral equivalent of home, this fact of American life gives that idea an urgency it might not otherwise have.

One century after Dewey's Chicago lecture the question has become, How can we create a moral equivalent of home in which children of all races, classes, and cultures feel at home? Surprisingly, those today who criticize our schools and make recommendations for their improvement have paid little attention to the transformations "the" American home and family have undergone in the last decades and have taken no account of the changed and changing composition of our nation's population. Instead, they have looked back with longing at the curriculum of their youth—a course of study designed for an earlier age and a different people. Impervious to our nation's pressing need for a new inclusionary concept of curriculum, they have allowed the inability of that old course of study to serve all our children to escape their notice.

But perhaps the extent of the violence in American society today casts doubt on the wisdom of conceptualizing school as home even if the diversity of our population poses no problem. Perhaps the metaphor is not robust enough, or is too removed from the reality to be of use.

Interestingly enough, one of the exercises of practical life that Montessori listed was conversation, a skill—some would say an art—not often nurtured in the American schoolhouse. When the Schoolhome finally opens, many of the children will be speaking English for the very first time and everyone there will have to learn to converse with people of other races, cultures, and nationalities. They will also have to learn to live with people who are very different from themselves, something that in this violent day and age is easier said than done. Dewey's question of what change in education suffices will undergo a double transformation in these pages. After discussing in Chapter 2 the importance of making all our children feel at home in school and in the world, I will turn in Chapter 3 to the question, How can we educate the next generation to live in the world together?

In May 1989 a courageous sixteen-year-old wrote to the *Boston Globe* expressing concern about the rise in teen violence. He said he had gotten used to kids carrying knives, but now they were carrying guns. "There are a couple of reasons for this rise," he said, "but the main one is to be tough or respected. They feel power when they have that deadly piece of steel in their hand. Another reason is that they are so easy to get." Since he had observed this change in just six months, he wondered what the world would be like in six years. Would it turn into "a combat zone" controlled by kids with guns?

Meanwhile, in song and story, dance and documentary, commercials and commentary, the electronic media teach our children far more about consumerism, violence, and sexuality than their parents ever knew at their ages and introduce them ever earlier to the possessiveness, jealousy, pugnacity, and greed that Woolf called uncivilized and that both she and Montessori believed were intimately related to war.

I am quite sure this electronic newcomer to our homes is capable of reinforcing and enhancing home's domestic curriculum. But sadly, television and video games are far more apt in actuality to transmit fear than serenity, mental stupor than joy, an attraction to peril to life and limb than to security. At last count, TV cartoons alone averaged 23 acts of violence per hour, with at least one program managing 122. Portraying mayhem as the norm, they make the three Cs of care, concern, and connection seem like symptoms of disability. Thus does the late-twentieth-century version of live-in "hired help" subvert the educative function that our culture has implicitly assigned to the hidden partner.

Historians have shown that when the Industrial Revolution irrevocably changed the American household by removing both work and workers from it, home—specifically the white middle- and upper-class home—came to be viewed as a haven in a cold, cruel world: the place to which men retreated after spending a long day in the greedy, pugnacious, possessive, jealous public arena. Its presumed ethos of love and intimacy and the values of care, concern, and connection it was said to embody were thought to be conducive to the rest and renewal required by the husbands and sons who were expected to reenter the fray each morning. But home's task was not merely to refresh and invigorate. It was expected to play a moral role as well. Besides inducting infants into human culture and teaching young children the basics of American life, it was supposed to provide its members with an education in the very kindness and cooperation, affection and sympathy that were also considered to be the prerequisites of life in a harmonious society.

Dewey told his Chicago audience that before the Industrial Revolution industry, responsibility, imagination, and ingenuity were the basic elements of home's curriculum. Perhaps so, but after that cataclysmic event it was considered home's particular function to teach what the psychologist Carol Gilligan, in her groundbreaking book *In a Different Voice*, has called an "ethics of care." Serving to curb the selfishness and dampen the pugnacity of those whose days were spent on the other side of the bridge, the moral education extended by the home was supposed to keep American society as a whole from slipping into a war of every man against every man. As the nations of nineteenth-century Europe were deemed able to keep the peace so long as the balance of power among them was maintained, the members of our society were considered able to live together harmoniously so long as the moral equilibrium between private home and public world was preserved.

Whatever efficacy that delicate balance of home and world might once have had, the changes in both and the arrival on the scene of the new household member make our continued reliance on home for a curriculum in an ethics of care anachronistic. "What the best and wisest parent wants for his own child, that must the community want for all children," Dewey said in *The School and Society*. Seeing the violence and knowing how hard it now is for home to accomplish its educative functions, will not wise parents want school to teach all children the ethics of care that was once home's preserve? Will not they sigh with relief when the American schoolhouse is converted into a moral equivalent of home?

But America's private homes probably never were idyllic sanctuaries, and at present they, like our streets, are sites of violence; is not home a dangerous model for our nation's schools? One advantage of models and metaphors is that they are selective. When William James developed the metaphor of a war against nature, the guns and cannons, the bleeding and dying all dropped out of his imagery. When I propose that our schools be homelike, I have in mind ideal, not dysfunctional homes. Another virtue of models and metaphors is that they can with impunity represent the ideal case. In likening the teacher to a gardener, Rousseau assumed a green thumb. In envisioning schools as communities, Dewey imagined not the worst case—not Salem, Massachusetts, in the days of the witch hunts, not Nazi Germany or James Jones's Guyana— but the best. In recommending that school be a moral equivalent of home, I also assume the best: a home that is warm and loving and neither physically nor psychologically abusive; and a family that believes in and strives for the equality of the sexes.

In the Casa dei Bambini in Rome both girls and boys carried those soup tureens. But listen to what a second-grade boy, vintage 1975, said to Rafaela Best: "I'll starve to death before I'll cook." Over the course of four years, Best watched a group of elementary school children in the Central Atlantic region of the United States learn what she called the "second curriculum"—the one that teaches each sex "how to perform according to conventional gender norms." Coming to know the children as intimately as Montessori wanted teachers to know their pupils, Best reported in *We've All Got Scars* that although most of the boys did not master this material by the end of first grade, in the next two years the majority became proficient in it. The ones who did not grasp the norms or were simply unable or unwilling to meet them were scorned by the other boys and excluded from their club. These outcasts were not necessarily shunned by the girls in the class, but they were perceived as losers by themselves as well as by those who had passed the various tests of masculinity. One of those tests was a scorn for things domestic. When asked how he planned to keep his house clean and have food to eat the boy who would die rather than cook replied, "I'll get a wife for that."

If Best's boys are representative, the Schoolhome will have to do more than teach children of all races, cultures, and nationalities to live in the same world. The boys will have to learn that domesticity is everyone's business. Or does the cultural denigration of home and domesticity make this prospect a utopian dream?

There can be no doubt that the cultural climate in the United States at the end of the twentieth century is a chilly one for both the work and the values of even an ideal home. However, this reality does not so much militate against the metaphor or model of home as it mandates a revaluation of domesticity. For when home and family are debunked, denigrated, and devalued, far more than equality of the sexes is at stake. The next generation itself is at risk. That is why, after elaborating in Chapters 2 and 3 the concept of a moral equivalent of home, in Chapter 4 I will discuss our culture's negative assessment of things domestic and ask what the Schoolhome can do to counteract it.

A concept of school as home may still seem utopian. Even if a revaluation of domesticity is accomplished, won't the world itself have to change before our schoolhouses can be turned into Schoolhomes? Can the kind of refocusing of attention and reorienting of practice that the metaphor of school as home requires occur if the nation remains as it is? An occasional Schoolhome can exist in the world as we know it, but a general transformation of American education will have

to be accompanied by a refocusing of attention and a reorienting of practice in the nation itself. That is why in Chapter 5
I explore and reinterpret in light of present realities the founding fathers' vision of this nation as home. That is why that
chapter also contains a remapping of the relationship of school
and world and a new definition of education for citizenship.

2

Culture and Curriculum

I [asked] Gale what the hearing people in town had thought of the deaf people.

"Oh," he said, "they didn't think anything about them, they were just like everyone else." "But how did people communicate with them—by writing everything down?" "No," said Gale, surprised that I should ask such an obvious question. "You see, everyone here spoke sign language."

Nora Ellen Groce, *Everyone Here Spoke Sign Language*

Describing how she and her schoolmates felt upon returning forty years later to the site of the Czech school in England that they had attended during World War II, Vera Gissing spoke in her memoir, *Pearls of Childhood*, of "an indefinable bond which makes us 'a family'—a special and unique group of brothers and sisters." Perhaps no children ever needed a moral equivalent of home as badly as Gissing and her friends, all of them refugees from Hitler and many of them in England without their families. Yet a school does not have to be a boarding school, as hers was, to be a surrogate home. It does not have to have been designed for a homogeneous population either.

Take out your binoculars and train them on the Schoolhome site. Do you see those people heading for the makeshift hut? With construction under way, parents have come to register their children, and some youngsters even seem to be registering themselves. Apparently word has spread that this school will be their second home. They do not seem the least bit daunted by the fact that the Schoolhome faces an enormous challenge since no common tongue binds all our children and no common culture makes them kin.

As long ago as 1983 the sociologist Sara Lawrence Lightfoot reported in *The Good High School* that at the public high school in Brookline, Massachusetts, a relatively affluent suburb of Boston, the 10 percent of the student body who spoke English as a second language represented fifty-five native languages originating in twenty-five countries. Thirty percent of the student body was minority, the largest proportion being Asian with that category including Chinese, Japanese, Korean, Indian, and Iranian. Twelve percent of the total was black. At the John F. Kennedy High School outside New York City, the student body was 40 percent Hispanic, 35 percent black, 2 percent Asian. Eight hundred students were enrolled in Spanish-speaking sections of its English as a second language program, but the program also accommodated native speakers of Russian, Albanian, Chinese, Vietnamese, Korean, and other languages.

In 1987–88, when Samuel Freedman entered the world of Seward Park High School, 155 freshmen required bilingual education or courses in English as a second language and nine of ten continuing students lived in non-English-speaking families. At the school in Holyoke, Massachusetts, that Tracy Kidder studied, 314 of 620 students were Hispanic. All told, less than 45 percent of the children were white.

As I write, California's population is 22 percent Hispanic and close to 40 percent nonwhite. In Massachusetts, only 23 percent of the students attending the Boston public schools are white. In 1990 the *New York Review of Books* began an article on the transformation of the American population: "Each year, this country becomes less white, less 'European,' and less tightly bound by a single language."

Dewey's question in 1899 was, What radical change in school suffices when home has been transformed? The question a century later is, How can we create a moral equivalent of home in which all our children feel at home?

Turn your glasses now on that group of teachers sitting under the big oak tree. In preparation for the Schoolhome's opening they are discussing a book by the anthropologist Nora

Ellen Groce. As Montessori's account of the Casa dei Bambini led me to the discovery of an idea of school very different from the one we now embrace, Groce's story of the deaf inhabitants of Martha's Vineyard suggested to me a very different model of culture and curriculum.

Driving Groce around the Vineyard in 1978, one of its oldest residents pointed out Jedidiah's house: "He used to fish and farm some. He was one of the best dory men on the Island, and that was pretty good, considering he had only one hand." "What happened to the other one?" Groce asked. "Lost it in a mowing machine accident when he was a teenager," Gale Huntington replied. As an afterthought he added, "He was deaf and dumb too." But this was not due to the accident. "He was born that way," Gale assured her. He then showed Groce Jedidiah's brother's house: "He was considered a very wealthy man—at least by Chilmark standards. Come to think of it, he was deaf and dumb too." How did people communicate with deaf people, Groce asked. Did they write everything down? "No," Gale said in some surprise at the question. "You see, everyone here spoke sign language."

The record shows that the deaf inhabitants of the island were fully integrated into Vineyard society: they were active in town government and the local militia, they owned stores, at least one was a minister. How is this possible? In the "up-Island" section of Martha's Vineyard the hearing people were bilingual. Instead of deaf citizens having to learn to negotiate the spoken language of the majority, or else resort to the written word, sign language was part of the hearing majority's curriculum. They learned at an early age to communicate with the minority in their own "tongue." Deaf people were not considered handicapped; indeed, were not even thought of as belonging to a group called "the deaf." Asked if she knew anything that was similar about Isaiah and David, a woman in her nineties replied that they were both good fishermen. Prodded by Groce about their being deaf she said, "Yes, come to think of it, I guess they both were."

"The most important lesson to be learned from Martha's

Vineyard," Groce wrote, "is that disabled people can be full and useful members of a community if the community makes an effort to include them." Hailing her for showing that "handicaps" are a culture's creations, reviewers agreed. To my mind, *Everyone Here Spoke Sign Language* contains an even more important lesson. I take the Martha's Vineyard story to be a parable for our time, its lessons pertaining to curriculum and culture, school and society.

I

Though we see the same world, we see it with different eyes.

Virginia Woolf, *Three Guineas*

A moving defense of American schooling is found in Richard Rodriguez's widely acclaimed educational autobiography, *Hunger of Memory*, published in 1982. Rodriguez grew up in California, the third of four children in a Spanish-speaking family. Upon entering first grade he could understand perhaps fifty English words. Within the year his teachers convinced his parents to speak only English at home and Rodriguez soon became fluent in the language. By the time he graduated from elementary school with citations galore and entered high school, he had read hundreds of books. He went on to attend Stanford University and, twenty years after his parents' decision to abandon their native tongue, he sat in the British Museum writing a Ph.D. dissertation in English literature.

Rodriguez's story is of the cultural assimilation of a Mexican-American and of his initiation into the "high" culture of the West. After learning to speak English he proceeded to acquire a liberal education. History, literature, science, mathematics, philosophy: Rodriguez studied these and made them his own, in the process becoming not just an unhyphenated American but, by any standard, a well-educated man.

Hunger of Memory is a success story, there is no doubt about it. When he went to school Rodriguez had his work cut out for him. This dark-skinned Mexican-American from a lower-class background had to learn to see the world through the eyes of another. Whether the lenses he had to get used to wearing were provided by science or the humanities, whether they were made for distance viewing or close work, they were all ground by the educated white man and for the educated white man.

To a lesser extent mine is also a success story. Long before Rodriguez entered college I studied roughly the same curriculum as he did and also tried to embrace it. For me, however, there were some recalcitrant subjects. As a government major concentrating in political theory, I found myself becoming increasingly alienated, although that word was certainly not in my vocabulary at the time, from almost everything I was reading. One day in my senior year my thesis advisor, genuinely puzzled, said to me: "Why don't girls understand politics?" Mortified, but knowing that he was right in my case and not at all sure that any of the other female government majors I knew—there were not very many of us—understood politics either, I had no ready reply.

Had *Three Guineas* been on our reading lists, I would at least have been able to say in my own defense and theirs that politics had always been and still was a man's profession. Had Emma Goldman's autobiography been assigned in my tutorial sessions along with Lincoln Steffens's, I would have been able to protest that I did after all feel kinship with some actors in the field. Had Charlotte Perkins Gilman's *Women and Economics* been required reading, I might even have been able to begin analyzing my plight. As it was, I had to wait well over a quarter of a century to do this. Only with the publication of Susan Okin's *Women in Western Political Thought* in 1979 did I learn what those great political theorists whose works I pored over as an undergraduate had said about people like me. Only upon reading an essay on women's rights by the Canadian philosopher Lorenne Clark did I discover that my field of concentration's very definition of the political realm placed me, along with children, in "the ontological basement." Only in doing my own research on the educational ideals held up for women by Plato and Rousseau did I see how lopsided my earlier instruction in their political philosophies had been.

In *The Road from Coorain* Jill Ker Conway described her curriculum as a student in the history honors program at the University of Sydney:

> I read *The Origin of the Family, Private Property and the State,* treating its subject as though it were about some distant and different race rather than my own sex. Certainly it reminded me of my mother's outraged complaints at her investments and the product of her labor being subsumed in my father's estate, but I had unthinkingly taken on the identity of the male writer and intellect present in all that I was reading, and did not take in emotionally that the subordination Engels wrote about applied to me. Obtusely, I did not pay heed to the fact that I was the only woman taking history honors that year, or how unusual I seemed to all my friends because I was aspiring to excel academically.

Engels's treatise on the family was not even on my reading lists. Having no teachers to identify with in college and no reading materials that spoke to me from a woman's point of view, I ended up blaming myself for my ignorance of the basic subject matter of my chosen field of study and admiring those men with whom I studied for my general examinations for being as self-confident and masterful as I was self-conscious and timid.

Rodriguez and I both became alienated without realizing it: he from his family, the Spanish language, his Mexican roots; I from my experience of growing up female in America and my heritage as a woman. I need hardly say that neither of us suffered as much from our educations as others have and still do. Just how many of those students in Chris Zajak's and Jessica Siegel's schools are unable to establish rapport with a curriculum that does not reach out to them no one really knows. But when I hear about young people retreating into their groups and themselves, I can readily understand why they have dropped out of school figuratively, if not literally. I can see why, having failed to find themselves reflected in the norm, they feel like—and in increasing numbers act and live like—outsiders in their own land.

Patricia, a low-income young woman in a New York City comprehensive public high school, told the sociologist Michelle Fine: "I just can't concentrate in school, thinkin' about my mother gettin' beat up last night. He scares me too but I just don't understand why she stays." How ill-matched her yearning to understand the world she lives in and her school curriculum! Even the excluded women and men who are not so disaffected as to become school's and culture's dropouts stand to suffer from a curriculum that assimilates all human experience and accomplishments to that of one relatively small group.

Trying to persuade Harvard University to strengthen its Afro-American Studies department, twenty students held a "sleep-in" outside University Hall one 1990 November night. "I honestly believed, until I was in around ninth grade, that Africans were running around in loincloths, waiting for Tarzan," a junior from South Carolina told the *Boston Globe* columnist Derrick Jackson. "Until I was 14, my only vision of Africans was being taught by white men in helmets how not to burp at the table and how to pray. I never questioned it," a student from Detroit confessed. A young woman who had attended Exeter Academy reported that, in all, three days of her American History course had been devoted to African-American affairs—two to slavery and one to Malcolm X. "I want to learn something about everybody," a junior from Los Angeles said. "That's why I came to Harvard. But I want to learn something about myself, too."

In 1895 the *Boston Sunday Herald* described life on Martha's Vineyard:

You make a neighborly call—they don't have such things as afternoon teas. The spoken language and the sign language will be so mingled in the conversation that you pass from one to the other, or use both at once, almost unconsciously. Half the family speak, very probably, half do not, but the mutes are not uncomfortable in their deprivation, the community has adjusted itself to the situation so perfectly.

Over on the promontory, at the Schoolhome, some eager teachers are planning next year's curriculum. Instead of allowing the greater part of the American population to feel uncomfortable and even deprived, they want to adjust the Schoolhome's course of study to the situation. That is why they are trying to design a curriculum that tells Juanita, Lun Cheung, Patricia, and these Harvard students about themselves and are seeking ways to insure that everyone else knows about them too.

Do you see that young African-American man? He is reading aloud from *Three Guineas:* "Though we see the same world, we see it with different eyes." He says to the other teachers, "By 'we' Virginia Woolf meant women, but her point holds equally for Asians, Hispanics, African-Americans, Native Americans, immigrants from the Near and Middle East." Reversing Woolf's sentence but not her sentiment, the teachers are now choosing as one of the Schoolhome's mottos: "Though we see it with different eyes, we see the same world." They are determined to fit themselves and their students with different cultural lenses much as the schoolhouse prescribed a physicist's, a psychologist's, an economist's, a historian's for Rodriguez. They believe, and I think they are right, that it is possible to treasure the uniqueness of a whole range of perspectives without losing sight of commonalities.

One teacher proposes that whatever cultures the various classes in the Schoolhome study, the focus should be on the great questions. He is telling his colleagues that issues such as life and death, good and evil, self and other, nature and culture, are not the white man's private property. Another teacher says that she wants her class to read Ntozake Shange's *Betsey Brown.* "Wouldn't it be exciting to juxtapose *Tom Sawyer,* or else *Huckleberry Finn,* and *Betsey Brown,*" a third teacher interjects. "If your class does Huck," another ventures, "mine will do *Little Women.*" "And if yours does *Little Women,*" another voice chimes in, "mine will do *A Raisin in the Sun.*"

African-American girl, St. Louis, 1959; white girls, New England, Civil War period; black family, Chicago ghetto, early

1950s; white boy, Mississippi River, slavery years. "Do we seek out the great questions or emphasize the theme that all four works share?" someone asks. "What theme is that?" a latecomer to the meeting inquires. "Growing Up," the first speaker offers. "Becoming Educated," another suggests. "Both of the above," the rest say in unison.

Can a course of study be coherent when the lives and experiences of so many different kinds of people are included? For a faculty that is willing to work together, curricular cohesion is not an insurmountable problem.

Not long ago I visited two extraordinary educational settings. The curriculum of Shakespeare & Company's Workshop for Theater Professionals was divided into four subjects— voice, movement, fight, and text—but, considering them conceptually interconnected, the faculty had arranged so much practical carryover from one class to the next that, as I heard a student say to a staff member, "You can't even tell when one class ends and another begins. One just bleeds into the next." In contrast, the curriculum of the summer institute for teachers held at the University of New Hampshire and sponsored by the National Endowment for the Humanities defied description in terms of separate subjects. Drawing its primary content from the fields of history and literature but also incorporating material from art and theater, sociology and education, the program on Women in Nineteenth-Century American Culture represented another kind of unity altogether.

Neither one of these breathtaking programs was designed for general consumption, and each had a specialized purpose that simplified the task of integration. But such examples demonstrate that if educators are determined to construct coherent, unified entities, they can do so. Besides, a nation with as diverse a population as ours does not need a unified curriculum nearly as much as it does a *unifying* one.

II

You all know why we are here, when we ought to be building our barns or mending our huts, when we should be putting our compounds in order. My father used to say to me: "Whenever you see a toad jumping in broad daylight, then know that something is after its life."

Chinua Achebe, *Things Fall Apart*

The most effective recipe one could invent for the fragmentation of culture is the curricular fragmentation we have come to know, one critic of American schooling has said. Has the curriculum of our nation's schools fallen apart? It is incontrovertible that it, like the American family and the American population, has changed enormously in the last decades. *The Shopping Mall High School*, a report of a five-year study of American secondary schools, leaves little room for doubt about the proliferation of courses at the secondary school level. The vivid portraits Lightfoot presented in *The Good High School* show that not all our secondary schools are shopping malls, their teachers salespeople, their courses products, their students consumers. But even her "good enough" high schools offer many more subjects than they once did and seldom, if ever, try to pull them all together.

One might expect the elementary school curriculum to be less fragmented, yet the accounts of elementary school language arts and mathematics in John Goodlad's *A Place Called School* make it clear that here too multiplication, or perhaps I should say division, is the order of the day. In 1987 the writer Cynthia Ozick noted that the hypothesis set forth by C. P. Snow almost thirty years before is no longer valid. His point was that science and the humanities formed two separate cultures. Hers was not that they have merged or even that, as Snow himself hoped would happen, scientists and humanists have begun speaking to each other. It was that instead of constituting a single culture, science has become a "multi-divergent venture—dozens and dozens of disciplines, each one nearly a separate nation with its own governance, psychology, entelechy." She described the humanities, too, as "multiplying, fragmented, in hot pursuit of split ends." Ozick might have been depicting language arts, a subject originally introduced to overcome problems of disconnection, rather than science and the humanities. Reading, composition, handwriting, spelling, grammar, speaking, listening may not quite be independent domains, but for the most part they are treated as autonomous subjects. If language arts seems to some to be an artificial subject that was never truly unified, one need but turn to elementary mathematics to discover more split ends. Reporting that our schools teach addition, subtraction, multiplication, division, fractions, decimals, percentages, money, measurement year after year, Goodlad remarks with regret though not surprise that "the common bonds relating each topic to the preceding ones were rarely revealed."

The reports of curricular multiplicity and disconnection cannot be ignored, but we need to ask ourselves if restoring the American curriculum of the past is the best policy. Critics of American education interpret the multiplication of courses in the last decades as a pandering to the baser instincts and provincial tastes of our youth. They say the new courses have been designed for lazy students with no ambition. They call these courses frills and imply that they are devoid of intellectual content. These critics would have us believe that only the subjects they themselves studied can yield genuine learning.

It scarcely needs saying that a more inclusive curriculum is not necessarily a better one. We have heard too many stories of subjects so banal, so trivial, as to be unworthy of study. Yet in a society in the process of changing color, can a course in Third World philosophy like the one at my university be considered frivolous? In a nation with a history of slavery and a continuing record of racial division and inequality, are the study of African-American history and literature, and the inclusion of slave narratives on the reading lists of American history and literature courses, the irrelevancies they are described as? In a land in which rape is rampant, most victims of sexual abuse in childhood are girls, and women are subjected to sexual harassment at home, at school, and at work, is it sensible to say that courses that represent and analyze women's history, lives, and experiences are parochial and take too subjective a point of view?

Focusing attention on the shattering of the curriculum they themselves studied, the critics ignore the issues that were primary for an earlier generation of educational reformers. From the late 1960s through the 1970s the American curriculum was damned for being irrelevant, not for being fragmented. Its remoteness from·the concerns of society was deplored, not the disconnection of the various subjects from one another. And when its completeness was questioned, the charge referred to the exclusion of subject matter relating to the background and experiences of students, not to a lack of internal cohesion.

As times change, so do perceptions of what is wrong. Nevertheless, the inward gaze of the present generation of critics keeps both them and us from noticing the gaps in the curriculum of their youth. The course of study they so admire had no space for portraying African-Americans as full human beings—in American history they were seen first as slaves and then as the objects of Lincoln's Emancipation Proclamation, elsewhere they were invisible. In it women were never seen crossing the bridge into the public world or even working in their own private homes or the homes of others. There was no room reserved for Native American cultures and no space in which the poor, whether male or female, of color or of no color, were accurately depicted.

The restorationist program of end-of-century educational reformers calls to mind the tale one of Okonkwo's wives tells her daughter in *Things Fall Apart* by the Nigerian novelist Chinua Achebe. She tells about the time all the birds were invited to a feast in the sky. Seeing their preparations for the great day, Tortoise decided to go too. "But he had no wings," interrupts the daughter. "Be patient," replies her mother. "That is the story."

Although the birds distrusted Tortoise he had such a sweet tongue that he soon persuaded each of them to give him a feather with which to make wings. Sure enough, on the flight to the sky Tortoise deceived the birds. Claiming that the custom at great parties was for guests to take new names, he chose the name, "All of you." Upon arriving he turned to the birds and said: "You remember that my name is *All of you.* The custom here is to serve the spokesman first and the others later. They will serve you when I have eaten." After Tortoise ate for all of them the angry birds, having had only the bones to pick on, flew home taking with them the feathers they had lent him. Tortoise then asked Parrot, the last bird to leave, to tell his wife—that is, Tortoise's wife—to lay out soft things for him to land on. But Parrot, upon arriving home, told her to bring out all the hard things in the house. So it was that when Tortoise jumped back to earth he fell and fell and finally crashed on his compound, making a noise as loud as a cannon. "Did he die?" asked the daughter. "No," replied the mother. "His shell broke into pieces but there was a great medicine man in the neighborhood. Tortoise's wife sent for him and he gathered all the bits of shell and stuck them together. That is why Tortoise's shell is not smooth."

Now Tortoise was a sly, ungrateful creature determined to make mischief. Knowing the trouble he caused and how he exploited others, his wife could have refrained from calling in the medicine man. Perhaps, however, Tortoise treated his wife well. Possibly she was able to discern in him the noble inner nature he said was his. Whatever the situation of Tortoise's wife may have been, the critics of education certainly love the curriculum of their youth and believe in its nobility. They have told us so repeatedly. They have said how well versed in the classics their generation was, how extensive its knowledge, how disciplined its minds. Core curricula, great books, lists for cultural literacy: even as they bemoaned the breakdown of the curriculum they had studied in school and college, they proposed strategies for repairing it. The mischief that curriculum did seems to have escaped their notice. And they are as unmoved by its inability to serve all of us as Tortoise's wife was by his betrayal of the birds.

What makes these restorationists so eager to piece back together a curriculum designed for another time and a different people? If they simply objected to the proliferation of subjects, or if what they minded was that the courses in the curriculum are not unified, they would not have to look back with longing at a curriculum that was in place when the overwhelming majority of American children were white and girls were supposed to spend as little time as possible on the other side of Woolf's bridge. They could ask our medicine men to pull the split ends together in some brand new creative way.

In *Liberating Education* Zelda Gamson and her coauthors described how the Federated Learning Communities experiment at the State University of New York at Stony Brook transformed "the nature of the undergraduate experience of academic and social fragmentation to one in which the meaning of community is felt vividly." Grouping a number of existing courses around a broad theme such as world hunger, it had students enroll in these as well as in a seminar and a team-taught core course specially designed to help them integrate the diverse content. Were culture transmitted biologically from one generation to the next, the critics might advise us to emulate examples like this. But it is passed down by education, not by our genes.

The problem the restorationists do not mention is that some of the new courses they disdain reveal Western culture for what it is: an artifact constructed out of materials that are neither as universal, as objective, nor as all-embracing as we once thought. The offerings in black history and women's history, for instance, make it clear that the comprehensive study of our nation's past, American history, misrepresents when it does not entirely neglect the lives, works, and experiences of women and minority men. Those on the psychology of women show that instead of being universal, as claimed, psychology's norms and its narratives of human development have been derived from studies of boys and men. Those on science and society document how the evidence for theories of intelligence has been manipulated so that white males invariably score the highest. The ones on gender and science demonstrate that biology's accounts of nature have mapped society's sex stereotypes onto the animal "kingdom," its studies of primates have consistently made the male the main actor of the troop and the linchpin of that small society, and its predominant account of human cultural evolution has done likewise although there is no more evidence for the theory named Man-the-Hunter than for the one called Woman-the-Gatherer.

This list does not begin to do justice to the situation. For the scholarship incorporated in some of those new school subjects—not all, just some of them—does not simply reveal biases and gaps in the knowledge accumulated by the different disciplines. It casts doubt on the very objectivity of the judgments by which some works of art, literature, history, science, philosophy have been included in the cultural canon and others have been put on the scrap heap. It is not merely that long-lost works by women and by men who are not white have been recovered. It is not even that recent research challenges the portrayals of both groups enshrined in science and history as well as in literature and the arts. Accepted definitions of what constitutes great art and literature and even good science have been called into question. It has been shown that the creation of works in the canon of Western culture has rested on the exploitation of the very people misrepresented in them. And the idea of canonizing any set of works is itself debated.

In *Things Fall Apart* one of the elders of Okonkwo's clan tells a huge crowd: "My father used to say to me: Whenever you see a toad jumping in broad daylight, then know that something is after its life. When I saw you pouring into this meeting from all the quarters of our clan so early in the morning, I knew that something was after our life." Self-appointed elders in our nation have seen a toad jumping in broad daylight. Just as, according to another kinsman, the white man put the knife in the things that held the Ibo together, the knowledge our elders would prohibit, if they could, has put it in the white man's creation. Revealing the incompleteness of Western culture's theories, the partiality of its claims, the bias of its narratives, its disfiguring portraits, this research cuts through the illusion that "the" classics speak for all of us. Exposing arbitrary norms by uncovering alternate ways of seeing, thinking, feeling, acting, and being in the world, it excises the myth that the canon of great works itself is eternal and immutable.

Although the school subjects the restorationists studied when young—mathematics, physics, biology, history, literature, and the like—were themselves treated as separate nations with their own governances, psychologies, and entelechies, they were ruled by an integrative principle as selective as it was unseen. In that former course of study every subject partook of the viewpoint belonging to the construct called Western culture. Our elders know that the new knowledge challenges the white man's definition of what constitutes Western culture. They know that the knowledge that has fallen apart is the white man's creation and that what has been described as "the crisis at the peaks of learning" is nothing less than the fragmentation of what all of us have been taught to call our cultural heritage. They also know that curriculum is what enables knowledge to survive. It passes along the cultural code from one generation to the next as DNA does the genetic.

From the point of view of our elders the problem is not so much the fragmentation of curriculum. It is that if the new scholarship is taught to our nation's young, the knowledge that casts doubt on the objectivity and universality of their definition of Western culture will take root and flourish. They reason that if the offending knowledge can be kept out of the curriculum of our schools and colleges, it will have a short life. Thus, by gluing together that earlier curriculum, they hope to be able simultaneously to pass along their version of Western culture to the next generation and to erase from our cultural memory the very knowledge that exposes its limits.

For better or worse this restorative project has a fatal flaw.

Okonkwo and his clan took the white man's differences from themselves to be disabilities, but there the parallel ends. Because the white man came to dominate and destroy, the Ibo learned to their sorrow that they should not have allowed him to stay. No foreign church or empire is trying to colonize us. In contrast to the Ibo, we have a longstanding commitment to religious pluralism and the toleration of diversity. So that their culture in the broad sense of the term—their social institutions, everyday practices, and belief systems—would not fall apart, the Ibo had to keep out those who looked and acted different, something they could not do. To preserve our own culture we have to ask, How can we find ways to make people who are different from one another feel at home in their own land? We also have to ask how we can make those precious few who meet the white man's norms realize that their home is our home too.

III

Nowhere else in the world could you see such singular pantomimes as are carried on daily from Chilmark back doors. Suppose you live in a lonely farm house and your nearest neighbor is an eighth of a mile away. Your men folk in both houses are fisherfolk, and so you have spyglasses. You go to your door at eleven, say, in the morning. Your neighbor is at hers. You signal to her in the sign language with your glass some question about the catch or the take from the lobster pots or a bit of womanly gossip and then you put your glass to your eye and she waves to you with her glass her reply.

Boston Sunday Herald, 1895

Warning that if American children do not all learn the same body of cultural facts they will not be able to participate in the activities that constitute culture with a small *c,* one educational critic, E. D. Hirsch, Jr., has exhorted the American schoolhouse to teach every child the information compiled by him and his associates. Constituting a concept he has named "cultural literacy," the extensive knowledge he says everyone must have "excludes nobody." Cutting across "generations and social groups and classes," it reaches "beyond the narrow sphere of family, neighborhood, and region" to the nation as a whole.

Hirsch's list is detailed enough to make even as educated a person as Rodriguez quake. Yet although it ranges from abolitionism and abominable snowman to zoning and Zurich, it perpetuates the curricular gaps of the past. How can it do otherwise when its creator assumes that what every American *needs* to know is what every literate American *does* know? True, the "mainstream culture" that the list is said to represent changes over time as new items like DNA enter the current and old ones like Harold Ickes are thrown off. It is, however, the stable elements of our "national vocabulary"— items like George Washington, the Tooth Fairy, the Gettysburg Address, Hamlet, the Declaration of Independence—that are "the most important contents of schooling." Susan B. Anthony and Frederick Douglass are said to fall in this category but, on the whole, women and nonwhite men are not well represented there. They could not possibly be, for literate Americans are only just beginning to learn their names and admire their works and many of those paragons have been strenuously resisting the process.

Dismayed at how little science the literati know, Hirsch breaks his own rule. Whereas cultural literacy is supposed to be a purely descriptive category, in this one case it is prescriptive. If literate Americans do not know blackbody and Brownian motion, escape velocity and lattice structure, wave-particle duality and white dwarf, they should. But why acknowledge only this gap in their learning? Is a shared knowledge of science—if that is what one should call everyone's knowing a set of items on a list—really more important to the nation's welfare at the end of the twentieth century than a shared knowledge of one another? Why require that literate Americans adapt to the special "subnational culture" of science but not to those of women and nonwhite men? Why say that if they do not know Mary Wollstonecraft, Catharine Beecher, Charlotte Perkins Gilman, Emma Goldman, Zora

Neal Hurston, Simone de Beauvoir, Lorraine Hansberry, Franz Fanon, so much the worse for those outsiders? Why not instead say that if they are not acquainted with those important people or with classic texts such as *A Vindication of the Rights of Woman, The Subjection of Women, The Origins of the Family, Private Property and the State, A Treatise on Domestic Economy, Women and Economics, Three Guineas, The Second Sex, Their Eyes Were Watching God, A Raisin in the Sun, The Wretched of the Earth,* they should be?

In Henry James's 1886 novel *The Bostonians,* Basil Ransom says that his interest is in his own sex:

> The masculine character, the ability to dare and endure, to know and yet not fear reality, to look the world in the face and take it for what it is—a very queer and partly very base mixture—that is what I want to preserve, or rather, as I may say, to recover; and I must tell you that I don't in the least care what becomes of you ladies while I make the attempt!

The question is, Do we care what becomes of the women and the nonwhite men who today constitute the greater part of our population?

Calling curricular inclusiveness "anarchy," the restorationists would exclude the very subject matter that would acquaint us with the differences of sex, race, class, ethnicity, religion. They equate curricular inclusiveness with chaos, although to make the curriculum of our schools and colleges receptive to voices and perspectives that have been excluded is no more a prescription for disorder than is any step toward democracy. The democratization of the curriculum undoubtedly introduces a degree of complexity. But complexity is quite different from chaos.

Are our elders justified in saying that the opening up of the American curriculum to a wide range of voices will mean the dilution of quality? No one who has read Achebe's *Things Fall Apart,* Woolf's *Three Guineas,* Zora Neal Hurston's *Their Eyes Were Watching God,* Lorraine Hansberry's *A Raisin in the Sun* can possibly think so. As for the complaint that the inclusion of these works would diminish content, the opposite is true. I, at least, know of no work on the restorationists' list of "the" classics of Western culture that shows the white man putting a knife into clans like Okonkwo's from the standpoint of the victim, none that discusses the white man's past exclusion of the white woman from both his education and his professions, none that represents an African-American woman's repudiation of the roles white society has written for her, none that portrays a ghetto family's agonizing decision to move into a white neighborhood.

Treating a problem of inclusion as one of exclusion, the critics worry about the intellectual purity of their subject matter as much as realtors once did about the racial and religious purity of the people to whom they sold property. Displaying the selfsame exclusionary bent in their recommendations, they equate giving curriculum space to research by and about women and nonwhite men with a lowering of quality and a diminution of content. Bewailing the lack of integration in today's curriculum, they endorse restrictive policies regarding the knowledge and perspectives to be included therein.

Can it be that as some thoughts are best left unspoken, some matters are so sensitive that they are best left unstudied in school? Might bringing new perspectives into the American curriculum hasten the fragmentation of our culture? Were the United States a society whose history held no traces of race, religious, ethnic, and gender discrimination, curricular silence on these issues might not now matter. Had a multiplicity of standpoints long since been incorporated into the construct called Western culture, the differences of race, religion, ethnicity, gender might require no comment. As it is, denial spells denigration. It also spells alienation.

Our elders are quite right to want to bind all of us together, but it is unlikely that the means they have chosen will have this effect. As the standard response to deaf people has been to expect them to conform to the culture of the hearing, the response of the critics of education to our nation's changed school population has been to expect everyone to adopt the white man's point of view, memorize his history, and cherish his achievement. Just as the off-Island strategy has for the most part relegated those who differ from the norm to lives outside the mainstream, so will the strategy the critics have chosen.

The story told in Groce's book is every bit as important for Americans to know as the items on Hirsch's list—far more important, I would venture, than Abominable Snowman, Tooth Fairy, or even Zurich. In fact, I would say that American society has suffered an incalculable loss because the treatment of the deaf population on Martha's Vineyard is one of those items about a minority that has never been considered a part of our cultural heritage. Had it been incorporated into that construct and passed on to the next generation by our schools, those who now persist in wanting to teach our young to see the world, themselves included, through the white man's eyes—the "able-bodied" white man, as it turns out—might be having second thoughts. If literate Americans knew about the Vineyard's response to people who diverged from "the norm" and realized that it had benefited everyone, they might now understand that the inclusion of new voices and viewpoints is precisely what is needed to keep our culture from falling apart.

I should emphasize that on Martha's Vineyard English and sign language were never merged into one single, unitary discourse. Rather, the shared knowledge of these two different ways of speaking—of these two distinct mediums for describing the world, stating intentions, expressing feelings—is what mattered. By fostering communication and social intercourse, this common knowledge managed to integrate into the larger community those who would otherwise have remained outsiders. Even so, in one important respect the Vineyard case does not match our own. There, everyone's knowing sign language made the difference. Although some deaf inhabitants may have been lip readers, the comprehension and production of spoken English were not required of all. The teachers in the Schoolhome, in contrast, realize that it is as important for everyone to have a knowledge of the white man's culture as it is for the white man to have knowledge of cultures and perspectives other than his. They believe that as he learns to look through our eyes at himself and the world, we can do no less for one another and for him.

On Martha's Vineyard, up-Island society was enriched by everyone's knowing sign language. As Groce discovered, its use "fostered a free and easy exchange of ideas and concerns among all members of the community." The community also gained because instead of an "outcast" population draining its resources, its pool of talent was significantly increased. In addition, the hearing had at their command an alternate mode of communication.

It is an understatement to say that Groce's tale belongs on the list of what every American schoolchild should know. If our nation took this model to heart and incorporated into the curriculum of its schools the lives, works, history, and perspectives of those who are now excluded, all of us might begin to feel at home. In addition, our "cultural capital" would more than double.

IV

All that is implicit is a commitment to what is thought valuable.

R. S. Peters, *Ethics and Education,* 1967

Over on the promontory, the Schoolhome's doors have opened and some students are becoming as wrapped up in Huck's adventures as the teenagers already are in the life of the Younger family. But in another room some boys are refusing to read *Little Women.* "It's stupid," one of them complains. "My father said he never read it and he doesn't want me to read it either," a second boy says. "He says I should be reading something good like *Huckleberry Finn* or *Moby-Dick.*" "My father told me not to read *Huckleberry Finn.* It calls my people 'nigger,'" a black boy interposes. "Huck's turn will come," the teacher reassures the one child. Turning to the other she says, "Some of the things we'll talk about are what reasons Mark Twain might have had for putting that word in Huck's mouth, how you and your father feel when you read it, and why it is a bad idea to use it in real life." Only then does she ask the first two boys, "What do you think is wrong with reading *Little Women*?" "It's about girls," several boys shout. The silence their outburst occasions is not broken until a girl plaintively says, "Well, Huck is a boy and the girls are going to read about him." "That's different," the first boy responds. "Everyone reads about boys. Only girls read about girls."

The boys have tradition on their side, but seeing them wriggle uncomfortably in their seats, one of the girls in the group blurts out: "What are you so afraid of? Jo isn't going to bite you." Her question finally releases the tongue of a boy who has been silent: "Jo's not so bad. I wish my sister was like her." The teacher sighs with relief and asks, "How many people here have sisters?" "I have four," one boy admits as the others groan their sympathy. "Are any of them like Jo?" "One is and one is stuck up like Amy."

Forgetting his announcement that he would under no circumstances read the book, one of the recalcitrant boys now takes the floor: "Do you remember when Amy went through the ice on the river and it was Jo's fault? Well, my mother told me to go to the store and made me take my baby brother along. And I got mad at him so I pretended I didn't notice when he started to cross the street against the light." "What happened?" someone finally says. "He almost got killed," is his barely audible reply. "Has anyone else had experiences like the March sisters?" the teacher inquires. "This is sort of like what happened to Meg with the jelly," a boy responds. "My mother gave me money to buy a pizza for supper and I put it in the oven to heat it up in the box." "In the box!" everyone gasps. "In the box and our house almost burned down because I turned on the TV and forgot."

Did those teachers who decided to place *Little Women* beside *Huckleberry Finn* in the Schoolhome curriculum anticipate resistance from the boys? They certainly should have.

Tracing the mastery of the second curriculum by those six-, seven-, and eight-year-old boys, Rafaela Best showed how closely the macho ideal to which they aspired was linked to a fear of feminization. The excluded boys "were regarded as being like girls and not like real men," she reported. For a third-grader to be called a sissy "was a fate worse than death." To be a crybaby or to be oriented to one's mother or female teacher was inexcusable. Kenny, one of the "losers" in the class, liked doing housekeeping tasks in school for his teacher and enjoyed receiving her hugs in return. Jason, another loser, cried frequently. And Edward, whose behavior in school was far too perfect, was not good at games. Fighting, or at least the willingness to fight when challenged, was one essential ingredient of masculinity in the "winners'" eyes. Playing well and playing rough was another. Engaging in "anti-establishment" activities ranging from throwing mudballs at houses and cars to stuffing paper in the school locks was a third. All three aspects of seven- and eight-year-old machismo were valued in large part because their opposites betokened femininity.

What is so bad about being like a girl? In 1989 Derrick Jackson told his *Boston Globe* readers about sixth-graders in a public school who had been asked to tell the first word that came to mind about the other sex. The girls said: "Fine. Jerks. Conceited. Ugly. Crazy. Dressy. Sexy. Dirty minds. Boring. Rude. Cute. Stuck up. Desperate. Sexually abusive. Punks." The boys said: "Pumping ('big tits'). Nasty. Vagina. Dope bodies (big breasts and behinds). Door knob (breasts). Hooker. Skeezer ('a girl who will "do it" with 50 guys')."

There is nothing idiosyncratic about those images the boys invoked. Here is what Margaret Clark, in *The Great Divide*, reported that primary school girls in Australia have to say on the subject:

There's a group of boys in our class who always tease us and call us—you know, dogs, aids, slut, moll and that.

This boy used to call us big-tits and period-bag and used to punch us in the breasts.

They take things off us and drag us into the boys' toilets.

They call us rabies, dogs, aids.

They reckon I'm a dog. My brother gave me to them. He said, "Oh, come here, I've got a pet for you. Do you want my dog?" And he gave me to them as a pet dog.

Perhaps the boys in the Schoolhome believe that people unconsciously adopt the attitudes and values of the characters in stories and copy their behavior. After all, in the Just State Plato outlined in the *Republic*, stories about heroes running away from battle were to be censored. Maybe these boys are genuinely scared that just by reading *Little Women* they will turn into girls. Possibly they are simply afraid of being found guilty by association with these fictional females. The truth of the matter is that in their eyes *Little Women* has two strikes against it: the protagonists are girls and the book's action takes place on the near side of Woolf's bridge. Meg visits a rich friend, Beth delivers gifts to a needy neighbor, Jo befriends the boy next door, Amy burns the book Jo is writing, the girls and their mother celebrate Christmas.

I wish I could say that those boys in the Schoolhome are unusual in asking to be excused from study of the domestic "sphere" of society. In fact, there is no place for this topic in the curriculum our elders want to restore. Filled with knowledge about the public world across the bridge, it has no space for the appreciation and understanding of the world of the private home. Take my own subject, philosophy. Although many of the great philosophers in the Western tradition— Plato, Aristotle, Locke, Rousseau, Hegel, Marx, for instance— have put forth views on the family, this topic was not included in course offerings in the past and rarely is even now. Consider politics. In this intellectual discipline the family exists in the ontological basement. Defining the very subject matter of politics in relation to the public or civic sphere, the field effectively rules the domestic out of its curriculum. Until very recently history followed suit: it considered the world across Woolf's bridge its only concern. And so it goes. Domestic arts, such as quilting and weaving, do not fall under the definition of "fine art" and, as a consequence, are excluded from general study. "Domestic novels" by women such as Alcott and Harriet Beecher Stowe are not considered good enough literature to be included in English courses. Domestic science is no more thought to be a science than a pink elephant is thought to be an elephant.

Does the silence regarding things domestic matter? That last big wave of educational critics directed the nation's attention to the hidden curriculum of schooling. Transmitted by school's architecture, its seating arrangements, its rules about how to walk in the halls, the language its teachers use, the art work on the walls, the instructional games children play—in other words, by any and everything but school's "formal" curriculum—its lessons convey attitudes and values to our children without their knowing it. With the advent of Black Studies and Women's Studies in the 1970s and 1980s we learned that negative messages are also sent by the silences of the formal curriculum.

The power of curricular silence is immense. The British philosopher R. S. Peters was right: whether or not what is taught in school and college is in fact worthwhile, in calling something "education" we place our seal of approval on it. Not that education always lives up to its reputation. Peters knew that some teaching is good and some bad, that some curricula are well designed and others are not. When he said, "All that is implicit is a commitment to what is thought valuable," his point was that although the content of education differs from one culture to the next, whatever it is that a culture chooses to call education will comprise the information it takes to be important for young people to know and the activities it considers worthwhile. Peters did not pursue the logic of his own argument but it is easily done. Just as the inclusion of something in the curriculum—a topic, a body of fact and theory, a perspective—signifies the value placed on it, exclusion bespeaks the culture's devaluation of it. In addition, the act of exclusion serves to reinforce that assessment.

The silences about domesticity constitute a hidden curriculum in anti-domesticity, one that I learned well in school. Why else did it take me, the daughter of a junior high school home economics teacher, such a long time—many decades, in fact—to admit that the processes and activities housed in the private home are capable of providing occasions for intellectual nourishment? Why did it take me even longer to realize that the reason home and family have been banished from liberal study is not that they are unimportant? On the contrary, one of the main reasons these topics are considered unimportant by people like me is that they have been banished.

No explanation for this gap in the American curriculum of yore is ever given, but one is not difficult to construct. Our society expects school to equip children for life on the other side of the bridge. Or, to put it another way, the function our culture assigns school is that of preparing the nation's young to carry out the economic and political tasks and activities located in the public world. Given this clear objective and the fact that children begin their lives in the private world of the home, school sees its mission as that of transforming inhabitants of the one world into denizens of the other. The outlines of this process are clearly discernible in Rodriguez's autobiography. Barely hidden beneath the success story he told lies a narrative of loss. As Rodriguez's educational journey progressed, as he learned to take his place in the public world, he experienced a diminution of intimacy in his family life, a distancing from family members, a turning away from the everyday world of home.

Given school's official function and the fact that in the fairly recent past we could count on most private homes and families to teach their own young about life on the near side of Woolf's bridge, the absence of domesticity from the curriculum of the American schoolhouse is understandable. Unfortunately, we can no longer count on home for this educational contribution. The curtailment of its services might not matter if we had entered an era of communal living and childrearing. But although in the United States at the end of the twentieth century men and women alike go out to work each morning, almost all of us go home again at night.

Those teachers over there on the promontory know that as a moral equivalent of home, the Schoolhome must take up the slack. That is why they have designed a curriculum that will prepare girls and boys alike for life on both sides of the bridge. *Little Women* did not offend the sensibilities of those young men merely because its action takes place in and around the private home, however. Its "problem" was that Alcott pulls her readers into a female world as seen through female eyes. Just as white readers of *Things Fall Apart* come to know the Ibo culture from the standpoint of black African men, male readers of *Little Women* are brought to see domestic culture in the Civil War period from the standpoint of white girls and women.

Should the Schoolhome be encouraging this sort of "gender crossing"? Does it not place boys at risk? The case is quite the opposite. Since the near side of the bridge has always been and still is inhabited by both sexes, it is unreasonable, if not actually irrational, to deny boys and men knowledge of it. Given that the ability to take the point of view of another is a basic element of morality itself, it is unconscionable—I would say positively immoral—to deprive them of the opportunity of identifying with the other half of humanity. Besides, how can girls feel at home in a culture whose curriculum excludes their perspective? How can boys respect girls if they are never encouraged to see the world as girls do? How in these circumstances can girls respect themselves?

Deaf people were integrated into Martha's Vineyard society because the up-Islanders were willing to count as part of their cultural heritage—their "cultural capital," some prefer to call it—what elsewhere was thought to belong to a different and inferior culture, or to fall outside the gates of culture altogether. The restorationist agenda treats domesticity in the way off-Islanders treated sign language: as not belonging to culture, or else as a quaint habit of that different and definitely inferior group called women.

There is an extraordinary irony here. In the name of preserving the achievements of our past and transmitting to future generations the knowledge that the West has accumulated, our elders have automatically discounted half of the West's heritage—the portion relating to home and domesticity and to the women into whose keeping culture historically placed them. Education's critics have also ignored the heritage accumulated by men of color. As a result, the capital that the restorationists want to pass down to the next generation is a small fraction of what has been amassed over the centuries.

V

> Don't say: "There must be something common, or they would not be called 'games'"—but look and see whether there is anything common to all.—For if you look at them you will not see something that is common to all, but similarities, relationships, and a whole series of them at that.
>
> Ludwig Wittgenstein, *Philosophical Investigations*

At a feast Okonkwo provided for the people of his mother's tribe, an old man said: "I fear for the younger generation, for you people . . . As for me, I have only a short while to live, and so have Uchendu and Unachukwu and Emefo. But I fear for you young people because you do not understand how strong is the bond of kinship. You do not know what it is to speak with one voice . . . I fear for you; I fear for the clan." The authors of those books on American education that were published in the 1980s expressed the same kind of fears for the younger generation. Claiming for their truncated construct of Western culture the name Tortoise took for himself, these elders attributed to the curriculum of their childhood an adhesive power it may once have had but that, what with our new population and the presence of so many women in the procession across the bridge, it certainly does not now possess. Excluding points of view other than the white man's, omitting aspects of the world he could not see, ignoring sites in which he did not feel at home, it does not reach out and touch all of us. Failing this, how can it bind everyone together?

At the University of New Hampshire Summer Institute on Women in Nineteenth-Century American Culture participants could not get over how relevant the subject matter was to their past existence and their present lives. Institute members described their experience there as "a homecoming." It provided "the missing link," they told me. It gave them back their "history." Clearly, that curriculum did far more than allot space to a group that has been systematically excluded. I can well imagine a curriculum's including women's voices and perspectives yet being so remote from students' lives and concerns as to be meaningless to them. This one spanned that seemingly unbridgeable chasm between private concerns and public knowledge.

Talking with Michelle Fine about Sylvia, a teacher said: "She is having some problems. She can't come to school because her boyfriend waits for her every morning and fights with her. He threatens her." From the standpoint of the curriculum of that urban high school, the domestic violence many students faced daily was a well-kept secret. Thought to be the business of the school psychologists and guidance counselors—each responsible for five hundred adolescents—the private lives of students were deemed irrelevant to the question of what should be taught. "I have to drop out to care for my grandmother," Portia informed Fine. When Fine consulted a guidance counselor about this she was told: "If Portia is concerned about her future she needs not to get so involved in her family but worry about herself."

Long ago the American schoolhouse adopted the unwritten policy that students should leave their worries on the doorsteps of their private homes. The point was not simply that in this way children would arrive in school with their minds clean slates for their teachers to write on. It also made possible the complete separation of the curriculum of school from that of home.

No doubt at the time it seemed a sensible division of labor for the hidden partner in education to help its own young work through their private problems. Did not school have its hands full preparing them to solve public ones? But if it was once warranted, the recent changes in home—especially the great domestic absence—call into question this institution's ability to handle such a task. That private problems so often originate in private homes makes me wonder how realistic the policy was in any case. So does the fact, recorded in that feminist slogan of the 1970s "The personal is the political," that so-called private problems are often rooted in societal practices. As if these were not good enough reasons to abandon a policy that purposely disconnects curriculum from the real lives of students, in assuming that school stands on the sunny side of the street, this plan presupposes that it is easy to cross the road. When a Sylvia, a Portia, a Lun Cheung, a Carlos Pimental, a Mary Tam cannot even make it out their front doors; when the sidewalks they travel to school are paved with violence; when their troubles are repeated in both school and society; when, if they are lucky enough to have gotten to school alive, they can see no relationship between the subject matter there and their own pasts, presents, or futures: the time for rethinking the American curriculum has surely arrived.

At the Schoolhome, the students in one room are reading *Huckleberry Finn* and are beginning to name a problem that the American schoolhouse glosses over. Huck is an abused child. No, the Widow Douglas is not the villain in the case—Huck's father is. After being kidnapped by "pap" and taken three miles down the river to a log cabin, Huck was a virtual prisoner. Locked in whenever pap went to the store to trade fish and game for whiskey, he "was all over welts" when pap "got too handy with his hick'ry." Once pap drank enough whiskey "for two drunks and one delirium tremens" and proceeded to chase Huck, knife in hand, saying he would kill him. Huck's response to this abuse was to run away, and the youngsters are now discussing its validity—for him and also for boys and girls today.

As students begin to cite their own experiences and those of friends who have ridden a bus to New York or San Francisco, the conversation becomes heated. The teacher is trying to bring students from many different backgrounds into the discussion. Now he steps in with a set of statistics and some good advice about how to interpret the charts. This discussion is not an idle interruption in a literature lesson. Rather it marks the start of a period of intensive interdisciplinary study that will illuminate Huck's life, the lives of the youngsters in the classroom, and perhaps the teacher's life too.

Plato said in the *Republic:* "We shall not admit into our city stories about Hera being chained by her son, or of Hephaestus being hurled from heaven by his father when he intended to help his mother who was being beaten." In general, he argued that children should not be exposed to stories that portray immoral or unvirtuous behavior. A firm believer that one learns by imitating what one sees and hears, including what one hears about secondhand, he advocated censorship on a large scale. If children are not even aware of the existence of undesirable behavior, he reasoned, they will not be in a position to emulate it.

Children in the end-of-century United States know about child abuse, however. They know about homelessness. They know about drugs, rape, violence of all kinds. The evidence of these evils is all around them. If they are so fortunate as to have escaped firsthand knowledge of them in their own homes, they have glimpsed them in their friends' families, seen them in their neighborhoods, watched representations on television, heard descriptions on the evening news. It is far too late to follow Plato's advice of protecting our young from the sight of evil, even if one shares his opinion that the beliefs they acquire "are hard to expunge and usually remain unchanged." Since the alternative the American schoolhouse has adopted of letting young children see evil, doing nothing, and hoping for the best has proved a dismal failure, the School-home has no choice but to follow a different course—one Plato did not consider.

Turning evil, whatever form it happens to take, into a bona fide object of study—of course, not only evil; good too—the Schoolhome plans to harness history, literature, anthropology, psychology, sociology, economics, philosophy, mathematics, and even the arts to the cause of introducing children to alternative patterns of behavior, benign ones that they might never otherwise encounter. Shedding light on what young children and teenagers have seen and heard firsthand, these studies will expand their limited horizons by revealing what else there has been and what there might be.

But what if, while the Schoolhome tries to broaden its students' horizons, each child there takes away something entirely different? Even if the exclusionary curriculum of the past did not have sufficient adhesive powers, could the critics be right that to be unifying the school curriculum must be the same for everyone?

On paper the idea that cultural unity requires a universal course of study is persuasive. Presumably, a common curriculum for all will result in enough commonalities—shared concepts, theories, beliefs, ways of seeing the world—to create the bonds of connection that a healthy culture needs. The example of the Casa dei Bambini suggests that children do not have to learn the same things at the same time in order to feel connected to one another. I would add that they do not have to learn them by the same methods. Even so, the question remains whether the American curriculum must be the same for all of us lest things fall apart.

Actually, the very concept of the same curriculum for all is plagued by a problem that I have yet to hear our elders address. People process what they are taught in different ways. As both a grade school and a university teacher I soon learned that what I said to my classes was not necessarily what my students heard and that, in fact, different students often heard different things. Moreover, even if they did hear the same thing they often placed different valuations on it. I also found out something literary critics know to be true: what an author has written will be interpreted differently by different readers. But then, even if American students leave their worries on the doorstep, because they bring very different selves to school and because their experiences in classrooms are themselves very different, what appears to be the same curriculum often results in very different learning. Add to this the fact that different teachers inevitably transmit very different messages about the same subject matter and the question of how common—how identical—any common curriculum can really be arises.

If there is no guarantee that mandating the same knowledge for all of us will give us all identical repertoires, if in fact the likelihood of this happening in a society as diverse and individualistic as ours is slight, then the argument that a unified people must study an identical curriculum collapses. Does this mean that the idea of a unifying curriculum is an illusion?

The assumption that all members of a culture must have vast amounts of shared knowledge—must own a great deal of cultural capital in common—is no more valid than the assumption that all those things we call by the same name must share a goodly number of characteristics. Consider the proceedings that we call "games," Ludwig Wittgenstein said in his *Philosophical Investigations:* "I mean board-games, card-games, ball-games, Olympic games, and so on. What is common to them all? . . . if you look at them you will not see something that is common to all, but similarities, relationships, and a whole series of them at that." Wittgenstein went on to mention chess, tennis, naughts and crosses, ring-a-round-a-roses. "Similarities crop up and disappear" as we move from one group of games to the next, he continued, so that "we see a complicated network of similarities overlapping and criss-crossing: sometimes overall similarities, sometimes similarities of detail." He called these "family resemblances."

Just as there are some categories—roses, for instance—all of whose members do perhaps have certain characteristics in common, there may be some cultures all of whose members have a body of knowledge in common. Perhaps all the members of Okonkwo's clan, including the women who appeared to lead such different lives from their husbands, did. However, the belief that those who belong to a culture as variegated and as open-ended as ours must possess the same knowledge is as misguided as the belief that all games have one or more features in common. If similarities crop up and disappear as we move from one game to the next, why not when we move from one American to the next? Just as there is a complicated network of similarities overlapping and criss-crossing in the case of games, why not in our case?

Since on up-Island Martha's Vineyard everyone spoke sign language, they at least had that in common. In the School-home that has just opened, everyone will soon be bilingual, with those who have come from other cultures learning English—or, if they are deaf immigrants, American Sign Language—and native speakers of English learning ASL if the need exists or else some other foreign tongue. But I do not draw attention to the Martha's Vineyard story here for the guidance it gives about language learning. It is the up-Islanders' desire to achieve the full integration of a minority into their society that first caught my eye. It is the Islanders' willingness to incorporate into the curriculum of the whole society the cultural capital belonging to relatively few and their determination that the dominant group adjust some of its mores to those of the few that is so pertinent. The Vineyard society's ability to adapt to the situation is all the more remarkable because, as Groce found out, it had its full share of feuds, dissension, and strife. Besides, the many jokes that are told about "off-Islanders" testify that up-Islanders are not "by nature" any more welcoming than the rest of us. Inhabitants of the island obviously cared deeply about the welfare of their deaf neighbors and kinspeople. They must also have taken great pride in maintaining the well-being of their small community to do what is normally so difficult: to put aside the suspicions and the false dignity that so often spur people who already feel at home to welcome only those who are exactly like themselves.

The main virtue of the Martha's Vineyard model is that it enables diversity and cohesion to coexist. For this reason alone I rejoice that the Schoolhome has embraced it. I am also thankful that the Schoolhome has chosen an experimental stance, for one of the many issues it will have to explore is the relative merits of curricular sameness and variety. I give thanks too that the Schoolhome is not relying on a common body of knowledge or information to establish kinship bonds among its inhabitants. These inestimable goods will be manufactured in other ways: by the inclusion of diverse voices and viewpoints; by the insistence that everyone take seriously the experiences and points of view of people unlike themselves; by the explicit rejection of stereotyping; by the working through of racial, ethnic, and religious as well as gender antagonisms; and, to top it all off, by a solid foundation in the three Cs. I think it fair to say that the curriculum of the Schoolhome does have a common core. It is equally important to note that that core is composed mainly of attitudes, skills, and values, not bits or bodies of knowledge.

3

Learning to Live

and blest are those
Whose blood and judgement are so well commeddled,
That they are not a pipe for fortune's finger
To sound what stop she please.

William Shakespeare, *Hamlet*

One November afternoon in 1990, as a boy named Larry left a Boston high school he moved an eight-inch switchblade from a sock to his jacket. "I haven't carried this thing in a few days, but I heard that there was going to be trouble today with some gangs and I wanted to be prepared . . . The way things are going these days, you never know if someone's going to come after you. If they do, they're going to be sorry 'cause I got my knife and I will use it, believe me," he said to a reporter. "I'm afraid to go out on the street with all the drugs and killings," a mother whose son had been shot by rival gang members had told the press the year before. And a twenty-five-year-old woman had said after being shot by members of a teenage gang in a city playground where she had taken her two-year-old son, "They can't cut me open anymore. The bullet is stuck in. They can't get it out."

The Ibo curriculum Achebe depicted in *Things Fall Apart* encompassed myth, ritual, and custom and initiated the young into ways of perceiving, feeling, thinking, acting, behaving toward others and toward nature itself. The glue it provided was composed not just of knowledge, or even of knowledge and skill combined. Mixed in were the three Cs of care, concern, and connection to others—the stuff the Ibo knew was needed to cement the bonds of kinship. Is end-of-century America in any less need of a broadly based curriculum?

Even if the project of reading the works in our cultural
heritage or getting our young to memorize a set of cultural
allusions did not cut off learning from thinking, even if all
the books on the list and items to be learned by rote could be
made meaningful to children, a set of books or a list of facts
that by its very nature rejects the interplay of thought and
action, reason and emotion does not have sufficient adhesive
power. Will a more representative reading list and course of
study suffice? In this large nation where kinship bonds, literally understood, cannot make us one, our young need to
learn to take care of their own bodies and those of others, not
mutilate them. They need to learn to live in this world, not
just know about it.

Dewey wanted us to educate "the whole child." I have been
talking about educating *all* our children in our *whole* heritage.
That valuable capital includes ways of living as well as forms
of knowing, societal activities and practices as well as literary
and artistic achievements. It is all too easy, however, for
school to instruct children *about* their heritage without ever
teaching them *to be* active and constructive participants in
the world—let alone how to make it a better place for themselves and their progeny. This is especially so in the United
States, where school is thought of as an instrument for developing children's minds, not their bodies; their thinking and
reasoning skills, not their emotional capacities or active pro-
pensities.

A nation that can no longer count on home to perform its
educative functions dares not settle for so narrow a definition
of school's task. What radical change in school suffices now
that home and the nation's population have both been transformed? Hamlet may be best known for his indecision, but
when he told the players to "Suit the action to the word, the
word to the action" and praised those who commeddle blood
and judgment, he could have been defining the goals of the
Schoolhome.

Perhaps at one time in American history our country could

afford schools that severed heads from hands and hearts. There may even have been a golden age when home taught children how to join together what school cast asunder. If so, that moment is past. In the Schoolhome over on the promontory, mind and body, thought and action, reason and emotion are all being educated. The studies that children pursue there integrate these elements so that they will be integrated into the lives those young people lead both in school and in the world. And the activities they engage in commeddle blood and judgment so well that if it should please fortune to pit white against black, African against Asian, Christian against Jew or Moslem, male against female, hearing against hearing impaired, able bodied against disabled, heterosexual against homosexual, she will find the souls of young folk unsuited to be her pipes. Need I say that the vision of an educated person the Schoolhome embodies stands in stark contrast to that of the restorationists?

I

It is an uneasy lot at best, to be what we call highly taught and yet not to enjoy; to be present at this great spectacle of life and never to be liberated from a small hungry shivering self—never to be fully possessed by the glory we behold, never to have our consciousness rapturously transformed into the vividness of a thought, the ardour of a passion, the energy of an action.

George Eliot, *Middlemarch*

"He has got no good red blood in his body," says Sir James to Mrs. Cadwallader as they discuss Dorothea Brooke's impending marriage to Mr. Casaubon in George Eliot's *Middlemarch*. "No," replies Sir James's friend, "Somebody put a drop under a magnifying-glass, and it was all semicolons and parentheses." A man who spends his waking hours collecting and classifying material for the Key to all Mythologies he is always writing and never finishing, Mr. Casaubon "dreams footnotes and they run away with all his brains. They say when he was a little boy, he made an abstract of 'Hop o' my Thumb,' and he has been making abstracts ever since. Ugh!"

The price Rodriguez's education extorted from him was not quite so high as that paid by Mr. Casaubon, but his narrative, like Eliot's, is a cautionary tale. Rodriguez tells a story of alienation: from the Spanish language; from his parents, for whom he soon had no names; from his Mexican heritage, in which he came to have no interest; from his own feelings and emotions, which all but disappeared as he learned to control them; from his body itself, as he discovered when he took a construction job after his senior year in college. Rodriguez depicts a journey from the intimacy of his private home to the isolation and distance on the other side of Woolf's bridge. Once he attended school, close ties with family members were dissolved, public anonymity replaced private attention, and he became a spectator in his own home as noise gave way to silence and connection to distance.

Had education turned Rodriguez into a mummified intellectual he could not have written so eloquent and revealing a book as *Hunger of Memory*. Yet if upon becoming educated Rodriguez possessed not quite the desiccated body of Casaubon and if his soul was not the "great bladder for dried peas to rattle in" that Mrs. Cadwallader believed her neighbor's to be, he too had learned to prize isolation over intimacy, to prefer "lonely" reason to fellow feeling, and even in his daily life to keep a scholarly distance from the mundane and not so mundane material world.

When on their wedding trip to Rome Dorothea asked her husband if he cared to see Raphael's frescoes he replied, "They are, I believe, highly esteemed. Some of them represent the fable of Cupid and Psyche, which is probably the romantic invention of a literary period, and cannot, I think, be reckoned a genuine mythical product." Even Eliot, who tries valiantly to enlist her readers' sympathies with the unlovable Casaubon, is moved at this point to comment on how depressing is "a mind in which years full of knowledge seem to have issued in a blank absence of interest or sympathy." Accumulating his own index cards in the British Museum, Rodriguez was fast becoming a Mr. Casaubon: "Whenever I started to write, I knew too much (and not enough) to be able to write anything but sentences that were overly cautious, timid, strained brittle under the heavy weight of footnotes and qualifications. I seemed unable to dare a passionate statement. I felt drawn by professionalism to the edge of sterility, capable of no more than pedantic, lifeless, unassailable prose."

Although he resisted one part of Mr. Casaubon's fate and wrote a widely acclaimed autobiography, Rodriguez seems to have succumbed to another. With the approach of age Mr. Casaubon decided to marry. "He determined to abandon himself to the stream of feelings," writes Eliot, "and perhaps was surprised to find what an exceedingly shallow rill it was." The obligations and agitations that his "close union" with Dorothea incurred were far more disturbing than this discovery was for him, however, "since this charming young bride not only obliged him to much consideration on her behalf (which he had sedulously given), but turned out to be capable of agitating him cruelly just where he most needed soothing." As a writer, Rodriguez confides, it is necessary to "avoid complex relationships—a troublesome lover or a troubled friend. The person who knows me best scolds me for escaping from life." After asking rhetorically, "Am I evading adulthood?" he goes on to reveal a self as wary of intimacy and entanglement as Mr. Casaubon and as fearful of the responsibilities that accompany connection to others.

Eliot admits to being sorry for someone "we call highly taught" who does not know how to enter into "this great spectacle of life." Some decades later on this side of the ocean and in far less passionate prose Dewey told school people not to separate mind from body, thought from action, or reason from feeling and emotion. Yet whether the devastating effects of these divorces be documented in fact, fiction, or philosophy, they seem to have little interest for education's critics. Savoring the memory of their undergraduate days, with one voice they have praised a curriculum that specializes in spectatorship.

The "Great Books" of the West: these are the works they would place at the center of the college curriculum so that students can address the "big questions" they say one must face in order to live a serious life. What kind of life is this? A spectator's. The natural sciences, the social and behavioral sciences, the humanities: these are the bodies of knowledge that our elders say should comprise liberal studies, and the secondary and primary education they advocate consist of simplified versions thereof. Carving up the world into separate domains, treating selected aspects of the one they claim to study, asking their own specialized questions of their subject matter and using their own technical languages, the various fields or disciplines of knowledge that fall under these three broad categories have spectatorship built into them from the start. Theirs is not to do or die. It is to tell the reason why the world is the way it is—or at least to describe what it is like and how it works. Thus, to base the curriculum of our nation's schools and colleges exclusively on these studies is to teach our young about life: to turn out observers *of* it not participants *in* it.

We need to ask ourselves if end-of-century America is well served by a population of onlookers. Before their marriage Mr. Casaubon was Dorothea Brooke's ideal of an educated man. She truly believed that he led the most serious and the best life there could be. Upon close acquaintance she changed her mind, preferring those who tried, however unsuccessfully, to make the world a better place in which to live. Some might say that Mr. Casaubon had too small a mind to ponder the big questions of reason-revelation, freedom-necessity, democracy-aristocracy, good-evil, body-soul, self-other, city-man, eternity-time, being-nothing. Were that maker of abstracts as self-critical as he was scholarly, he would respond that one big question the restorationists have forgotten to ask is how education can inform life if it is only devoted to turning out spectators thereof.

It has been said in defense of an education for spectatorship that, whatever a teacher does, "Life will happen to students." How true. The most academic study in the world will not prevent them from living some kind of life or other on the two sides of Woolf's bridge. The question is, what kind? In her letter to the *Boston Globe* that teacher who asked if her adolescent boys would live to remember her lessons said that her students "became attracted to gang involvement, much like a magnet is to steel . . . The power of the streets is too appealing to ignore."

Mindless imitation is the easiest path for someone to follow who has not been trained to bring intelligence to bear on living. In the best of cases education for spectatorship teaches students to lead divided lives. Instructing them to apply their intelligence in observing the world, it teaches them by default if not design to be unthinking doers—pipes for fortune's finger. In the worst it consigns them to the nasty, brutish, and short life that the philosopher Thomas Hobbes long ago attributed to the state of nature.

II

> The spectator's judgment is sure to miss the root of the matter, and to possess no truth.
>
> William James, *On a Certain Blindness in Human Beings*

The curriculum Rodriguez studied divorced education from life. Even when the object of concern was a form of human conduct or a mode of living, he remained an onlooker. Domestic politics, war, finance, international relations, social service, the arts: he was invited to inspect, think about, analyze, understand these from the vantage point of one or another observer—a historian, perhaps, or a political scientist, a psychologist, an economist.

Believing that the individuals and groups they analyze are subjects in their own right who actively give meaning to the world in which they live, many practitioners of the social or human sciences make a concerted effort to get "inside" those other minds. Historians try to capture the feel of times past and enter into the thoughts of their historical subjects, or at least reconstruct their conceptual frameworks and their reasons for acting. Psychologists try to discover how the individuals they study see others and themselves. Anthropologists try to understand other cultures from the point of view of the people in them. Yet even if these researchers adopt the standpoint of their "objects" of study successfully—and success is a matter of degree here since mere human inquirers can never shed all the preconceptions of their own time and place, let alone comprehend those of another—their goal is still understanding and their perspective still that of a spectator. Human science methodologies that resonate with Montessori's try to close the gap between observer and observed, but the observer nonetheless remains just that.

"The spectator's judgment is sure to miss the root of the matter, and to possess no truth," William James once said. Since children are experiencers, doers, agents, performers and will remain such throughout their lives—in other words, will participate in living—and since they are not born knowing how to do the things and perform the activities that constitute human life, it can only be perverse to teach them to be nothing more than competent watchers, perceivers, observers, critics. We should not forget that students can get inside some of their subject matter not just to see the world as other people do but to *learn human activities*. Besides teaching our young about drama's historical development, its societal function, its aesthetic qualities, besides trying to get them to see the world as Shakespeare or Euripides did, it is possible to teach them to write, perform, and produce dramatic works. In addition to conveying knowledge about voting patterns, alternative models of democracy, the history of revolutions, the intricacies of parliamentary government, educators can teach their students to run for office, lobby legislative bodies, participate in political campaigns, work on the staffs of elected officials.

In education, as in life, participation in a human activity is not always a desirable goal. History, psychology, and physics are worthwhile activities for students to engage in. Occupations like drama and politics—or at least selected aspects of these—are too. But if health care, protecting the environment, and preparing nutritional meals are valid additions to our list, drug dealing and gang warfare, polluting our air and rivers, abusing young children and battering their mothers, denying jobs and housing to people of color and persecuting them and other minorities are not.

The trouble with the critics' recommendations for improving American schools is not that all forms of human activity and behavior belong in our children's education and only one—spectatorship—is included. It scarcely needs saying that we should avoid teaching mugging and killing, extortion and terrorism. The point is that their proposals give little or no curriculum space to the enormous range of ways of acting and forms of living that the young of any nation need to learn. Supplying students with different kinds of lenses for different occasions—now those of a physicist, now those of a historian, a psychologist, a philosopher—and also with ones of different strengths so that a slice of life past and present can be seen from a distance or close up, they turn them into more versatile spectators of the world than Mr. Casaubon ever was. But although there are many views from outside and although glasses for distance as well as close work have their rewards, an education that is devoted to spectatorship is not an appropriate one for the young of any society. Certainly not for the young of a society in which violence is rife.

Activities of living are, in fact, to be found in the American schoolhouse, but the ones admitted into the "curriculum proper"—the formally sanctioned curriculum—are almost as divorced from thought as spectatorship is from action. While Rodriguez was receiving the liberal education that turned him into a disembodied mind, other youngsters were undergoing a vocational training. As they were learning to work in the world, they had to put their intelligence in cold storage. Someone who did not know the American school system might imagine that since one part of the curriculum was designed for heads and the other for hands, every child would be educated for both thought and action. But having divided American education into two parts—the one called general or liberal and the other technical or vocational—and assigned one the goal of educating heads and the other the goal of educating hands, our culture has asked school to place each child into one or the other section, not both. In other words it has instructed the schoolhouse to turn out two different kinds of fragments—people like Rodriguez and others like Bob Walters.

There is a scene in Frederick Wiseman's documentary film *High School* in which a teacher reads to a student assembly a letter she received from a former pupil now in Vietnam. But for a few teachers who cared, she tells her audience, Walters, a below-average student academically, "might have been a nobody." Instead, while awaiting a plane that would drop him behind the DMZ, he had written her to say that he had made the school the beneficiary of his life insurance policy. "I am a little jittery right now," she reads. She is not to worry about him, however, because "I am only a body doing a job." Measuring his worth as a human being by his provision for the school, she overlooks the fact that Walters is taking pride in being an automaton.

Endeavors that fit Hamlet's bill do exist in the American schoolhouse but they rarely lie on either the liberal or the vocational track. Where are they to be found? Ones that not only unite head and hand but link both of these to heart reside in the extra-curriculum, not the curriculum proper. That is also where there are activities in which connectedness to others is a fact of life. It is the place where students work so hard and so enthusiastically that disciplinary problems rarely arise and motivation takes care of itself, where they take initiative, carry enormous responsibilities, solve problems, think critically—in sum, do regularly all those things our elders say our nation's youth should be learning.

Theater and newspaper are just two of the many extracurricular activities that repeatedly perform these miracles. What is the meaning of the prefix "extra"? As in "extra-terrestrial," "extra-marital," "extra-territorial," it means "outside" or "beyond." Why, if integrative endeavors work such wonders, are they relegated to the margins? Another irony of the restorationist program is that despite the negative value its supporters attach to images of falling apart, their ideal of a truly educated person is a fragmented individual—a Rodriguez.

Given the importance of educating children to live in the world it would be ludicrous to glue back together a curriculum designed for the production of partial human beings. But let me change the image. Instead of thinking of the old curriculum as a shattered mirror or bowl in need of restoration, why not consider it a worn-out piece of fabric that we should be turning inside out? Not all the activities now located in the extra-curriculum belong at the center of the Schoolhome by any means. Chess and cheerleading are not sufficiently integrative. Photography may possess that virtue but its practice does not require enough collaboration. Orchestra is integrative and has mutual dependence built right into it but it demands too high a level of technical expertise. Theater and newspaper, in contrast, are integrative group pursuits that can successfully be undertaken by rank amateurs, they have the added advantage of directing students to the widest imaginable range of studies, and they are also capable of illuminating life on both sides of the bridge. This is why, right now, they are my own candidates for occupying the center, which is not to say that others could not make a good case for farming or animal care or child nurture or the building of a historical museum.

Although my favored enterprises quite naturally point students toward the study of language and literature, they lead directly into social studies too. Do you see those children in the Schoolhome who are preparing to stage their own adaptation of *Betsey Brown*? They are inquiring into the post–World War II era and are also embarking on a study of the history of African-Americans in general and school desegregation in particular. And the older youngsters who are rehearsing a version of *Huckleberry Finn* have already studied slavery and racism as well as life on the Mississippi and, of course, child abuse.

A director of dramatic productions at an Ivy League university once said that the best training an actor could get was a sound liberal education: that history and literature are what give you insight into time, place, and character. In the Schoolhome, where the object is not to train actors but to educate children for living, the flow is in the other direction. When theater is at the center of curriculum, instead of liberal studies feeding into drama, drama feeds into liberal studies.

Put journalism at the center and it has this same power. A group of students on the promontory are planning a feature story for the *Schoolhome Journal* on the composition of the student body. They are already beginning to compile statistics, make charts, draw maps, and absorb a mass of historical, political, and economic information about the different cultures represented in the school population.

Newspaper and theater do not only lead students back to language, literature, and social studies. In both cases there are ethical and legal questions to be investigated: should anyone be allowed to play any role or in theater are gender and race differences that make a difference? Is all news fit to print or are there limits to what a Schoolhome newspaper should publish? Since everyone on the *Journal* is involved in the final product, mathematical, scientific, and technical knowledge also loom large in the lives of its staff. Science, math, and technology bear on dramatic productions as well, and environmental questions inevitably crop up in both pursuits. The students are even now discussing what materials can safely be used in constructing the sets, whether printed programs constitute a waste of paper, which kind of paper is best for the *Journal* to use, and how to recycle it.

When activities like journalism and theater are located at the margins, school deprives them of the illumination that the disciplines of knowledge can yield. Students in the schoolhouse are too busy publishing a newspaper in their spare time to be able to study the history of free speech or the role of the fourth estate in democratic societies. They are too frazzled trying to keep up with their studies while putting on a full-scale dramatic production to wonder about the playwright's literary sources or the history of drama itself. And in any case, these practical pursuits and the goal of spectatorship stand worlds apart.

When students in junior and senior high school take part in dramatic productions, why don't their English and social studies teachers take advantage of the rich subject-matter potential of the plays being performed? When a school puts on a production of *Camelot,* why does not every class study some version of the King Arthur legend? Why do the teachers not make it their business to discuss the rule of law and compare it to the theory of might makes right? Why do the show's directors not conduct a cast discussion of the open sexism in one of the songs? The reason is that whatever is in the extra-curriculum is considered by definition to fall outside the concerns of teachers *as* teachers.

But theater and newspaper belong at the center of the Schoolhome's curriculum not just because they spin a web of theoretical knowledge. Threads from these pursuits also reach out to skills and activities such as reading, writing, speaking, listening, drawing, designing, and building, and to every human emotion. In theater it is not just the play that engages the feelings of students. Putting on a performance, carrying the project through to completion, does too. In newspaper, besides the emotional responses that many stories call forth, there is the emotionally wrought task of getting out an edition. If in the role of news reporters the girls and boys remain observers of that portion of the world contained in the Schoolhome, they are nevertheless full-fledged participants in managing the school paper. If as stage actors they do not literally live the scenes they portray, they exhibit genuine agency in performing the play.

The web of curriculum that an activity like theater or newspaper can weave might by itself justify placing it at the center of curriculum. The claims of theater and journalism are enhanced, however, by the fact that their products—the plays performed, the newspapers published—can be designed to speak to everyone's experience and to be seen or read by everyone. Tying the inhabitants together with invisible threads spun by shared emotions that derive from common experiences, they can thus weave young people of different races, classes, ethnicities, religions, physical abilities, sexual orientations into their own web of connection.

III

Is there any greater evil we can mention for a city than whatever tears it apart?

Plato, *Republic*

"Today a youngster said a group of guys was after him, and they drove up outside of the school. They may have had guns, I'm not sure. I make sure my kids are inside and are safe," a Massachusetts high school principal told the press in 1989. In 1990 the headmaster at Boston's Hyde Park High School acknowledged to a reporter that "the weapons situation is starting to get epidemic." "Just like pens and notebooks, knives are a part of a lot of kids' school supplies," one school police officer said. "We have gangs from all over the city coming to these schools," said another. "And the contempt that some of these kids have for each other does not end at the school door." Shortly after, their worst fears were realized: a seventeen-year-old boy was stabbed to death in a Boston high school.

In 1651 Hobbes described the state of nature as a state of war. War consists not in battle only or in the act of fighting, he said in *Leviathan*. Comparing war to weather, he wrote: "For, as the nature of foul weather lies not in a shower or two of rain but in an inclination thereto of many days together, so the nature of war consists not in actual fighting but in the known disposition thereto during all the time there is no assurance to the contrary." Answering the objection that there never was such a time or condition, he pointed to "the savage people in many places in America."

Hobbes had his facts wrong. Native Americans were not fierce or ferocious, uncivilized or barbarous. They were not mercilessly cruel and did not live in a "brutish manner." The weapons students carry to school in the 1990s in order to protect themselves on their city's streets suggest, however, that in many places in America three and one-half centuries later there is a known disposition to fighting. "They want to carry something that will put them on the same level if they encounter a group of hostile kids," the chief of the Boston school police force explained. "It gives them a feeling of confidence knowing they have a knife in their pocket." Or gun, he should have added.

In a war of every man against every man, Hobbes said, there is "no knowledge of the face of the earth; no account of time; no arts; no letters." As if in echo, the headmaster of Boston's West Roxbury High School complained: "Having to deal with kids with weapons takes time away from teaching and learning."

The headmaster of Madison Park High School indicated more or less in passing that girls as well as boys come to school armed: "I asked her what she was doing with a knife and she said that some kids in her neighborhood were harassing her and she didn't want to be victimized anymore." It is impossible to tell from the news account who the victimizers were, but the media's tendency to indulge in "false gender neutrality," to use Susan Okin's felicitous phrase, should in any case be noted.

Headlines such as "City Tries to Stem Youth Violence," "Boston Tries to Stem Violence among Young People," "Youths Revise Survival Code" and talk of "kids," "students," "teen violence," "the weapons situation" mask male mayhem. It is boys and men who are killing one another on our nation's streets to such an extent that homicide is now a leading cause of death for teenage males—*the* leading cause for African-American males. In our homes it is men who are beating their lovers and spouses and abusing their children.

Statistics on domestic violence in the United States vary considerably depending on which reports one reads. It seems safe to say, however, that at least two million women are beaten by their husbands each year and that as many as six hundred thousand are severely assaulted by them four or more times a year. In the state of Massachusetts alone, a woman is killed by an abusive partner every eighteen days. Violence in the other direction—by women toward their husbands and lovers—occurs too, but in comparison to these figures its incidence is negligible. Studies also indicate that 38 million adults in the United States were sexually abused as children and that, in all, 22 percent of Americans are victimized, with this proportion quite possibly on the rise. Investigators have discovered that boys as well as girls are victims of sexual abuse in childhood and that women as well as men are the victimizers. But there is not equal representation in the two categories. Female victims far outnumber male and the great majority of offenders are men.

Some might think it amusing that in an age when boys and men do so much violence, our cultural images portray girls and women as the ones who are less than fully human. While billboards, bus placards, store windows, and public art have turned urban space into what the historian Dolores Hayden has described as a "landscape filled with images of men as sexual aggressors and women as submissive sex objects," comic books, pop music, films, videos, and the multibillion-dollar pornography industry have turned each person's psyche into a vista filled with images of female bodies and body parts. Some might find it entertaining that girls and women are the ones thought of as creatures of nature instead of intelligent, moral beings. Even Woolf, who accused the men practicing those professions across the bridge of having lost sight, speech, sense of proportion, and humanity, might smile at the reversal. What then remains of a human being? she asked. Sending man back to his first private home, she answered: "Only a cripple in a cave." But this subhuman perception of the "opposite" sex is no laughing matter.

A purist will say that a causal connection has yet to be established between the degrading imagery and the abusive treatment of girls and women in end-of-twentieth-century American culture. He or she will also argue that it has yet to be shown that the messages transmitted by the media correspond to the perceptions of Derrick Jackson's sixth-graders or exert any negative influence on male behavior. A realist is compelled to reply that violence toward girls and women is to be expected in a society unwilling to acknowledge its own misogyny, let alone admit that it is perpetuated in school.

While scholars in the 1970s and 1980s were unearthing the negative portrayals of women across the disciplines and finding enormous gaps in their fields' texts, studies of coeducational classrooms were discovering what the classroom climate is like for half the school population. In *The Classroom Climate: A Chilly One for Women?* published in 1982, Roberta M. Hall and Bernice R. Sandler let college women students speak for themselves:

> You come in the door . . . equal but having experienced the discrimination—the refusal of professors to take you seriously; the sexual overtures and the like—you limp out doubting your own ability to do very much of anything.

> I was discussing my work in a public setting, when a professor cut me off and asked me if I had freckles all over my body.

> In classes, I experienced myself as a person to be taken lightly. In one seminar, I was never allowed to finish a sentence. There seemed to be a tacit understanding that I never had anything to say.

> I told my advisor I wanted to continue working towards a Ph.D. He said, "A pretty girl like you will certainly get married. Why don't you stop with an M.A.?"

When I volunteered the fact that I was a politics major [the professor] expressed surprise and asked "Now why would you want to do that?" when he had commended the same information just minutes before to one of the men.

Does the classroom temperature suddenly become chilly when girls enter college? The attitudes of Best's and Jackson's boys suggest otherwise and so do Margaret Clark's reports on how the "second curriculum" that teaches gender norms affects girls. Obviously, findings about the construction of gender in Australian primary schools do not necessarily hold true for the American case. Yet Clark's girls' descriptions of the boys' language call their American cousins to mind. The girls were not the boys' only targets, however. This is what the female teachers in Clark's report had to say:

I've been here for four years, but at the beginning of this year the whole school blew up with some problems. Boys that I had visited at home, taught in my class and been on camp with—I thought I had a good relationship with them—put their fingers up at me and then stood there as if to say, "What are you going to do about it?" I was horrified. I could not believe it.

I used to spend a lot of time on the basketball court, to get the girls involved but last year I was bullied off the court, by one of my boy students. I was in tears. He bullied me off.

Almost any day of the week I see boys using sexuality as a way of exerting power. You know boys going up to a female teacher and sticking two fingers up at her.

Female teachers are nothing to some male children.

By comparison, the experience of sixteen-year-old Kathy, an Inner London comprehensive school student cited by Dale Spender, seems mild:

Sometimes I feel like saying that I disagree, that there are other ways of looking at it, but where would that get me? My teacher thinks I'm showing off, and the boys jeer. But if I pretend I don't understand, it's very different. The teacher is sympathetic and the boys are helpful. They really respond if they can show you how it is done, but there's nothing but "aggro" if you give any signs of showing them how it is done.

The teacher's complicity in creating the chilly classroom climate matches the Australian experience, however. "There's no point telling the teachers 'cos they just say 'they're just teasing,' or 'they didn't hurt you.' You feel like you're wasting their time," said one group of girls in Clark's report. According to another, "When we told one teacher about these incidents she just ignored us."

Other reports cited by Spender confirm these estimates of their situation given by Clark's girls:

A group of year 6 students were walking across the school yard from the library to the classroom. One of the boys ran up behind one of the girls, rammed a rule between her legs and called her a slut. A female teacher's aide saw the incident and since there was no teacher nearby called the boy over to reprimand him. A male teacher then arrived and enquired what was going on. The aide told the student to return to his class and recounted the incident. The male teacher commented, "She probably asked for it. She's as rough as they come."

Well, as the music started, without a word spoken, the girls lined up at the back and the boys all moved together and sort of faced the girls. The girls started to move and sing but the boys stood in the line and started singing very loudly and moving in a very sexual way, you know swinging their hips and their arms and legs and walking slowly towards the girls as they did it, staring at them. It was an aggressive and threatening situation.

The girls immediately stopped moving, stopped singing and just looked at each other with very stunned expressions.

The student teacher saw it as a form of teasing.

Now that we know about them, what should we do about the misogynist messages that are sent and received in school and college classrooms? One response to a hidden curriculum is to do nothing, to pretend that it does not exist. Is nonaction defensible when the hidden curriculum dehumanizes half the population? Not if one agrees, as I do, with the male primary teacher in Clark's study who said: "I think people have just not put the obvious together when it comes to boys' violence and the denigration of girls when they are young, and domestic violence and gun shootings when they are older."

To turn the schoolhouse curriculum proper inside out is not by itself an adequate response to the problem posed by the chilly classroom climate for girls. It may fill Dewey's prescription of educating the whole child, but whole children are quite capable of perceiving and treating others as not wholly human. It is one thing for school to provide integrative activities that unite mind and body, thought and action, reason and emotion. It is quite another for it to teach each child to interact with every other child—and every adult too—as one fully human being to another. But an education for living can do no less. A man is not apt to treasure a woman's good red blood if he places her and her whole gender far beneath him on the Great Chain of Being. "Is there any greater evil we can mention for a city than whatever tears it apart?" Plato asked in the *Republic*. On both sides of Woolf's bridge our cities now reap the consequences of one sex's doubting the other's qualifications for membership in the human race.

IV

Now it is with emotions and actions that virtue is concerned; excess and deficiency in them are wrong, and a middle amount receives praise and achieves success, both of which are marks of virtue. It follows that virtue is a sort of middle state.

Aristotle, *Nicomachean Ethics*

In a 1990 survey of educators around the United States, one person, commenting on the sexism ingrained in everyday thought, ventured the opinion that the children can keep teachers honest. Maybe so, but the Schoolhome's teachers will also have to keep the children honest, its girls will have to keep the boys honest, and its boys will have to police themselves.

Clark reported an interview in which a group of young Australian boys were asked why they had been so mean to Janine:

Boy 1:   To show we're tough.
Int.:   Does it take courage to be mean?
Boy 1:   Yeah.
Friends: Yeah.
Boy 2:   No it doesn't. That's weak. It takes courage to treat girls nicely. You have to be really brave to do that.

A similar conversation is taking place in the Schoolhome. Mocking laughter follows the comment of Boy 2, as it did in the interview. But one of the girls in the Schoolhome, even at her tender age, seems to understand what is at stake: "They have to be mean to us because otherwise they will turn into girls or something—I don't know." Echoing a child in Clark's study, she manages to cut through the snickering. And lo and behold! Although a number of boys sound angry, several gather up the courage to agree that she is right. I am not sure how the conversation ends, but I know that, in keeping with a tradition of the Schoolhome, the conversation will be continued the next time the occasion arises. It seems that everyone there agrees that keeping the atmosphere loving is everybody's business. Everyone also seems to know what to do after angry words have been exchanged. The group says in unison, "Peace, love, and respect for everyone," and on the last beat of that benediction the children and their teacher extend their arms as if to embrace the whole world.

As the children begin to think about their own behavior, as the boys are led by their teachers and challenged by the girls to question the assumptions about girls and themselves that are implicit in their language and their actions, with a bit of luck and a lot of effort they can begin to resist stereotypical images of male and female. Despite the women's movement of the 1970s and the early 1980s, these still wreak havoc on us all.

I had started to think that American culture was no longer in their clutches. Then a drama was enacted in my own classroom that made me change my mind. In all the years I have taught philosophy of education I have only once had a class that I could not tempt into lively discussion of the issues. Every day I tried to get my students excited about the subject but nothing worked until, in conjunction with our reading of Rousseau's *Emile*, I played "William's Doll" from the recording *Free To Be You and Me:*

> When my friend William was five years old
> He wanted a doll to hug and hold.
> "A doll," said William, "is what I need
> To wash and clean and dress and feed;
> A doll to give a bottle to,
> And put to bed when day is through;
> And any time my doll gets ill,
> I'll take good care of it,"
> Said my friend Bill.

As the song proceeded and William continued to ask for a doll against his father's wishes and his friend's taunts, the young men in my class began exchanging looks. By the time William's grandma came to his rescue, they were beside themselves:

> So William's grandma, as I've been told,
> Bought William a doll to hug and hold.
> And William's father began to frown
> But Grandma smiled and calmed him down, explaining:
> "William wants a doll so when he has a baby someday
> He'll know how to dress it, put diapers on double,
> And gently caress it to bring up a bubble
> And care for his baby as every good father should learn
>   to do.
> William has a doll! William has a doll!
> 'Cause someday he is going to be a father too."

These lyrics occasioned the greatest outburst I have ever witnessed in a college classroom. The young men in my course were unanimous that if you give a small boy a doll to play with—not a GI Joe but a baby doll—he will grow up to be homosexual, in their eyes something definitely unnatural and abnormal. That he will ultimately contract AIDS seemed also to be a foregone conclusion. A few women in the class agreed with them. Most of the women, however, were incensed by the illogic of the argument and aghast that men of their own generation, their schoolmates in fact, should hold fast to what they had thought were discarded and discredited stereotypes.

Although I did not know this at the time, a decade earlier Rafaela Best had played the same song for the young children she was studying and to similar effect. The boys in grades one to three did not look askance; they crawled under their desks and hid under the coats on the rack. Commenting that some years later those boys could listen to "William's Doll" "without experiencing trauma," Best said that for fifth-graders gender "stereotypes were no longer so urgent." No doubt her ten-year-old boys were beginning to like girls and make some accommodations to them, but the scene in my classroom attested to young men's abiding scorn of females. Because it also demonstrated their fear of feminization, it made me realize that intellectual study of misogyny, although better than nothing, is not enough. If one step in diminishing the violence and misogyny in our culture and in weaving a web of human connection is to acquire a cognitive understanding of these phenomena, another is to accept on an emotional and behavioral level that the three Cs of care, concern, and connection are everyone's business.

While Best's boys were learning to be "real men," her girls were on their way to becoming "true women." At six years old they were helping those classmates—almost always boys—who were in trouble. When Martin was distraught because no one liked him, Jeannette came to the rescue. Anne comforted Michael when a film made him cry, and Meg did the same for Tony. In a testing period in which many of the first-grade boys did not seem to understand the instructions, those girls who finished early immediately looked around the room, saw who needed assistance, and went to their sides. No boy offered to help another child, and almost every child who received help from the girls was male. Remarking that the boys did not thank the helping girls, Best concluded, "Helping behavior was already expected from them." It obviously was not expected from the boys.

A gender-based division of labor is anathema in the Schoolhome whether the work be physical or emotional. Is it possible that teaching boys to share the emotional labor both in the classroom and in the world is a prescription for the very feminization that so alarmed my college men? If boys in the United States today forswear violence, aggression, and their scorn of girls and women must they fear for their masculinity? When I thought of applying Aristotle's doctrine of the "golden mean" to these questions, our culture's male and female stereotypes appeared in a new light. Establishing beyond any reasonable doubt that in its representations of gender our culture mistakes vice for virtue, an Aristotelian analysis reveals that an education in the three Cs for boys entails the *debrutalization* of America's image of masculinity, not emasculation.

In saying that excess and deficiency in emotions and actions are wrong, and that virtue is a sort of middle state, Aristotle did not suppose that the golden mean lies at some precise mathematical point between two extremes or that it consists in middle-of-the-road, wishy-washy action. Rather, it involves feeling the right emotions and doing the right thing "at the right time and on the right occasion and towards the right people and for the right motives and in the right manner."

One of Aristotle's examples was courage. "The middle state as regards fear and boldness," courage stands between the vice of deficiency that is called cowardice and the opposite vice of excessive fearlessness and boldness that is called rashness or foolhardiness. Now think about our macho ideal. Equating courage with its excess, it legitimates a perversion of that virtue, not the genuine article. In America today a "real man" exercises no judgment about when to stand his ground, accept a dare, go into battle, test his mettle. Afraid of being called a coward, he takes every time as the right time and every occasion as a reason for risking life and limb.

The virtue of loyalty suffers the same fate. The middle course between the defect of betrayal and the excess of blind allegiance is not incorporated into our male stereotype. A perversion of this virtue is. In our culture's eyes a "real man" is not one who, using moral judgment and discretion, says no to the immoral directives and illegal commands of friend, employer, or country. The label is reserved for one who carries out requests and follows orders whatever they may be. The virtue of self-assertion is similarly distorted. The middle way between the twin offenses of meek passivity and overaggressiveness does not enter into our macho ideal. A "real man's" aggressiveness knows no bounds. He makes his presence felt on the wrong occasion, in the wrong manner, or to the wrong people, or all three together.

Turning courage, loyalty, and self-assertion into vices, our cultural construct of a "real man" brutalizes the character traits that our society has traditionally assigned to boys and men. Making the mistake of assuming that only one alternative to an obvious evil exists, our macho ideal substitutes for the clear offense of deficiency the less apparent but equally egregious one of excess. Scorning cowardice, it applauds a devil-may-care attitude toward life and limb. Spurning betrayal, it promotes a disregard for morality and law. Despising passivity, it endorses violence. Calling the perversion of the virtue by the virtue's name, our manly ideal thus honors what it should condemn.

But our macho ideal does more than substitute excess for genuine virtue. Although Aristotle did not discuss the care, concern, and connection that our culture attributes to women, his doctrine of the golden mean can be applied to the three Cs as well. The historian Barbara Welter pointed out in the 1970s that in the nineteenth century, white middle-class

America defined a "true woman" by her piety, purity, submissiveness, and domesticity. These are no longer considered the measures of womanhood, but we still think we know a "true woman" when we meet one. In our eyes she is a person who does not exercise judgment about when to help others and when to stop, when to worry about their well-being and when to ask them to reciprocate, when to feel their joys and sorrows and when to remember her own, when to try to meet their needs and when to allow them to do things for themselves. She is one who thinks that every intimate needs comfort, every occasion demands indulgence, every relationship requires self-sacrifice.

Look at our gender stereotypes from Aristotle's perspective and it is easy to see that just as our ideal of a "real man" incorporates the excesses of courage and loyalty, that of a "true woman" also replaces virtue with excess. The virtue of caring can be viewed as the midpoint between the deficiency of coldness or lack of warmth, on the one hand, and the excess of indulgence on the other. The virtue of concern falls, in turn, between disinterest and self-sacrifice; connection to others between total separation and a loss of all sense of self; nurturance between separation or neglect and smothering. Staying away from the vices of deficiency—lack of warmth, indifference, total separation, and neglect—our female stereotype mistakes the opposite evils for the virtues themselves.

What stance is a "real man" expected to take toward the three Cs? Even as our male stereotype embraces the excesses of those virtues we call "male," it appropriates the deficiencies of the ones we call "female." It is true that passions can run high when males root for the home team or enlist in the Marine Corps. Nevertheless, it is the very distance, the indifference, the disinterestedness, the coolness that are held against females in this society—that in their case are considered vices—which are generally counted in men's favor.

One beauty of an Aristotelian analysis is its demonstration that the virtues named by the three Cs imply *going beyond* stereotypical femininity, not succumbing to it. Although in *name* they are culturally associated with females, in *content* they transcend our gender categories. Happily, then, men can renounce the macho ideal without losing their masculinity.

Since a culture that constructs masculinity around the vice of excess is almost inevitably headed toward violence and misogyny, the Schoolhome has a lot to do. Not only must it eradicate the hidden curriculum that boys and girls now study. It will have to teach boys genuine virtue. In one of the homerooms on the promontory, a boy is standing beside his desk looking defiant. No, he is not disobeying the teacher. A schoolmate who has lost some money is demanding the right to search everyone's possessions. Bobby refuses to open his desk, and the rest of the group begins to accuse him of theft. It is a situation that might turn ugly. Then the teacher comes to stand next to Bobby and rivets the children's attention by asking questions: "Do you know what a vigilante is? What due process is? Have you ever heard of McCarthyism? Can you tell me what the Fourth Amendment says?" In an instant he has turned a case of classroom bullying into a lesson in constitutional law. Capitalizing on real-life experience, he is also teaching a lesson about true courage. Bobby may or may not be the thief; the teacher does not know. The lesson he is teaching is not about one boy's actual guilt or innocence, however. It is about the myriad forms violence can take. It is about political freedom. And it is about new tests of male courage.

V

With a view to having women guardians, we should not have one kind of education to fashion the men, and another for the women.

Plato, *Republic*

Where have all the girls gone? Surely the boys in the Schoolhome are not alone in having to work on genuine virtue. The answer is that since they already know how to reach out to others, the girls are concentrating on their own issues. A group of them are deep in conversation with a teacher. They are asking her how to curb their tendency to help others at too great cost to themselves. Whereas the boys have to learn to substitute acts of kindness for deeds of violence, the girls have to learn to think about their own good. And while the boys' education will have to counteract our male stereotypes and stress their becoming the givers and not just the recipients of care, the girls' instruction will have to reverse the emphasis. Just as boys now quickly learn to admire the associated deficiencies of the three Cs, girls are taught to relish the corresponding excesses. To the extent that girls arrive in school already predisposed to shoulder the classroom's emotional labor and boys come prepared to reap the benefits, the immediate goals of education must therefore be different.

The goals for girls and boys will have to differ also when genuine courage, loyalty, and self-assertion are at stake. Just as our culture turns into male virtues what are perceived to be obvious vices of deficiency when females possess them, it incorporates in the female stereotype the timidity, passivity, and deceitfulness that when males possess them are rightly called defects. The symmetry ends here, however. In the process of assigning the baser qualities of coldness, disconnection, and distance to men, our alchemists have deftly transmuted them into objectivity and neutrality, the valued currency of science and politics, scholarship and the law. Leaving the deficiencies that are now built into the female stereotype in their original state, they have put women in an unenviable position. The traits that our culture says are theirs expose them to scorn and make them exceptionally vulnerable to the violence, bullying, and exploitation of those who are their polar opposites.

All this means that while boys in the Schoolhome are learning to replace violence to others and themselves with positive acts of courage and self-assertion, the girls will have to learn to speak their minds and stand up for themselves. Will this detract from their femininity? Like the boys who have to learn

that in making the genuine virtues of the three Cs their own
they sidestep femininity, the girls have to learn that they
bypass masculinity in taking possession of the genuine virtues
of courage, loyalty, and self-assertion. Whether or not they
know their Aristotle, both sexes have to learn that although
in name these virtues are associated with males, in content
they too transcend our gender stereotypes.

By coincidence this issue is under discussion in a homeroom
at this very moment. A girl and boy have just performed the
scene about the sun and the moon from Act IV of Shakespeare's *The Taming of the Shrew:*

Petruchio:	Good Lord, how bright and goodly shines the moon!
Kate:	The moon! the sun: it is not moonlight now.
Petruchio:	I say it is the moon that shines so bright.
Kate:	I know it is the sun that shines so bright.
Petruchio:	Now, by my mother's son, and that's myself, It shall be moon, or star, or what I list, Or ere I journey to your father's house. Go on, and fetch our horses back again . . .
Kate:	Forward, I pray, since we have come so far, And be it moon, or sun, or what you please: An if you please to call it a rush-candle, Henceforth I vow it shall be so for me.
Petruchio:	Say it is the moon.
Kate:	I know it is the moon.
Petruchio:	Nay, then you lie: it is the blessed sun.
Kate:	Then, God be bless'd, it is the blessed sun: But sun it is not, when you say it is not; And the moon changes even as your mind. What you will have it named, even that it is; And so it shall be so for Katharine.

The teacher asks them why Petruchio forces Kate to say
what is patently untrue. One of the onlookers in the class
mutters, "No problem. He's a practical joker." But the boy
who is going to play Petruchio in another scene of the play

says: "I am not. I'm trying to get her to obey me." "You're right," one of the girls interjects. "Petruchio says, 'I will be master of my own.'" "She is my goods, my chattels," the students recite in unison. Then the teacher asks, "What happens to people if you are constantly telling them that what they see isn't really there?" "They think they are crazy," a girl says; "My father does it to my mother all the time." "When this happens to someone," the teacher asks, "can she speak her mind?" "She doesn't even know her mind," the girl answers.

The ensuing silence has more meaning for the students than any words. And now the teacher tells those in the final scene of *Taming* to begin. How will Kate do the long submission speech that starts:

> I am ashamed that women are so simple
> To offer war where they should kneel for peace,
> Or seek for rule, supremacy and sway,
> When they are bound to serve, love and obey.

Will she "accidentally" send Petruchio sprawling at the end, as was done in a recent star-studded production in New York, or will she play it straight? The actors, who have been in a huddle, tell the teacher and their schoolmates that they have decided to do their scene twice—once ironically and once seriously. The teacher is very pleased. He congratulates the students on their ingenuity and good sense. After the scene is over they will talk more about male-female relations, he promises.

And so they do. They have a long conversation about how Kate's submission, whether genuine or not, is achieved. Is Petruchio by any chance brainwashing Kate? They discuss what effects male dominance has on the two parties. Does he drive her crazy or simply underground, turning her into a wily manipulator? Is he a joker or is he practicing a form of domestic battery? They ask what gives him the right to call her his goods, his chattels. Before her marriage was she her own person or her father's? And whose person is Petruchio? Tomorrow the teacher will bring in materials from history, psychology, law, economics to illuminate these issues. Then there will be more scenes, this time occasioning a discussion of Kate in relation to both her former self and her sister Bianca. These "three" female characters and the male characters' perceptions of them will lead naturally into an analysis of the deficiencies that even now define femininity and of the dangers girls face when they try to speak their minds.

Because of its sexual politics, *Taming* has been called one of Shakespeare's problematic plays. Petruchio's treatment of Kate has even made educators wonder if it is an appropriate one to read or perform in school. In a universe where children had never seen women beaten or humiliated or driven crazy by men, the policy of shunning the play might make sense. Why expose them unnecessarily to such unhealthy behavior? In the American schoolhouse where sexual politics is considered a personal problem, hence unworthy of curricular attention, this policy might also be wise. Like it or not, evasion of the issues in the play functions implicitly as support for Petruchio. In the Schoolhome, however, the only thing problematic about *Taming* is whether the play should be called a comedy.

In this safe atmosphere where students can talk about the domestic violence in the play's action and the misogyny in its language, sense Petruchio's sadism, and feel Kate's pain, *Taming* does not represent an embarrassment that must be gotten round. The very features that in other contexts make it problematic make it an especially effective educational vehicle here. Like other Shakespearean plays it illuminates some of those big questions that sooner or later all of us must confront. Its special virtue is that it raises questions that girls and boys in our culture face here and now: What is it to grow up female or male at this time and in this place? What happens to women who speak out? What are masculinity and femininity anyway? Can boys and girls, men and women live and work together without the one sex being dominant and the other submissive? Does marriage have to be an abusive institution?

The American schoolhouse has shut its eyes and, in the process, the eyes of our children to the workings of gender, but this blindness is a luxury the Schoolhome cannot afford. How can boys make the three Cs their business if their teachers belittle the very people our culture calls the bearers of these virtues? How can they acquire the belief that the nation belongs to girls and women as well as to themselves—and that both sexes equally belong to it—if their texts cast women as extras? How can girls know their minds and speak them if both they and the boys believe that in so doing they renounce their femininity? And how can teachers know when to teach the boys and girls separately and when together?

Before I began to study women and education, I was firmly committed to coeducation. As someone who had been brought up to believe in the Platonic dictum that sex—or gender as we would now say—is a difference that makes no difference, I thought it obvious that males and females should have the same education and that they should be educated together. When I read the *Republic*, it seemed so self-evident that "we should not have one kind of education to fashion the men, and another for the women" that I did not even discuss the issue in my philosophy of education courses. My research made me alter my position. I read the literature on the radically different socialization of males and females from infancy, on the higher valuation our culture assigns the traits and tasks considered masculine, on the differential evaluation of traits associated with one sex when they are possessed by a member of the other, on the differing effects on the psychological development of boys and girls of the fact that women are their primary caretakers, on the way girls and women think about others and themselves and about knowledge itself, on the chilly classroom climate for girls. This body of scholarship convinced me that educators cannot ignore gender with impunity.

When I first came to the conclusion that in education gender makes a difference, colleagues were quick to say: For the sake of women, forget what you have learned! It has taken centuries to prove that women are as capable of governing the state as men. Do not trifle with history! Believing that the only alternative to a gender-blind form of education is one in which girls and boys are routed onto separate tracks leading to different destinations, they cautioned me against publicizing the workings of gender in education. But to accept their reasoning is to fall prey to a false dilemma. The Schoolhome does not face an either-or choice: gender blindness or outright gender bias. It can choose to be *gender-sensitive*—to adopt a policy that takes gender into account when and where it makes a difference and not otherwise.

In the best of all possible worlds we would have a rule at our fingertips specifying precisely when and where gender makes a difference. In this world, however, there is nothing self-evident about the difference gender makes to education. It is not something you just intuit. Enough work has been done by now, however, to make it clear that gender affects the temperature of the classroom and that a chilly one for girls and women lowers their confidence and self-esteem.

In my philosophy of education courses I have taken to asking students if they, as parents, would want their sons and daughters to attend coeducational or single-sex schools. The response to my latest poll was paradoxical to say the least. After reviewing the arguments pro and con, the majority decided that they would want single-sex education for their daughters and coeducation for their sons. I could not disagree with this admittedly incoherent scenario. Early advocates of coeducation, Dewey among them, frequently justified it on the grounds that it civilizes boys and young men. At this moment in American history it certainly seems that boys can benefit from the civilizing influence of girls. Studies suggest, however, that to gain courage and confidence girls may profit from learning environments that are boy-free. Still, those students in my class were right who insisted that girls must learn how to maintain their self-confidence in the presence of boys. And although no one made this point, it could reasonably have been argued that boys might find it easier to resist the brutalization of masculinity if they could talk about the issues by themselves.

If boys and girls are given different educational experiences, what becomes of coeducation? Does not the policy of gender-sensitivity undermine what our culture has struggled for more than a century to achieve? No, it simply demands from the Schoolhome a flexibility about the issue and an imaginativeness that our nation's schoolhouses lack. It poses the challenge of how to design environments in which boys and girls can do some things together and others separately without replicating the old, stereotypical curricular divisions of shop and auto mechanics for boys, home economics and typing for girls and without slipping into those ill-fitting mantles of manhood and womanhood that replace virtue with both excess and deficiency. Will the Schoolhome be able to meet this challenge? I am not worried. Given its overarching aim of educating children not just for living but for living together, its motivation is great to find a middle way in which the values of both coeducation and single-sex education can be preserved.

When the object is to teach children to stand inside and keep in good repair a web of connection that includes all of us, is gender sensitivity enough? Definitely not. Sensitivity to race, class, ethnicity, religion, physical abilities, sexual orientation, and the other salient dimensions of American children's lives is also required. And it is as necessary in relation to the question of who should teach in the Schoolhome as in other matters. For how can the next generation learn to live and work with one another if they are not taught by people who are doing just that? The issue of what differences make a difference to education cannot be settled in advance, however. Since it calls out for inquiry and investigation, I again consider it fortunate that an experimental attitude is part of the Schoolhome's constitution. This moral equivalent of home is in the happy position of being able to learn from the relevant research, and also from its own successes and mistakes, how to teach our young to treasure their own good red blood and that of everyone else.

4

Domesticity Repressed

> The resistance shown by patients is highly varied and exceedingly subtle, often hard to recognize and protean in the manifold forms it takes.
>
> Sigmund Freud, *A General Introduction to Psychoanalysis*

One of the most memorable scenes from education I ever witnessed took place in a day camp, not a school. "It never rains for the Arts Festival," a parent with hubris had said that July. Now it was August and the two hundred or so children in the Charles River Creative Arts Program in Dover, Massachusetts, were driven indoors by a storm just as they were to present their production of an original musical play. For two hours sisters and brothers, parents and friends waited in a hot, humid, cavernous indoor tennis court as campers and counselors together created a performance area, worked out new stage directions, set up makeshift lighting and sound systems, and generally did what had to be done to put on the show. Their success gave the audience an object lesson about the disciplinary value of a love that has been harnessed to constructive activity. Not one adult that night found it necessary to enforce quiet. Not an unkind word was uttered, not a single fight had to be stopped. It is a myth, I realized as the performance began, that large groups of children can only be governed by force and fear.

That momentous night I felt as if the camp's educational practice was being put to the test. Like those crucial experiments by which scientists hope to confirm their theories, the event validated—and could have invalidated—a whole way of life. Yet I did not grasp all that was at stake. I had once asked the camp director how she managed to create such a warm, loving atmosphere for children that parents would look forward all year to summer so that their sons and daughters could begin learning again. "I don't do a thing," Priscilla Dewey had replied inaccurately. "It's the staff. They're all such wonderful people." Having read my John Dewey, her distant relation by marriage, I knew that night that his philosophy of freedom was being enacted. Because I had not yet read *The Montessori Method,* let alone reread "casa" as "home" or understood the Casa dei Bambini as a moral equivalent, I did not realize that what was being subjected to the most rigorous of tests was actually a fusion of the love Montessori built into her idea of school and the social activity that Dewey built into his. Nor did I then understand that the camp constituted a moral equivalent of home.

How could it be that I, who taught university courses in the philosophy of education, had not read Montessori? And why, for that matter, did the reports on American schooling and the reform proposals that were issued in the 1980s say almost nothing about the three Cs and neglect home's educative function altogether?

Nobody but Dorothy Canfield Fisher seems to have been listening when in 1907 Montessori said that "casa" meant "home." When Fisher tried to insist on this rendering, no one paid heed. No one noticed when, in 1984, John Goodlad said in a widely discussed study of American schooling, "One thing expected by parents is the safe care of their children and another is that they be seen as individuals . . . As I see it, this expected nurturing is, in part, residue from the once implicit assumption that the school should be during its hours of responsibility what good homes are expected to be the rest of the time." Nobody paid attention, either, when Sara Lawrence Lightfoot reported that one of our nation's best high schools had actually written into its statement of philosophy that "the schoolhouse must be a kind of home."

Read the other reports on American education issued in the 1980s. It does not matter if the subject is higher education, lower education, teacher certification, professional preparation; Dewey's insight into the relationship of school and home is ignored. One finds repeated demands for proficiency in the three Rs, for clear, logical thinking, and for higher standards of achievement in science, mathematics, history, literature, and the like. One searches in vain for discussions of love or calls for mastery of the three Cs of care, concern, and connection. Forgetting that home is a partner in the educational enterprise and focusing exclusively on school's role in the education of our nation's youth, these documents do not think to ask what the contribution of that silent collaborator has been or if it is still fulfilling its function.

As the idea of school as a moral equivalent of home began to take hold of me, I started to wonder why Montessori's translators had misread "casa" and educational experts so many decades later were silent on the subject of home. Could these closely related oversights be attributed to mere coincidence? Coming across the book that, according to Montessori's biographer, was responsible for dealing her ideas "a telling blow," I saw in the preface that the author thanked Dewey for reading the manuscript and making valuable suggestions. When I told a psychologist friend that I seemed to have discovered a pattern of cultural repression, she advised me to read Freud.

According to Freud, "the essence of repression lies simply in the function of rejecting and keeping something out of consciousness." The process of repression is not one over which a person has control. When we repress some unbearable idea—and it is the unbearable ones that get repressed—we do not know we do so. Indeed, the aim of psychoanalytic treatment is to bring what is submerged to consciousness. So that the symptoms will disappear, "all gaps in the patient's memory must be filled in, his amnesia removed." The analyst's task is not easy, for "there is knowing and knowing." When the physician tells the patient the repressed idea, this is not the end of the matter but the beginning of the treatment. Once the therapy has started, the patient exhibits resistance, which is "highly varied and exceedingly subtle, often hard to recognize and protean in the manifold forms it takes." Needless to say, the patient manifests resistance without recognizing it as such.

When the patient is a society, then culture is consciousness, the heritage that is passed along from one generation to the next is what is remembered, and curriculum is the process or "faculty" of memory. As curriculum plays the role of DNA on a biological model, on the psychological one it serves as the mechanism by which remembrances of things past are retained over time and a sense of cultural identity is thereby preserved. If it is difficult to fill in the memory gaps in the case of an individual, think how much more so it is when the patient is a culture like ours and the amnesia is a function of rejecting and keeping something out of that social construct. Yet when home has changed so radically that society is in danger of losing the benefits it can yield and the repressed idea is domesticity, we can but try. For in this, surely, Freud was right. If we do not "work through" the highly varied and exceedingly subtle resistances to home and domesticity that are manifested not just in America's educational thought but in its culture at large, we are bound to repeat them. Forgetting the lessons to be learned from Victor's case, we will overlook home's domestic curriculum. Denying home's educative role, we will neglect Dewey's insight into the relationship of home and school. Ignoring the recent transformation of home and family, we will not even perceive the need for school to step into the breach.

I

The question of a permanent contribution turns on whether there have been presented original points of view capable of guiding fruitfully educational practice . . . We owe no large point of view to Madam Montessori.

William Heard Kilpatrick
The Montessori System Examined, 1914

Freud would tell us to begin the therapeutic task by naming the manifold forms resistance takes. At the top of my list of our culture's resistances to domesticity are the doorkeeping activities that kept Montessori's idea of school out of our cultural consciousness. In the early part of this century, as I learned from Rita Kramer's biography of Montessori, William Heard Kilpatrick, an assistant professor of philosophy of education at Teachers College, Columbia University, launched "a devastating attack" on her ideas. By 1912 Montessori's work was known throughout the United States and in November 1913 she sailed to America, making triumphant lecture appearances in New York, Boston, Washington, Philadelphia, Pittsburgh, Chicago. Returning in 1915, she demonstrated her work to spellbound teachers who were attending an international exposition in California. By then, however, the man who was attracting so many students to Columbia that he was known as "the million-dollar professor" had delivered his fateful address to the International Kindergarten Union and had published a book based on it.

Besides thanking Dewey, his former teacher, Kilpatrick said in the preface to *The Montessori System Examined* that he wanted to ascertain Maria Montessori's contribution to American education. He then proceeded to break down the Montessori "system" into seven "characteristic elements." After analyzing and evaluating each one he asked, "Where among other systems does this one belong? What is the relation of Madam Montessori to the world's educational thinkers?" Had Kilpatrick done no more than say that Montessori belongs in the Rousseau-Pestalozzi-Froebel group he could not be faulted. But in his introductory chapter he asserted of the physician and world traveler he called "Madam": "If she had known more of what was being thought and done elsewhere her discussions would have been saved some serious blemishes and her system some serious omissions." This charge of ignorance was repeated later: "Doubtless if Madam Montessori had herself known more of better educational practice elsewhere, she would have incorporated some, perhaps all, of the features the absence of which we here regret." Worse still, Kilpatrick impugned Montessori's ability to think logically. Summing up his criticisms of her doctrine of education as development he wrote: "It would not be fair to Madam Montessori to say that she herself draws all of these objectionable conclusions from her doctrine of education. She does not. She has not thought consecutively enough."

There are periods, said Freud, when the patient evinces a "desire to put the analyst in the wrong, to make him feel his impotence, to triumph over him." In the last pages of his book Kilpatrick determined that Montessori "belongs essentially to the mid-nineteenth century, some fifty years behind the present development of educational theory." What reasons did Kilpatrick give for this assessment? One was that she had "confessedly been most influenced by Séguin." Kilpatrick did not say why the connection tainted her, but the disdain he exhibited toward Séguin, and through him toward Itard, shows how little he understood Victor's significance. When the patient dislikes anything, Freud commented, "he can defend himself against it most ingeniously; but when anything suits his book he can be credulous enough." Comparing Montessori's work to that of Dewey, of whom he once wrote in his diary, "Sometimes I am vexed with myself that I find so little to object to in John Dewey's position," Kilpatrick then brought in his final verdict: "they are ill advised who put Madam Montessori among the significant contributors to educational theory. Stimulating she is; a contributor to our theory, hardly if at all."

Acting as doorkeeper to the pantheon of educational philosophers, Kilpatrick took it upon himself to bar from the canon of Western educational thought not only Montessori's idea of school but the bearer of the tidings. Whether or not he is solely responsible for her exclusion from the texts and anthologies that comprise our collective memory, her banishment is by now a fait accompli. Remembered for the teaching materials she devised and for her individualized mode of instruction, Montessori is thought of as someone to whom "we owe no large point of view." Why that night at the camp's Arts Festival did I barely know of the existence of *The Mon-*

tessori Method? My ignorance was a function of a cultural amnesia that consigns far more than this one woman's work to oblivion.

How could Dewey, a man with insight into the interdependency of school and home, have endorsed a book that disparaged the ideas and achievements of a woman who was acting on that central understanding? *The School and Society*, the volume whose first three chapters comprise the lectures Dewey gave in Chicago, has been on the syllabus of my philosophy of education course for a long time. I used to tell my students that there was a gap in the title: Dewey should have called it *School, Home, and Society*. After reading *The Montessori Method*, I realized that I was wrong. The gap is in the text.

Freud said that one of the many forms resistance takes is the production of "derivatives." If an idea is sufficiently remote from what is repressed, it will have "free access to consciousness." Dewey apparently found it possible to remember home only by producing a heartless derivative thereof. In his eyes the household of an earlier generation was a place of work. Focusing on its disciplinary features—the industry, responsibility, habits of observation it taught—he paid no heed to the intimacy and affection of family relationships and to the shared day-to-day living that constitutes domesticity. In consequence, in recommending that the occupations of home be transplanted into school, he was tearing them from their domestic roots just as surely as the Industrial Revolution had done when it moved production out of the private home. Wanting to distinguish his program from contemporary movements whose aims were strictly vocational, Dewey insisted that the occupations to be placed in the school curriculum should be free from any economic motive or stress. He did not say, presumably because he did not realize, that in the ideal school he envisioned they would also be free from the domesticity associated with home.

Dewey's repression of domesticity is all the more interesting because an alumna of the Laboratory School of the University of Chicago, also called the Dewey School, wrote:

> We were a large family, anxious to put forth our kindest manners, happy to help the child who was slower to grasp the problem at hand, knowing that when we needed help it would be as gladly given. A most remarkable spirit of normal cooperation existed, the kindliest tolerance, an inspiring pride in work and play. There every child felt as much released, as happy and as unself-consciously contented and at ease as in his own home.

In their published account of the school that was under Dewey's guidance from 1896 to 1903 two teachers said, "a common center was found for the laboratory school in the idea of a school-house as a home."

Repressing the domestic aspects of the earlier American home, Dewey could not have understood what Montessori saw so clearly: by sending both mothers and fathers out to work the Industrial Revolution was creating a dangerous vacuum in poor children's lives. Lacking even a rudimentary comprehension of the problem the Casa dei Bambini was intended to solve, he could not have realized that it was Montessori's answer to the question of what radical change in school suffices when home has been transformed.

II

> We have of late been hearing much of the philosophy of tenderness in education . . . *Soft* pedagogics have taken the place of the old steep and rocky path to learning. But from this lukewarm air the bracing oxygen of effort is left out.
>
> William James, *Talks to Teachers*

If Montessori had gained entry to the pantheon for herself and her school, would the critics of American education have responded with alacrity to the parental wish reported by Goodlad that "Teach my child with tender loving care" be posted on the school bulletin board side by side with "Knowledge sets the human spirit free"? I doubt that her inclusion would have been enough to counteract the scorn of "soft pedagogics" to which William James gave voice in his *Talks to Teachers*.

Equating tenderness in education with a smoothing away of difficulties so that a child need never expend effort to achieve some result, and insisting that learning is hard work and involves intense effort, James concluded that in education

> the fighting impulse must often be appealed to. Make the pupil feel ashamed of being scared at fractions, of being "downed" by the law of falling bodies; rouse his pugnacity and pride, and he will rush at the difficult places with a sort of inner wrath at himself that is one of his best moral faculties. A victory scored under such conditions becomes a turning-point and crisis of his character. It represents the high-water mark of his powers, and serves thereafter as an ideal pattern for his self-imitation.

The metaphor of learning as war has seldom been developed so fully. Yet who has not been counseled that learning can be hell? That blood, sweat, and tears are necessary to gaining mastery over mathematics or some other hated school subject? True, most philosophers have shied away from calling pride and pugnacity "potent spurs to effort" and from casting the teacher in the role of a military officer whose job it is to inspire his men to capture a strategic fortification. Gardener, sculptor, guide: these are the preferred images. They clash, however, with the widespread opinion shared by many parents and some teachers that the process of learning is essentially painful. When ideas are seen as hostile forces to be "grappled with" in hand-to-hand combat, and the happy outcome of the struggle is described as getting the new subject matter "under one's control," the teacher can scarcely escape comparison to Teddy Roosevelt on San Juan Hill.

The contempt of softness and the intrepidity that James called martial virtues were in his eyes the rock upon which to build education as well as our nation. In the eyes of many

Americans still, a love imbued with tenderness and the three Cs leads to indulgence rather than "true" learning.

Yet think of the children in the Casa dei Bambini. The effort they put into their own learning was a constant source of amazement to observers and so was their perseverance. Shame, fear, the fighting impulse, inner wrath were not the spurs, however. Montessori compared her charges to hermits in the desert oblivious to surroundings and immensely happy, but I prefer Fisher's image of practitioners of yoga. It has been said that the beauty of yoga lies in its intensity. An activity that eschews the very martial attitudes that James wanted to put in classrooms, yoga depends for its successes on serenity and concentration. The total concentration, intense effort, and resultant joy the children of the Casa dei Bambini experienced constitute a peaceable alternative to the martial approach to learning James promoted.

Think also of how, in *Little Women*, the mother of Meg, Jo, Beth, and Amy acted when they told her they did not want to do any work that summer. Marmee, a wise fictional educator, allowed her daughters to remain idle for an entire week. With the hired woman's help she "did their neglected work, keeping home pleasant, and the domestic machinery running smoothly." But when Saturday came, Marmee and Hannah disappeared and the girls, who had already tired of their experiment, were left to learn through bitter experience how much effort goes into making day-to-day living comfortable and how inept they were at even getting food on the table.

Like good soldiers, the students envisioned by James were supposed to meet the enemy head on. Children in the Charles River Creative Arts Program did not think of themselves and were not pictured by others as in combat. The good schoolteachers I have known do not use war imagery to represent learning either. For one thing, they realize that, in education, indirection is often far more effective in the long run than confrontation.

Resistance "employs arguments as weapons," Freud said. Thus, one should not be surprised to hear those who deem love an insufficient motive for learning also arguing that it is unequal to the task of maintaining discipline. James himself was of two minds about whether the troops respond better to fear or love. After saying to teachers, "Fear of punishment has always been the great weapon of the teacher, and will always, of course, retain some place in the condition of the school-room. The subject is so familiar that nothing more need be said about it," he turned equally briefly to the subject of love. "The teacher who succeeds in getting herself loved by the pupils," James commented, "will obtain results which one of a more forbidding temperament finds it impossible to secure." The differences between James's concept of love in the class-room and the kind evinced in the day camp are striking. He spoke of students loving their teachers, not teachers loving their students. In his ideal case students loved their teachers, not one another. And he seems to have viewed love merely as a useful tool or technique to be adopted by the teacher in order to obtain results. When it constitutes a way of living and learning, however, by no stretch of the imagination does it make the children disorderly.

Remember those little vandals in Rome? Every report con-firms that when they and their brothers and sisters attended the Casa dei Bambini they were extraordinarily well behaved in school, not because harsh disciplinary measures were taken and not because the teacher had lured them into loving her. Engrossed in what they were doing, doing what was neither so easy as to be boring nor so difficult as to be frustrating, and doing it out of interest and desire, they almost never needed to be chastised, let alone punished. Made to feel secure by the love that enveloped them, they struggled mightily to do by themselves what in another classroom an adult would have done for them. According to James, "'Come and let me show you how' is an incomparably better stimulus than 'Go and do it as the book directs.' Children admire a teacher who has skill." The alternative of figuring out how for oneself appar-ently did not occur to him. Yet it worked for Montessori, and the children accomplished what at their age no one but she expected them to. Those three- and four-year-old writers and readers were not prodigies. The children carrying tureens of soup had no special genes for poise and balance. These were ordinary children, poor as Eliza Doolittle to boot, who felt safe and secure enough in school to outdo themselves.

However, the children in Rome were very young. Would older ones wreak havoc on a school governed by love? Not by a love that eschewed overindulgence—provided that the children were fully engaged in what they were doing.

In *Experience and Education,* a book written in 1938 to clear up misunderstandings of his philosophy, Dewey said that if a teacher repudiates the role of "external boss or dictator" and does not fully understand "the only freedom that is of enduring importance," pupils will very probably take advantage of the situation. "The commonest mistake made about freedom," he added, is "to identify it with freedom of movement, or with the external or physical side of activity." Not that he wanted young people to sit still all day. Far from it. But the schools modeled on his teachings were gaining a reputation for allowing children to run wild in halls and classrooms like ignorant little vandals and he was finding it necessary to remind his followers that freedom of movement is a means that is to be prized for bringing about the inner freedom we call self-control.

The self-discipline that Dewey had in mind, that some progressive educators in the 1920s and 1930s were finding it hard to translate into practice, and that was embodied in the campers at the Arts Festival that steamy August evening is not a function of obedience to the commands of some external authority. It derives from activities whose inner "logic" exerts its own demands on participants.

The activities need not be as complex as producing a play or an original musical show. Serving the soup can fit the bill. The rules or norms of the activity itself (carry the tureens to the tables, do not spill); the expectations of the other participants (serve everyone, make the portions equal); and the limitations imposed by the material conditions at hand (the hot soup, the long walk from the kitchen, the size of the tureens) all contributed to solving the problem that consumes teachers in our schoolhouses. Or perhaps I should say that activities like serving the soup *dissolved* the discipline problem. Of course, most older children would not find serving soup a sufficiently engrossing activity. For them, however, the intricacies of a theatrical production or of publishing a newspaper would impose the right kind of demands. So, for that matter, would the production of a full noontime meal for an entire school.

The discipline I saw enacted at the Charles River Creative Arts Program was not merely a function of the children's engaging in an engrossing activity, however. As the little ones in Rome felt for the boy who was struggling with his napkin and stayed with the young girl until she began rewriting her composition, the older youngsters at the day camp gave one another moral support and sympathy while working for a common cause.

Looking back upon my own experience as a child in a school that subscribed to Dewey's and Kilpatrick's philosophies, I can see that Kilpatrick's doorkeeping activities cost Dewey's disciples and their pupils dearly. I adored my school and I think most of my classmates did too. Yet although at a recent reunion—our first ever—we remembered our past with pleasure, we vividly recalled how unloving many of our actions and relationships had been and asked each other why our teachers had not taken better care of us. Did they not know how badly we were treating one another? One of the gifts our school bestowed on us was a care, concern, and compassion for the different peoples of the world outside its doors. How ironic that it did not require us to embody these virtues in our personal relations! When I think of Kilpatrick's resistance to Montessori, I understand the oversight. Through the years our school had tried to develop the strong sense of community that he and Dewey extolled. Their theories had no dealings with a concept of school as a domestic environment permeated by a family affection that influences not only the way activities are done in classrooms but behavior in the halls, the lunchroom, the playground.

The barrage of arguments continues. Why did a night of parachuting into France and the few months of actual combat "mean more to me than the ensuing years of college and work, happiness, sorrow, and love, marriage and children?" asked the author of a newspaper column published in 1985 on the eve of the fortieth anniversary of D-Day. James would have assured him that "the element of precipitousness"—of "strength and strenuousness, intensity and danger"—is what gives life its "moral style." The Harvard philosopher who had always prided himself on being "a so-called cultivated man" acknowledged ruefully that upon leaving the peaceful Chautauqua he exclaimed, "Ouf! what a relief! Now for something primordial and savage, even though it were as bad as an Armenian massacre, to set the balance straight again." Demonstrate that love in the classroom is capable of bringing order in its wake, and the many Americans who share James's predilection for precipitousness will protest that a loving, nurturant, peaceful environment is deadly dull; that such an insipid milieu will breed boredom if not disorder.

Is the rack necessary for excitement? Cross-cultural studies assure us that no one is born with a predilection for life in the fast lane. There is nothing intrinsically dull about safety and love, nothing inherently exciting about physical danger. This is an acquired taste. Introduce the three Cs into our schools, make classrooms into nurturant settings, and will children be bored to distraction?

The children of Rome did not find life in a Casa dei Bambini dull, but the end-of-twentieth-century United States is a very different place. Youngsters today grow up in a world in which the earth itself is at risk of life and limb, nations regularly engage in primordial and savage acts, and five-year-olds carry guns to school for protection. As if this were not enough to induce them to seek excitement in precipitousness, that new member of American households—the electronic media—habituates them to the sounds and images of violence and death.

I would not be at all surprised if newcomers to the School-home pronounced it too tame. As I found out in my three years of elementary school teaching and rediscovered as a mother, however, children's judgments about what is boring and what is exciting change as their knowledge, expectations, interests, and goals change. That young people do not initially find excitement in safety and love does not mean that they cannot learn to.

When you stop to think about it, despite its loving, nurtur-ant environment, there was plenty of excitement for the camp children that August night. Even if the weather had lived up to its reputation there still would have been enough thrills to go around. Theater is an exhilarating and inherently risky enterprise in which players can muff lines and forget entrances as well as bring themselves and their audiences to new emo-tional heights, stagehands can misplace props, the lighting crew can miss cues, and playwrights can be accused of a dozen sins. Every parent and teacher knows, however, that one child's source of endless fascination is another's occasion for boredom. This homely truth was understood at the Charles River Creative Arts Program where, had the Arts Festival not coincided with the last day of the season, the youngsters who put out the daily newspaper would have had their work cut out for them the morning after the storm. The photographers in the group would have been facing new risks and challenges too, as would the gymnasts and the hand bell ringers.

Freud talked about the ways patients project their problems onto something else. Boredom is a fact of life in American classrooms but love is not its source—at least not the kind of love that honors children, respects their abilities, and encour-ages them to take responsibility. Rather, this perennial school-house problem is a function of the mindless repetition of meaningless tasks. As workers on assembly lines are be-numbed by having to perform a single motion over and over, children are rendered insensible in school by having to mem-orize facts that have been detached from real-life contexts, fill in answers on worksheets that turn living, throbbing ideas into inert, disconnected facts, and hear the same old story again and again—nouns, the Pilgrims, Patrick Henry, state capitals, the multiplication facts. I was fortunate when young. My schoolmates and I were rarely subjected to this indignity. But as a public school teacher I was expected to subject my pupils to it, my sons in turn were its victims in school, and when one of them was for a brief period a substitute teacher, he was expected to carry on the tradition.

III

They were almost at the top of the hill now. Perhaps they would turn there and wave to her.

No, of course not, she was foolish to think of such a thing. Children never remembered the people they were leaving behind.

Dorothy Canfield Fisher, *The Brimming Cup,* 1919

"The intellectual resistances are not the worst," Freud said. In the case of domesticity repressed, one form more difficult "to get the better of" is a set of linguistic conventions deriving from the logical geography of education. These tell us that homes do not *educate* children, they *socialize* them; mothers do not *teach* their young, they *raise* and *train* them and in the best of cases *foster* their growth. When R. S. Peters mapped the educational terrain in the 1960s and 1970s, I did not notice that home's educational role is systematically slighted. No one then did. In fact, it was only after I began to see that domesticity is repressed in educational thought that I realized how differently we as a culture assess the contributions of home and school. It was not until I saw the relevance of Dewey's insight to our own situation that I understood just how damaging this way of speaking and thinking is.

In his memoir Rodriguez does not link learning to war. Yet, like James, he considers pain an inevitable accompaniment of education—a consequence of the journey children take in school from the world of their private homes to that public world across the bridge. Hidden between the lines of *Hunger of Memory* there lies a story of domesticity repressed. This tale is not uniquely Rodriguez's. Implicitly dividing social reality into the same two parts that Woolf could see from the bridge, we Americans take it for granted that the function of education is to transform children who have heretofore lived their lives in the one place into members of the other. Assuming that the private home is a natural institution and that, accordingly, membership in it is a given rather than something one must achieve, we see no reason to prepare people to carry out the tasks and activities associated with it. Perceiving the public world as a human creation and membership in it as something at which one can succeed or fail and therefore as problematic, we make the business of education preparation for carrying out the tasks and activities associated with it.

In those reports on the condition of American education published in the 1980s the preoccupation with life on the other side of the bridge that governed Rodriguez's schooling was amply demonstrated. Giving home the silent treatment, they viewed children as travelers to the public world, and school as the place they stop en route in order to acquire the knowledge, skill, attitudes, and values that they presumably will need when they reach their destination—a kind of wayside inn.

Once children enter school, according to this unexamined scenario, they do not go home again; not ever, not even as adults. Whereas Woolf told readers to watch the procession of men leaving home each morning to walk across the bridge into the public world, the authors of these volumes forgot that life is lived in both places. True, they expected children to do something called "homework," but the term is a misnomer. Designed by teachers as part of the work of the classroom, these assignments have no more to do with the business of the home than the briefs a lawyer reads on the commuter train each evening or the papers a teacher corrects after dinner. Homework is schoolwork done after school hours. The worksite may be the private home, but the home represented in the script is a house in which the silence of school prevails and parents are required to act as proctors for their offspring.

There is a stunning reversal here. The very aspects of home that have made it an effective partner in the educational enterprise—the intimacy of its atmosphere, the informality of its ethos, the daily life that is lived in it—are viewed by the authors of those reports as obstacles to a child's education. In consequence, their analyses and proposals pay no attention to the kind of environment that children need for growth and development. This break with reality is as self-defeating as these authors' total disregard of the transformation of home and family. The two oversights are connected, of course. Deny school's dependence on home for the domestic curriculum children require and the affectionate atmosphere they crave, and there is no reason to take into account even the most earthshaking changes in those institutions.

Turning school's partner in the educational enterprise into an antagonist ever ready to subvert its mission, the reports advised parents to support the teacher's authority and warned them against dereliction of their duty to monitor homework. The idea that because home had changed school might have to change did not occur to the authors of these tomes. The thought that school should take over its partner's responsibility of preparing young people to live in those private homes and families from which they exit each morning first to go to school and then to go to work in the public world was the furthest thing from their minds. And why not? As Dorothy Canfield Fisher made so clear in her novel *The Brimming Cup*, one unstated premise of American culture is that domestic life is the very thing we must learn to go beyond:

> Marise stood for a long time looking after the children. They were climbing up the long hilly road now, growing smaller and smaller. How far away they were, already! And that very strength and vigour of which she was so proud, which she had so cherished and fostered, how rapidly it carried them along the road that led away from her!

They were almost at the top of the hill now. Perhaps they would turn there and wave to her.

No, of course not, she was foolish to think of such a thing. Children never remembered the people they were leaving behind. And she was now only somebody whom they were leaving behind. She felt the cold penetrate deeper and deeper into her heart, and knew she ought to go back into the house. But she could not take her eyes from the children. She thought to herself bitterly, "This is the beginning of the end."

In the United States today almost all children who go off to school continue to live in homes and be members of families of one sort or another, and so do the adults who cross the bridge and take their place in the world at large. Americans know that to go beyond is not necessarily to leave behind. Nevertheless, as a culture we think of becoming educated not just as a process of acquiring new ways of thinking, feeling, and acting. We also assume that it is a matter of casting off the attitudes and values, the patterns of thought and action associated with domesticity.

Why were the schools my sons attended not moral equivalents of home? Why did the report that parents want their children taught with tender loving care go unacknowledged? The reason is not that Montessori was kept out of the pantheon. The intellectual resistances to domesticity are minor obstacles compared to the way our culture thinks about home, school, and world. We basically agree with Woolf that life on the other side of the bridge is competitive and that the people there have to be pugnacious and possessive in order to succeed. But then it follows that if education is to do its culturally assigned job properly, the insertion into school of any traces of the love, the nurturance, or the three Cs of care, concern, and connection associated with home and domesticity will be regarded as counterproductive. It follows that to expose children to "soft pedagogics" will be seen as a failure to prepare them for the world.

It also follows that the heritage school teaches will be one-sided. It is no accident that history, literature, and the other subjects of the American school curriculum give short shrift to the world of the private home. The logical geography of education demands no less. Think for a moment about the strikingly similar cases of politics and education and their very different treatment in the curriculum that the critics of American education favor. Activities in the real world around which institutions have grown up, education and politics are both suitable subjects for a vocational or professional curriculum. Nevertheless, space is reserved in the general or liberal curriculum for the one but not the other. In taking its place there the activity called politics is converted from an occupation to be undertaken into an object of study. Students are taught theory, history, research *about* politics, not politics itself. In the interests of spectatorship, success in the subject that often goes under the name "political science" or "government" is judged by the comprehension of a body of knowledge and perhaps the ability to undertake relevant inquiries, not by the efficacy of action taken in the real world. But the activity we call education can also be recast. It too has inspired its fair share of theory and research, some of it as enlightening and profound as one could wish. From the standpoint of both the individual and society, not to mention the future of the planet, it is surely as vitally important a set of activities and institutions as politics.

Why does the curriculum our elders praise welcome politics and shun education? Despite disclaimers, the one is not intrinsically more interesting and important than the other. The advantage politics has is that our culture situates it in the public world and places it in men's care. The problem education has is that although school has managed to move education out of the private home and into the public world, its "natural" site is still considered to be the near side of Woolf's bridge and its "natural" practitioners are still assumed to be women.

Freud spoke of repression as a topographical process. The logical geography of education reveals that, conceptually

speaking, home and family fall outside the educational realm.
In that enlightened country where the citizens are teachers,
school administrators, and pupils, school is the dominant institution. At once a product of culture in the broad sense of
the term and an institution expected to transmit high culture,
school is the site of the educational realm's primary activities—teaching and learning. Where in this territory do mothers and fathers, daughters and sons reside? In the place called
education there is no room for family members. Only unencumbered individuals are welcome. Nor is home to be found
here, not even as an object of school study. To meet those
people and become acquainted with that institution you must
cross the border into the domestic realm. Should you decide
to do so the inhabitants of the educational realm will tell you
that you will enter a region close to nature. In that less civilized domain the main commodity is socialization, they will
add, not education. And the main activities on behalf of children are so effortless and so lacking in direction and purpose
that they do not constitute teaching, they will say, but are
simply instinctual responses to nature's urgings.

Once I read the maps of this terrain for myself, I realized
why Fisher alone grasped that the Casa dei Bambini was intended to be a surrogate home for children: a home away from
home I am tempted to say, except that it was located in the
very building in which the children lived and the parents—or
at any rate the mothers—were expected to make frequent
visits. Writing as a mother for mothers like herself who were
loath to send their own preschool-age children to school in
the outside world, Fisher shared Montessori's belief in the
values of domestic life. On the one hand attuned to Montessori's domestic imagery, she was also better situated than her
peers to step outside the paradigm that imprisoned their
thinking. Had Kilpatrick and Montessori's other academically
inclined interpreters acknowledged her domestic metaphor
and its implications, they would have had to rethink their
assumptions about the relationship of school and home and

acknowledge home's contributions to the maintenance of culture itself.

IV

I reckon I got to light out for the territory ahead of the rest, because Aunt Sally she's going to adopt me and sivilize me, and I can't stand it. I been there before.

Mark Twain, *Huckleberry Finn*

In Fisher's novel school carries children away from home. In the works that are said to define American culture—the ones that constitute the American literary canon and that regularly appear on school and college reading lists—the private home is represented as something to run away from.

Seven years before Victor emerged from the forest, Thomas Jefferson's *Notes on the State of Virginia* was published. In that book, as jam-packed with facts of geography and natural history as the computer file of a late-twentieth-century protector of the rain forests of Brazil, he took up the complaint that America "has not yet produced one good poet, an able mathematician, a man of genius in a single art or a single science." Citing George Washington as one "whose memory will be adored while liberty shall have votaries" and Benjamin Franklin as a man "than whom no one of the present age has made more important discoveries," Jefferson called the reproach "unjust as it is unkind." Look at how small our population is in comparison to those of France and England and consider what a short time we have existed, he added in our defense. We have good reason to believe that America "can produce her full quota of genius," he concluded, before going on to list ninety or so indigenous birds.

Jefferson's faith in his countrymen was not misplaced. Before his death in 1826 Washington Irving's *The Sketch Book* appeared. Three years later came James Fenimore Cooper's *The Pioneers*, with *The Last of the Mohicans* following soon after. If these works do not quite qualify as poetry they have nevertheless passed the test of time. What makes their presence on the literary scene shortly after Jefferson's defense of American letters so interesting is that while both authors set their stories against the nature Jefferson described in such literal detail, neither one celebrated the domesticity that he valued so highly. Locating their protagonists as far from the "mobs of great cities" as Jefferson hoped his fellow Americans would remain, Irving and Cooper combined his admiration of the land with his mistrust of so-called civilization. But whereas Jefferson wrote to his grandson in Washington, "Your situation, thrown at such a distance from us, & alone, cannot but give us all great anxieties for you," Irving and Cooper founded a literary tradition that has utterly repressed home and family. The literary hero they constructed has been called a man on the run. Rejecting Jefferson's belief that "those who labour in the earth are the chosen people of God," he heads into the forest, down the river, out to sea, to find adventure in nature and with luck gain redemption. From what is he fleeing? The usual answer is "society" or "civilization." But if you read *Rip Van Winkle*, the Leather-Stocking Tales, *Walden*, *Moby-Dick*, *Huckleberry Finn* with domesticity on your mind, you quickly see that the reply masks home's role in the drama.

Long before he experienced anxiety about a grandson's leaving home, a widowed Jefferson wrote his eleven-year-old daughter Martha: "After four days journey I arrived here without any accident and in as good health as when I left Philadelphia. The conviction that you would be more improved in the situation I have placed you than if still with me, has solaced me on my parting with you, which my love for you has rendered a difficult thing." After laying out for her a daily schedule of study he said: "I expect you will write to me by every post. Inform me what books you read, what tunes you learn, and inclose me your best copy of every lesson in drawing . . . I have placed my happiness on seeing you good and accomplished, and no distress which this world can now bring on me could equal that of your disappointing my hopes."

Rip Van Winkle also had a young daughter, but Irving did not endow him with Jefferson's concern for her welfare. The first of a long line of American protagonists to withdraw from the world, Rip walked into the woods where Hendrick Hudson and his men were playing ninepins in order to get away from home: "Poor Rip was at last reduced almost to despair; and his only alternative, to escape from the labour of the farm and clamour of his wife, was to take gun in hand and stroll away into the woods."

By no means do all our literary landmarks explicitly portray a man in flight from domesticity, but Irving made Rip's trajectory crystal clear:

> In a word, Rip was ready to attend to anybody's business but his own; but as to doing family duty, and keeping his farm in order, he found it impossible . . . If left to himself, he would have whistled life away in perfect contentment; but his wife kept continually dinning in his ears about his idleness, his carelessness, and the ruin he was bringing on his family. Morning, noon, and night, her tongue was incessantly going, and every thing he said or did was sure to produce a torrent of household eloquence.

Listen now to the words Mark Twain put in his leading character's mouth on the very first page of *Huckleberry Finn:* "The Widow Douglas she took me for her son, and allowed she would sivilize me; but it was rough living in the house all the time, considering how dismal regular and decent the widow was in all her ways." No doubt the home Huck was forced to share with his alcoholic father is the immediate cause of his escape, but before setting out in his canoe Huck acknowledges that he cannot abide the Widow Douglas's version of domesticity either: "I did not want to go back to the widow's any more and be so cramped up and sivilized, as they called it." In fact the book ends with Huck saying that he has to get away because Aunt Sally is going to adopt and civilize him "and I can't stand it. I been there before." Huck runs not from society as such but from that part of it called home.

The protagonist of *Walden* also perceives home and domesticity as something to be discarded. We think of Thoreau as having separated himself from the corrupting influences of the city and town; from the luxuries and comforts of civilization that "are not only not indispensable but positive hindrances to the elevation of mankind." And so he did. Yet in the very first pages of his account of living alone in the woods for two years and two months he wrote: "I see young men, my townsmen, whose misfortune it is to have inherited farms, houses, barns, cattle, and farming tools . . . Better if they had been born in the open pasture and suckled by a wolf." Thoreau did not stop to ask how his new world Victors would acquire the rudiments of culture, let alone elevate the species. Instead, after giving an abbreviated history of human shelter, he remarked:

> At last, we know not what it is to live in the open air, and our lives are domestic in more senses than we think. From the hearth to the field is a great distance. It would be well perhaps if we were to spend more of our days and nights without any obstruction between us and the celestial bodies, if the poet did not speak so much from under a roof, or the saint dwell there so long. Birds do not sing in caves, nor do doves cherish their innocence in dovecots.

Borrowing an ax in order to build "a tight shingled and plastered house, ten feet wide by fifteen long, and eight-feet posts, with a garret and a closet, a large window on each side, two trap doors, one door at the end, and a brick fireplace opposite," Thoreau left home only to recreate a domestic environment for himself on Walden Pond. Natty Bumppo lived in the woods too—for forty years in a hut of his own, he confides in *The Pioneers,* although in other volumes of the Leather-Stocking Tales he seems to be perpetually in transit.

"Providence placed me among the Delawares young," says

Cooper's hero. To judge from the admittedly sparse evidence, the domestic circle in which he had spent his first years was a far happier one than Huck's. Experiencing "a rush of childish recollections" when in the second chapter of *The Deerslayer* he enters a room inhabited by two sisters, Natty finds that the resemblances to home "opened a long hidden vein of sensations; and as he quitted the room, it was with a saddened mien." In the book's final chapter the man who would hence-forth be called Hawkeye tells one of those sisters: "If father and mother was livin'; which, however, neither is—but if both was livin', I do not feel towards any woman as if I wish'd to quit 'em in order to cleave unto *her*."

Choosing a life of adventure over the home and family Judith offers him, and friendship with the Delaware chief Chingachgook over marriage, Hawkeye rejects domesticity just as surely as Huck does. "And do you so delight in violence and bloodshed?" Judith asks when Hawkeye—or Deerslayer, as she knows him—says he is going to pursue the Huron so long as the war lasts: "I had thought better of *you*, Deer-slayer—believed you one who could find his happiness in a quiet domestic home, with an attached and loving wife, ready to study your wishes, and healthy and dutiful children, anx-ious to follow in your footsteps, and to become as honest and just as yourself." "Lord Judith," he replies. "What a tongue you're mistress of! Speech and looks go hand in hand, like; and what one can't do, the other is pretty sartain to perform! Such a gal, in a month, might spoil the stoutest warrior in the colony." In response to Judith's query, "And am I then so mistaken? Do you really love war, Deerslayer, better than the hearth and the affections?" this "fair-dealing" man for whom truth is the "polar star" turns the question away from hearth and home and launches into an abstract justification of war.

"Where is our *Madame Bovary*, our *Anna Karenina*, our *Pride and Prejudice* or *Vanity Fair*?" asked the literary critic Leslie Fiedler. Most of our classic novels "avoid the facts of wooing, marriage, and child-bearing." We might add to his list the facts of childrearing, intergenerational relationships, and the day-to-day interactions between the sexes. But our American classics are not merely evasive. Implying when not actually saying that the domestic is a realm of tedium, constraint, and even cruelty, they represent home as that which a boy or man must leave behind in order to seek adventure and ultimately find fulfillment.

Huck felt bored and cramped up at the widow's. Rip was reduced almost to despair by his wife. Ishmael, the narrator of *Moby-Dick*, has just one recollection of home: that of his stepmother whipping him for "cutting up some caper or other" and then packing him off to bed where he was forced to stay for sixteen hours. Near the book's end Ishmael says of Captain Ahab, "The step-mother world, so long cruel—forbidding—now threw affectionate arms round his stubborn neck, and did seem to joyously sob over him, as if over one, that however wilful and erring, she could yet find it in her heart to save and to bless." But this redemptive echo of memory scarcely dilutes the earlier message of child abuse.

In the moral terrain of our literature as in the "logical geography" of education, the domestic realm is an arid, unfertile region. Yet although these two quite different areas of culture both view home as a place on which to turn one's back, they espouse opposing ideals. Educational thought makes the flight from domesticity a prerequisite of civic responsibility: children have to turn away from home in order to take their places in the public world as workers and citizens. In American literature that flight augurs irresponsibility. Instead of initiating our literary heroes into the tasks, duties, and frames of mind of adulthood as the schoolhouse is supposed to, the woods, the river, the sea keep them eternally young.

At least one literary critic has described Hawkeye as infantile and presexual, but there is no reason to single him out. Rip, Hawkeye, Huck, Ishmael, even Thoreau are Americanized Peter Pans who, whatever their chronological ages, find or create their own Never Never Lands. On the river Huck, the only teenager in this group, leads a life as packed with adventure and empty of obligations other than the ones he chooses to honor as Peter himself could desire. Before his escape Rip, a middle-aged husband and father of two, spends his days with the other men of the village sitting on the bench in front of the inn "talking listlessly over village gossip, or telling endless sleepy stories about nothing." When he awakens from his twenty-year slumber his wife is dead and his children full grown. Resuming his life of idleness "with impunity," he returns to his place on the bench at the inn. Ishmael, a schoolmaster by trade, is in the habit of packing up a shirt or two and going to sea as a way "of driving off the spleen, and regulating the circulation." To be sure, life on the *Pequod* turns out to be no lark. Still, if Captain Ahab's desire for revenge far exceeds Captain Hook's, and if Ishmael is less successful than Peter in eluding the rule of a monomaniac, the American protagonist nevertheless manages to spend three years as one of the boys in a world almost as far from Manhattan as Never Never Land is from Kensington Gardens. Even that Harvard graduate Thoreau constructed a world in which obligations to others disappeared and the only rules he had to obey were those he legislated for himself: an adolescent boy's dream if there ever was one.

J. M. Barrie saw to it that domesticity had an important part to play in his hero's life. Attracted to the bedtime stories Mrs. Darling told her children, Peter Pan carried off his Wendy to be a mother for the lost boys whose captain he was and a housekeeper for himself. Girls and women are at best occasional visitors to the worlds inhabited by our American Peters, and the usual contributions of home and family are conspicuously absent. Fiedler referred to the "sacred marriage" of Huck and Jim, Hawkeye and Chingachgook, Ishmael and Queequeg, but the derivative of home in *Huckleberry Finn*, the Leather-Stocking Tales, and *Moby-Dick* is far more distant from the repressed idea of domesticity than the one invented by Barrie. Irving's concept of a man who sleeps away the long childrearing years and returns to the inn bench only after his wife has died is even more remote.

The narrative of a man on the run from domesticity is as familiar to late-twentieth- as it was to mid-nineteenth-century readers. The western, the detective story, the space saga, the adventure genre are variations on the theme. Our new age heroes are not presexual, far from it. But that is because in the postmodern world sex is no longer attached to love, marriage, and procreation, all or any of which create ties and establish obligations. Perceived as marks of independence rather than signs of entanglement, the sexual forays of the descendants of Huck and Hawkeye signal the very freedom from domestic responsibility that forced those earlier protagonists into a presexual mold.

The dream of escape encoded in our literary canon is not just a figment of the American imagination, however. Enacted daily by the man who disappears from home leaving wife and children to fend for themselves, it is lived also by the runaway adolescent held hostage on the streets by drugs, crime, prostitution, AIDS. Turning fantasy into nightmare, our latter-day Rip Van Winkles, Huck Finns, and Henry David Thoreaus expose the gaps in the stories told by Irving and his successors and the fatal flaws in their underlying philosophies. "I've had 4,000 arrests on nonsupport, and this guy was the smoothest I've seen. All he talked about was how he loved sailing and couldn't wait to get back to it," a State Department of Revenue investigator told a news columnist. The man's ex-wife, who at one time had held two jobs so as to stay off welfare, said, "Now, I hope Chip can finish college. He's such a nice kid. I just do not understand how a father could leave a child like that."

Calling Rip "an obedient, hen-pecked husband" and Dame Van Winkle "a termagant wife," enlisting our sympathies with his unhappy domestic existence and making light of her concerns about Rip's "idleness, his carelessness, and the ruin he was bringing on his family," Irving never lets his readers ask how Rip's family could have survived economically during his twenty-year sleep in the woods. Nor does he allow the question to arise of how Rip's daughter could have grown in that period from a "ragged and wild" child into a woman with "a snug, well-furnished house, and a stout, cheery farmer for a husband" who is willing and able to take care of her still idle father. Cooper, in turn, makes Hawkeye such a romantic figure that one does not stop to wonder how a man who has spent the better part of his life in the woods and who feels closer to nature than to other human beings could be so different from Victor, so thoroughly human in his manners and mores. And Mark Twain spins his tale so well that we do not think to inquire how a child who was dreadfully abused by a drunken father and who had no mother, sisters, or brothers to comfort and care for him could have consorted with base criminals without becoming one.

Beneath the unasked questions in our literary canon there lies a world of domesticity. Who cooked the substantial fare of meat, potatoes, and dumplings that was served up to Ishmael that first night at The Spouter-Inn? What were Captain Ahab's young wife and child doing during that long voyage of the *Pequod*? How large were the families of the whaling men of New Bedford whose tombstones Ishmael remembers so well, and how did the mothers, the widows, the children left behind manage to survive? How did Rip stay alive those twenty years without food and shelter? When and where did Huck acquire the sensitivity to the feelings of others he sometimes displays? Equating domesticity with the mundane, the commonplace, the trivial, the banal, the fiction writers whose works have come to define the American literary tradition have kept its positive contributions to human development and self-fulfillment a well-guarded secret. Representing the activities, values, and relationships of home as unworthy of a hero's respect, "the" American classics—the literary works that are said to stand at the very center of our cultural heritage—teach us to forget what it is necessary to remember.

V

The symptoms—of course we are here dealing with mental (or psychogenic) symptoms, and mental disease—are activities which are detrimental, or at least useless, to life as a whole.

Sigmund Freud, *A General Introduction to Psychoanalysis*

Freud pointed out that "repression leaves symptoms in its train." Our culture's repression of domesticity does just this. In 1989 Anne Machung reported on a survey of the expectations of graduating seniors at the University of California at Berkeley. The overwhelming majority of those studied hoped to marry, have children, and pursue a career. Of the women, nearly nine-tenths planned to acquire graduate degrees and half thought they would earn at least as much as their husbands. Few anticipated getting divorced or raising their youngsters alone. Each one believed she would rear two or three children and expected to interrupt her career for anywhere from six months to twelve years to do so. While in Machung's words the women were "talking career but thinking job" in order to be in a position to take care of the children they wanted to have, the men were talking family but thinking career. They were willing to "help out" at home but they did not want to be told what to do or have their contributions measured against those of their wives, let alone share housework equally. As for child care, most not only believed it to be the wife's responsibility; they could barely see themselves making daycare arrangements or missing work when the children were sick.

Come stand with me on the bridge and watch the procession again, this time to see with our own eyes just how well the expectations of these young men and women are being realized. I notice how racially and ethnically diverse the procession has become since Woolf's time, and how all social classes are represented. I am also keenly aware that whereas in 1950 less than 30 percent of married women in the United States walked across the bridge to work each day, by 1995 80 percent of mothers will do so; that two-thirds of all our children under six years old will then have mothers in the procession. I know too that, on the average, women at all levels of employment earn far less than men. But I want to find out what has happened to that woman whose child was sick. I do not see her anywhere. If she has had to miss work to care for her daughter, her law firm will not be pleased. And where is the woman who with her husband was close to tears? I fear she may have left the procession for good.

One thing that is clear is that it is mainly women who miss the morning march on account of a sick child. It is also mainly women who at day's end are carrying heavy bags of groceries, arriving home and starting to cook before they even remove their coats. And who is taking charge of the children? I fear it is that irresponsible new household member. I wonder why fathers do not take care of their sons and daughters while the mothers work in the kitchen. I wonder why in so many of those homes I see no signs of men. And why, in the others, the men either have not yet arrived back from work or are too wrapped up in the evening news to give the children their attention.

Machung's men—who sound to me like Best's boys grown up—have history as well as literature on their side. From the very beginning of American society the domestic arena has been considered women's place. The tasks and activities associated with home and domesticity have changed dramatically over the years. As the historian Laurel Thatcher Ulrich has shown, one of the most basic household skills in colonial days was building and regulating fires for cooking, while slaughtering, cider making, and spinning were standard activities. Still, despite the enormous differences from one period to the next, the assignment of housekeeping tasks to women has remained an unwritten rule even as the assumption that women have primary responsibility for nurturing and bringing up the children has persisted as a fundamental cultural premise. For rich and poor the place called home has differed dramatically and so have maternal duties and responsibilities. But whether a woman has been a white mistress or a black slave, a Boston Brahmin or an Irish immigrant servant, a middle-class employer or a black maid, the work of the home and care of the children in it have been hers.

The women in our past were not barred from all participation in the public world, but their place on the other side of the bridge was narrowly circumscribed. Ulrich has reported that in the colonial period a wife might act for her husband in his absence, planting the corn, minding the shop, administering the estate, suing his debtors. And it is now common knowledge that textile mills in the nineteenth century were "manned" by women and girls. During all those years, however, women had no role to speak of in politics; and insofar as they entered into business, they did so mainly as their husbands' deputies. A whaler's wife may have looked after some of his commercial interests but she did not sign on the *Pequod.*

With women now acting as their own deputies and working outside their homes as hard as the men in our past ever did—which is, of course, far harder than our literary heroes—the question is, how do they manage to do their new work and their old? To judge from the look of those women on the bridge I am not so sure that they are managing well. Some of them are barely dragging themselves along. Instead of stepping onto solid ground as they walk off the bridge, they are disappearing from view. Like the woman with a husband and three children who in a letter to Ann Landers described herself as "bone-weary," they seem to be sinking in the quicksand. But not all of the women going under are married. Whether married or not, women are the ones working full time in the public world and returning home each evening to another job.

Of course not all the women are allowing themselves to get caught in the bog. Like their foremothers in the early part of this century who had to choose between a family and a career, some are deciding to hold onto their sanity by forgoing motherhood. As for the others, one dressed in designer clothes is saying that she does not plan to run herself ragged any longer. Instead, she will resign her hard-won managerial post and stay at home with her children during the day. To earn pocket money she will work as a waitress three nights a week. Another woman is turning down a promotion in state government in order to work part time while her daughter is young. What are the chances that these women's positions will be waiting for them when they decide to reenter the public world some years hence? I wonder if the arduous graduate study they underwent will still be relevant, if the on-the-job skills they learned will remain up to date, if their colleagues are planning to keep their places open.

In a letter to Ann Landers, a woman wrote that in leaving a lucrative career to become "a stay-at-home wife and nurturing mother," she "adopted a whole new set of values and put aside pride, envy, competitiveness and the need for recognition." The unconscious echo of *Three Guineas* might have pleased Woolf, but she was far too attuned to the psychic damage self-sacrifice does to accept at face value the woman's claim to be "truly content" in her new life—really woman's old life. Woolf knew that a heavy toll is exacted by a cultural ideal that defines a "true woman" as one who devotes herself to those who do not dream of returning the favor. I do not doubt that some women are genuinely happy refusing promotions and leaving careers, but I wonder how many can afford to take this step. Poverty is now a woman's problem. I also worry about the women who have second thoughts. Will their anger and frustration stay pent up until another Betty Friedan comes along?

In the American literary tradition one of the many variations on the theme of escape from domesticity is men—sometimes even boys—coming to women's rescue. It is painfully evident that women now need saving and that the Roberts, Juanitas, Mary Tams, and Lun Cheungs do too.

Instead of looking to boys and men for help, can we not ask the Schoolhome to take over all the tasks of the private home?

154 / The Schoolhome

It is not equipped for this. Its loving atmosphere should keep
mothers from feeling guilty about leaving home each morning.
Its domestic curriculum can provide boys and girls with the
knowledge, skill, and behavior patterns their mothers and
fathers have no time to teach. With the medical profession's
help, it can even have physicians and nurses on call. But the
Schoolhome cannot buy the groceries, do the housework of
the private home, tend the children during their waking and
sleeping hours there. It is not designed to do all those things
both great and small that maintain life on this side of the
bridge.

James intended his war against nature to be a replacement
for war itself. My moral equivalent differs fundamentally from
his in just this regard. Convinced that modern war was essentially immoral and hence should be eradicated, James proposed that it be abolished and a substitute be found for it.
Believing that the private home is potentially, if not always
in actuality, a moral institution—a force for good in children's
lives—I propose that benign versions of it be preserved and a
new institution be created to lighten its load. Collaborating
with the variegated forms of the new private home, the
Schoolhome will take on some of the functions the latter can
no longer carry out on its own, but only some. Insofar as it
can help save mothers and their children, it is not because it
will undertake all the domestic work that is now done by
women. The reason is that the education it provides will teach
boys and girls alike that domesticity is everybody's business.

Ultimately, the rescue operation will have to be carried out
by men and boys who display not the heroics of a Hawkeye
delivering a timid female from danger only to embark immediately on another adventure, but a new kind of courage.
Acting as friends and co-workers of women rather than as
protectors and patronizers, the males who come to their rescue will have to be brave enough to defy society's stereotypes.
As the boys over there in the Schoolhome are now learning,
genuine male courage today means doing with grace, not re-
sentment, what our culture has traditionally, but nevertheless

arbitrarily, labeled women's work, and sharing responsibilities that have long been assigned to the opposite sex.

Does our culture's domephobia—its devaluation of and morbid anxiety about things domestic—make it hard to imagine that boys and young men will be willing to learn the values, virtues, responsibilities, and processes of domestic living? "I have a little difficulty being a househusband," an unemployed coal miner told Melissa Ludtke. "But I love being with the kids. I also believe it is good for them to see me doin' housework, so they don't keep believin' that outside work belongs only to the man and inside is the woman." I have high hopes that by raising to consciousness the hidden curriculum in anti-domesticity of both school and society and making it a topic of study in the curriculum proper while adopting a gender-sensitive approach, the Schoolhome will be able to work through, instead of repeating, the myriad resistances to home and family.

Right now the students in one of those homerooms on the promontory are discussing the question of whether the United States is a domephobic society. "What's that?" one boy asks. "Do we hate home," another says. "No, do we *fear* home," a girl corrects him. "Do we hate *and* fear home," a peacemaker suggests. "I don't know if we hate home," another girl volunteers, "but I know that Americans look down on domestic work. Look who does it." "Women," say the boys. "You mean black women," three African-American girls mutter. Hearing them, the teacher introduces the inevitable history and statistics. "We've already talked about the fact that in the South in pre–Civil War days slave women and children did the domestic work. But do you realize that as late as 1940, 60 percent of working black women in the nation were domestics?" "Wow," an African-American boy groans. "I read somewhere that W. E. B. Du Bois talked about a despised race being joined to a despised calling. Now I know what he meant." "I don't see why the fact that black people have done it means that we hate domestic work," an Asian-American boy ventures. "Look," says a girl. "I don't want to change the subject but both my great-grandmothers were domestics, and they were Irish." I am glad to hear the teacher gently tell her that she has not changed the subject and remind the others to listen closely to what she is saying. As the authors of *Women's Ways of Knowing* have documented, all too many girls and women become trapped in silence. "Immigrants, I bet they were," her best friend, who is from Cambodia, says. "Yeah, you're right." "In my house there are no domestic servants," someone announces. "In mine either," the shout goes up. But one girl says quietly, "Yes there is. Your mother is one."

Again some squirming and a long pause, after which the teacher and her students start exploring their own attitudes on the subject. I happen to know that the next time it meets this group will pursue the connection it discovered today between women and domesticity to see if any light can be shed on the phenomenon of domephobia.

Meanwhile, in another part of the Schoolhome, a book by Erma Fisk called *Parrots' Wood* is under discussion. "Look," says one boy, "we agreed that Huck was running away from home, but here's this old woman and isn't that exactly what she's doing? Isn't going off to those jungles, in I don't know where, just as escapist as Huck going down the river on the raft?" "Where?" the teacher asks incredulously. "Let's map Erma Fisk's journey before we say another word." "Can we call her Jonnie?" a girl asks. "It says on the back of the book that her friends did." "I can't say that I like her that much," someone interposes. "She's okay," a boy says. "I'd like to see you walking around Belize, wherever that is, catching birds in nets at almost age eighty." "No more of this geographical stupidity! I can't stand it," the teacher almost shouts. "Who wants to make the map? We'll hang it beside Huck's." "Belize is where I was born. I'll work on it if someone helps me," a girl offers, "but I want to say something first. Jonnie is not like Huck. He left home behind but she took domesticity with her. I couldn't believe how much cooking she did for all those bird people . . ." "Ornithologists," a boy interrupts. "Spell it," everyone yells, and they do, or at least they try to.

"As I was saying before I was so rudely interrupted: Jonnie did a lot of the cooking for all those people on the expedition and the food shopping and she even washed other people's clothes." "Yeah," a boy muses. "When a woman is on the run, she takes the housework with her."

In the Schoolhome both domesticity and domephobia are objects of study. But students there do not only learn *about* these phenomena. They learn *to be* domestic—to live and work together in a homelike environment. I can see teenage boys and girls diapering the infants some mothers have brought for a visit and taking charge of the toddlers. Besides occasional contacts like this with the very young, each older student cares for at least one much younger child. I also see girls and boys planning, preparing, and serving breakfast. The Schoolhome is capitalizing on the fact that our society can no longer take it for granted that children will arrive in school well fed and toting a nutritious lunch. Making its students responsible for feeding their extended family and rotating the tasks so that each student does his or her fair share, it teaches by example that domesticity is everyone's business.

Vocational or professional training is not the issue here. Citizenship is. Each day, every child does some domestic work, not in order to be qualified for careers in food-related industries but because the daily life of the Schoolhome requires this commitment. But won't children do this "housework" grudgingly? I see a group washing dishes. They are singing work songs that the music teacher has taught the whole school and making up one of their own to perform at a school assembly. Once they finish the breakfast dishes they will be done with their domestic labor for the day, but not with the issues it raises.

The manual labor that students in the Schoolhome perform daily does not make it a site of anti-intellectualism. The members of this dishwashing crew know that their job is essential and why. Like every other domestic work brigade, they are trying to figure out ways to solve the school's—and by extension the world's—problems of food, energy, and waste disposal. Like theater and newspaper, domestic activities spin their own webs of knowledge. After a short break in the gym these youngsters are headed for the library where they will do research on the ecological issues related to their present job. The meal planning team will be there too.

The kitchen squad is now talking earnestly to a teacher. "Should we be serving red meat?" several youngsters asked her yesterday. "Why ever not?" she replied. Today, after having done some reading and thinking on the subject, both children and teacher know that the question is not easily answered. "What should we do?" a boy wonders. "We could pretend we never asked," says one girl. "We could plan a week's worth of meatless meals and our consciences would be clear," another suggests. "Or you could investigate the ethical, nutritional, social, political, and economic aspects of meat eating, knowing that your findings might ultimately affect all of us," says the teacher. "You mean our group could do the research and report back to the whole school?" a girl asks with suppressed excitement. "Can we make a recommendation?" a boy continues. "Great!" they all roar. "But what do we do about meals until then?" a realist groans.

Activities relating to that basic human need, food, are not the only ones that give inhabitants of the Schoolhome a healthy respect for domestic work. The children have heard all about those American schoolhouses that are falling apart and they do not intend to let that happen here. They know about the cracked ceilings and broken windows, the freezing buildings and the failed plumbing. They also know—and are learning more about the fact—that shelter is a basic human need. Actually, these young people have a particular stake in keeping their building intact because they took part in the planning. They were the ones who proposed that the larger classrooms resemble living rooms and the smaller ones dens or studies, and who insisted that even from the outside the school should appear homelike. They realize, of course, that there is no one ideal or single "correct" floor plan for a Schoolhome; that the way a moral equivalent of home organizes its space will depend on local needs and factors such as climate, site, size. However, they would be the first to say that although even a standard schoolhouse building can be turned into a Schoolhome, in the process it will have to acquire the look as well as the feel of home.

Do you see those boys and girls carrying screwdrivers and hammers? They are one of the Schoolhome's repair teams. On call in emergencies, they periodically check the condition of the furniture and fixtures in each classroom. That other group roaming the building works mainly on heating and plumbing, the crew now walking out the front door is in charge of the grounds, another squad tends the building's exterior, and there is a paint crew for inside work. The personnel on these work forces rotates, so that everyone in the Schoolhome gets a chance to be on each squad. However, since some students definitely prefer and are more adept at one kind of job than another, plans are in process for the older ones to have the opportunity to work in their area of choice.

Freud said that in certain cases of neurosis "the rejected idea is replaced by a displacement-substitute, often by displacement on to something utterly trivial or indifferent." Today's fixation on the facts our young do not know by rote, instead of on the plight of those women on the bridge and the children left at home, certainly fits this description. In our nation's relatively recent past it was home's function to teach Americans to live in private homes, and it discharged this duty by replicating fixed gender roles. While mothers taught daughters to cook, sew, clean house, and tend babies, fathers taught sons to take out the trash, repair leaky faucets, and mow the lawn. Without doubt an uneven division of labor, but then both sexes knew that boys would eventually walk across the bridge to work and that their sisters would stay at home. The transformations in home and family make this system untenable. The procession's new composition makes a mockery of this separate and unequal apportioning of domestic labor.

Freud also told us that the neurotic is in some way tied to

a period in his past life in which he was happy, and that his symptoms do not relate to external reality. Harking back to their boyhood and college days, our elders put forth educational proposals that bear no relation to reality now. But while Freud called the neurotic's symptoms "detrimental, or at least useless, to life as a whole," I would say that the symptoms produced by our culture's repression of domesticity are more serious. The amnesia about home's educative function places rigid constraints on educational thought. With Dewey's insight under lock and key, we cannot ask the right questions. With Victor's case impounded, we cannot even see the dangers. Worse still, the erasure from memory of home's role in educating our children causes us to discount learning that is even more basic than the three Rs. With the contributions of home's domestic curriculum forgotten, we scorn the virtues that are essential to civilized life. I would say that the symptoms of domesticity repressed are not merely useless to our nation's life. It is not even accurate to call them detrimental. With the fear of things domestic uppermost on our minds, we cannot possibly solve the problem of how to educate the generation of children who are being left behind each morning when their parents walk across the bridge.

What radical change in school will suffice? The desperation of the women who must sacrifice self by forsaking newly established careers or else risk drowning, and the domestic vacuum experienced by the children who are left behind when the adults in their private homes go off to work, call for a transformation of the American schoolhouse that is premised on the remembrance of domesticity.

5

Home and World

We the people of the United States, in Order to form a more perfect Union, establish Justice, insure domestic Tranquillity, provide for the common defence, promote the general Welfare, and secure the Blessings of Liberty to ourselves and our Posterity, do ordain and establish this *Constitution* for the United States of America.

Whenever I discuss innovative educational proposals in my philosophy of education courses, a number of students are quick to condemn the practice even though they approve the theory. Intrigued by Rousseau's pedagogy or Dewey's concept of curriculum, they nevertheless dismiss the ideas saying they will not prepare children for the real world, which is, by their account, a ruthless place. Is that what education should do, I ask—prepare children for the "real" world no matter how heartless it is, no matter how competitive and pugnacious? What about attempting to change the real world?

The qualms demonstrate my students' firm grasp of the logical geography of education. No matter how badly American society needs schools that are moral equivalents of home; no matter how important it is to transmit this nation's whole cultural heritage to the next generation; no matter how essential it is to teach the three Cs: without a remapping of home, school, and world the requisite reforms do not stand a chance. So long as our culture agrees that the function of school is to equip children for life on the other side of the bridge and accepts as norms what Woolf considered flaws in the men who worked there—the possessiveness, jealousy, pugnacity, and greed that she feared would contaminate women— the Schoolhome will be called counterproductive. So long as the logical geography of education remains the same, the

Schoolhome's efforts to remember domesticity will be perceived as dysfunctional.

Does this mean that the idea of the Schoolhome is doomed to die aborning? Has school no choice but to dissociate itself from home? As those students of mine who challenge their classmates to think about changing the "real" world intuitively know, there is another option. We can remap the public world. Instead of renouncing the Schoolhome because its values, attitudes, and patterns of behavior conflict with those on the other side of the bridge, we can try to make the values, attitudes, and patterns of behavior that belong to the public world conform to those of the Schoolhome. What my students do not know, because it has for so long been repressed, is that there is a historical precedent for doing just this.

Just as "a moral equivalent of war" has become part of our lexicon although its place in James's philosophy has been ignored, "domestic tranquillity" is invoked today by those who have forgotten that the phrase is from the Preamble to the United States Constitution. I asked a historian why the framers included the words "domestic tranquillity" in the Preamble. Shays's Rebellion, was his reply as he directed me to Marian Starkey's wonderful history, A Little Rebellion.

The elders who perceive our country as being in imminent danger of falling apart do not tell us that we have been there before. For many citizens, Abraham Lincoln among them, the issue over which the Civil War was fought was not slavery but unity. "Is there any greater evil we can mention for a city," Socrates asked, "than whatever tears it apart?" There is not, Northerners said as the secession of the Southern states split in two what in their eyes was meant to be a single whole. Three-quarters of a century earlier the question had also preyed on American minds. At that time the new nation had appeared to be on the brink not so much of losing a portion of itself as of falling completely apart.

Upon declaring independence from Britain the thirteen American colonies drew up the Articles of Confederation establishing a loosely organized form of government in which each state remained its own master and national power was minimal. There was no real executive branch of government, and although a Congress was instituted it could not act directly on individuals and had no powers of enforcement over the states. For example, taxes were collected by state governments, which were then expected to hand over to Congress a share proportionate to their population. They could and sometimes did pay late or not at all. Under this system foreign affairs could hardly be conducted. It was impossible to get the separate states to speak to England or Spain with one voice let alone to act as one either in honoring the treaty that had ended the Revolutionary War or in paying the debt incurred during the war. Their interests often conflicting, the states treated one another much as independent nations do, taxing each other's imports and claiming one another's land.

Ten years after breaking away from its motherland, America was in trouble. Beset by problems both foreign and internal that it could not solve, it was being pulled apart by the private interests of the separate states. Shays's Rebellion was the last straw. In the summer of 1786, frustrated by high taxes, high interest rates, declining farm prices, farm foreclosures, and the imprisonment of those who could not pay their debts, Massachusetts farmers began protesting the actions of their legislature. By the fall and winter their protests had become armed confrontations, albeit with almost no bloodshed. By February 1787 Daniel Shays and his men were routed by state militia, but the fear of further rebellion—if not in Massachusetts then in Virginia or New Hampshire—haunted those who had previously been unconvinced that a new system of government was needed.

Before the disturbances in Massachusetts a constitutional convention had already been called although it was not then known if the states would attend. After Shays's Rebellion, George Washington, James Madison, Alexander Hamilton, and other leaders of the nationalist cause had relatively little difficulty persuading the states who had shunned an earlier conference to send delegates. That the idea of a strong national government would be accepted at the convention in Philadelphia was still by no means assured. Yet it is fair to say that

Daniel Shays and the debt-ridden farmers of Massachusetts had a good deal to do with the adoption of this concept by our founding fathers.

Historians are in accord that we owe our present form of government to Shays and his men. We are also indebted to them for the inclusion in the Preamble to the Constitution of the two words that bear directly on our present plight. Yet how many today remember that one of the founding fathers' objectives in framing the Constitution was to insure domestic tranquillity? The goals of liberty and justice set forth in the Preamble have a time-honored place in public learning. The common defense and the general welfare turn up regularly on the political agenda. But our culture's amnesia is so severe that even in the bicentennial celebration of the writing of the Constitution, domestic tranquillity was slighted.

"Law and order" has achieved slogan status. Legal scholars regularly remind us, however, that the language of the framers outlives the immediate concerns of 1787. That is what makes the United States Constitution a great document. That is why it is still applicable some two hundred years after its drafting. Thus, domestic tranquillity is no more to be equated with law and order than it is with the absence of armed insurrection. Knowing what significance the domestic tranquillity clause had when the Constitution was written, we should ask what significance it might have now.

I

Crowned with wreaths they will hymn the gods and enjoy each other, bearing no more children than their means allow, cautious to avoid poverty and war . . . So they will live at peace and in good health, and when they die at a ripe age they will bequeath a similar life to their offspring.

Plato, *Republic*

Even for the founding fathers the phrase "to insure domestic tranquillity" meant more than the prevention of rebellion.

Had they spoken of *civic* tranquillity, we might conclude that they were only interested in insuring governmental stability. Indicating on the one hand that internal as well as foreign disturbances can constitute threats to that stability, their use of the term "domestic" also cast the new nation in a special light. In selecting that word our founding fathers were signaling that if England had once been home to the colonists, they were now to consider the United States of America their home.

This is noteworthy in itself. Although both press and politicians regularly contrast foreign and domestic affairs and Americans abroad speak of returning to their homeland, the relativity of the domestic—the fact that what one takes to be the domestic sphere will vary according to one's point of view—is seldom noticed now. In the last decades the concept of the domestic has been retrieved by scholars doing research on women and has played a central role in their investigations. But adopting the perspective of a single society, this work consistently contrasts the domestic sphere or realm—what Woolf called the world of the private home—with the public, political, or civic realm, different writers giving it different names. Current scholarship is not of one mind about how universal or useful the two-sphere distinction is, yet on this point there seems to be no dispute: it locates the domestic *within* a society. In contrast, our founding fathers adopted an international perspective. Viewing our country as but a part of that larger whole they considered the world, they saw the United States as a site of domestic affairs. For them what people today call the public or civic realm *was* the domestic realm.

Still, the significance of the framers' language is not merely academic. Two centuries after Shays's Rebellion the domestic tranquillity the founding fathers sought to preserve is relatively unproblematic. I do not mean that the fear of insurrection is entirely a thing of the past. Yet, although the *civic* form of domestic intranquillity that worried our founding fathers is by no means extinct, another kind of domestic intranquillity—an *antisocial* form that seems to have been relatively unproblematic for them—is by far the greater danger today. Tearing the social fabric as surely as rebellion unties civic bonds, domestic violence writ large and small violates the very rights of life, liberty, and the pursuit of happiness that the United States Constitution was meant to protect.

In the true city, said Plato—and by this he meant not a feverish luxurious one but a healthy one—people will build houses and be adequately clothed and shod in winter. Working at what they can do best and have been trained to do well, they will feast together on cooked dishes with their children and they will enjoy each other: "So they will live at peace and in good health, and when they die at a ripe age they will bequeath a similar life to their offspring."

The homeless in America, who by some estimates will soon number nearly nineteen million, know neither peace nor good health. Many do not live to a ripe age, and their offspring, to whom they would if they could bequeath a very different life, succumb in numbers far exceeding the national average. Those millions who, though not homeless, are too poor to be adequately fed and clothed or are so hard at work attaining these ends that there is no time or energy left to feast together with their children and enjoy each other do not know domestic tranquillity either. Neither do those living in private homes where violence and abuse are rife. Nor, indeed, does any inhabitant of a city or town whose public spaces have become war zones or wastelands, whatever the condition of their private homes.

If ever there was a time to remember the domestic tranquillity clause of the United States Constitution, it is now. If ever there was cause for increasing *our* vision of the domestic to match that of the framers while enlarging *their* understanding of tranquillity to meet present realities, we have it. If ever there was reason to educate our young to insure domestic tranquillity on both sides of Woolf's bridge, the condition of the public world and our private homes provides it.

Look again at the Schoolhome. The children are now crowding around the bulletin board, waiting eagerly to find out whose turn it is to work on the buildings and grounds squads. In the American schoolhouse, where each child calls one classroom home, the halls, cafeteria, auditorium, playground constitute a public world and are often ruthless places where each person had better look out for himself or herself. There is as little incentive for students to make these areas pleasant and comfortable as there is for parents to pick up the litter on city streets. But students at the Schoolhome, having learned to think of school itself as home, gladly take on responsibility for the upkeep of all its spaces. In fact they consider it an honor to do the painting and carpentry and do not even seem to mind the daily cleanup chores.

A high school English teacher was in the news not too long ago for resigning a relatively well paying post. As I recall, she resented the "irrelevant" demands being placed on her, especially having to pick up trash in the hallways and keep order in the lunchroom. Were I an English teacher in the American schoolhouse I would not like to do those things either. If I had wanted to be a prison guard or a garbage collector I would not have gone into teaching. Yet even as I admire her courage to speak her mind, I am aware of how the dichotomy between domestic and public informed her protest. As she saw it—as perhaps most teachers in the schoolhouse see it—the job of an English teacher ought to stop at the classroom door. Implicitly dividing school into the world of the private classroom and the public world beyond its doors, she took it for granted that only the former sphere is a teacher's domain. Learning recognizes no such boundary line, unfortunately. What transpires in the halls and in the lunchroom may fall outside the standard school subjects, but its educational impact is not thereby diminished. Nor is the lesson lost that the way people live together and treat both one another and their surroundings is not nearly so important as how well one knows the facts of history and the formulas of physics.

Strict adherence to a public-private split contradicts the

very idea of school as a moral equivalent of home. Just as the private home's public spaces, however large or small—a hall, a living room, a dining room, a kitchen, a game room, a TV room—belong to every family member and everyone is supposed to take responsibility for the quality of life in them, the halls and kitchens and eating rooms of the Schoolhome are everyone's responsibility. The dichotomous mode of thought also conflicts with the goal of teaching children to be citizens of a nation that is itself a moral equivalent of home. For if teachers refuse responsibility for school's public arenas, why should their students act differently? And if the students do not care for and cherish their school's physical environment and accept responsibility for the quality of life lived there, how can we expect them to insure domestic tranquillity in the world outside?

I am not advocating a rigid law and order regime. The last things I have in mind for the Schoolhome are passes to leave the classroom, authoritarian vice-principals, up and down staircases, silence at meals. I want litter in the halls and chaos in the lunchroom to be perceived by everyone as fruitful opportunities for moral education—occasions for developing a sense of domestic community and a protective feeling for the environment, not for punishment and repression.

Am I nonetheless condemning the Schoolhome's teachers to being split personalities—both subject-matter experts and moral educators? Schizophrenia is not the issue. Since all education is moral education, no teacher can safely hide beneath the cloak of subject-matter expertise. Whether one turns the litter into a lesson or ignores its existence, one is transmitting norms. Whether one patrols the halls with despotic fervor or brings the students to the kind of feeling for their environment that is daily growing in the children of the Schoolhome, one is teaching patterns of conduct. One is also teaching citizenship. Deny that the condition of the halls, the walls, the cafeteria is your business and your students may well think that they need not take responsibility for public environments in school or society. Turn over the caretaking work to custodians, lunchroom supervisors, and other specialists and your students may become convinced that they can forget about it in school, home, and world. Train them to make and keep their physical environment a safe, healthy, comfortable, civilized place and who knows how many will learn to shoulder responsibility for the nation's environment as well as those of school and their own homes.

When not just school but the nation is thought of as home, the safety of our public spaces and the protection and upkeep of the physical and natural environment will be considered everyone's responsibility and will be made the occasions for national pride or disgrace, as the event may prove. Our country's worth is measured today by its economic power and military might. Take to heart the domestic tranquillity clause and we will have to rate ourselves on the quality of our housekeeping: the mayhem in our public spaces, the vandalism, the littering, the messages of violence and sadistic sex transmitted by the media, the dumping of industrial waste, the use of toxic building materials, the car exhaust, the indiscriminate laying of highways will all enter into the equation.

In 1910 James wrote that the term "peace" had been stripped of positive connotations and was being used simply to refer to the absence of actual war. Montessori made a similar observation a quarter of a century later. How can we keep "domestic tranquillity" from that fate? Denoting the absence of intranquillity whether in our public spaces or our private homes, the phrase also holds out the promise of health and happiness to all family members. Suppose that the violence in our streets and our private homes could be quelled through police action alone—something social workers and police today agree is highly unlikely. Intranquillity would be eradicated, but domestic tranquillity would not prevail if a state of anxiety comparable to that obtaining in a cold war among nations—or even the "quiet desperation" Thoreau attributed to the lives of the mass of men—ensued.

Besides the cessation of violence and violation, domestic tranquillity in the positive sense of the phrase requires that the growth and development of young and old, male and female, black, white, tan, yellow, and red, able-bodied and physically disabled be nurtured. It means Schoolhomes for the young, support groups for the troubled, halfway houses for the disturbed, medical care for the sick, prenatal care for the pregnant, provisions for the elderly, better housing conditions for the poor and the homeless, recreational facilities for everyone. It also means a radical shift in the way we see ourselves in relation to our progeny.

In his 1970 book *Two Worlds of Childhood* the psychologist Urie Bronfenbrenner told of an unforgettable encounter on a Moscow street:

> Our youngest son—then four—was walking briskly a pace or two ahead of us when from the opposite direction came a company of teenage boys. The first one no sooner spied Stevie than he opened his arms wide and calling "Ai malysh!" [Hey, little one!], scooped him up, hugged him, kissed him resoundingly, and passed him on to the rest of the company, who did likewise, and then began a merry children's dance, as they caressed him with words and gestures.

Attributing the teenagers' behavior to the "diffusion of maternal responsibility" in Soviet society to people other than parents, Bronfenbrenner remarked: "similar behavior on the part of any American adolescent male would surely prompt his parents to consult a psychiatrist."

There are things in Bronfenbrenner's account of the upbringing of Soviet children that a nation like ours would not want to emulate; for instance the invariable subordination of private loyalties to whatever is considered to be the public good. But although what he called "the concern of one generation for the next" will inevitably take different forms in different cultures, a form appropriate to our own culture is nevertheless mandated by the goal of domestic tranquillity. That such concern did not characterize American society at the time Bronfenbrenner was writing is made clear in his book. The most cursory reading of our daily newspapers and weekly magazines reveals that as a nation we still have not learned to love our children as ourselves or to do for them what the times demand. When new life is breathed into the domestic tranquillity clause our lack of concern for the next generation becomes a family matter, the issue being not how much individual mothers and fathers love their biological offspring but how much all Americans care about the health and happiness, the growth and development of all the nation's children.

The goal of domestic tranquillity also changes our perception of what is important and worth doing. The domestic realm is often called the site of the mundane. Understanding this term to denote the earthly as opposed to the spiritual and the commonplace in contrast to the extraordinary, we conclude that one must leave home for both excitement and the sake of one's soul. In truth, everyday life is filled with challenges as difficult and as demanding of courage and moral fortitude as any faced by Huck, Hawkeye, or Captain Ahab's crew.

To maintain a roof over one's head and put food on the table is no simple feat when jobs are scarce and costs are inflated. To find an occupation that is personally fulfilling and economically viable is a rare accomplishment in this postindustrial age. To feed the family properly requires the knowledge of a chemist, the pocketbook of a banker, and the willpower of a saint. To protect the health of oneself and one's loved ones demands a degree of financial security, an awareness of environmental hazards, and an eternal vigilance regarding the side-effects of medications and the ins and outs of hospitals that are not easily obtained. To keep one's young sons from running wild is a full-time occupation when both the electronic and print media teach violence and guns and drugs are readily available in school and on the streets. To keep one's young daughters from being raped or abused sexually is no small achievement when violence is rife and when in comic books and television, on billboards and in family newspapers girls and women are made into sex objects and sex is made unloving. To keep them from becoming pregnant is a major struggle in a culture at once obsessed by sexuality and devoid of concern for its children.

Political scientists are wont to think of the citizen as a consumer: someone who picks one candidate for office over another much as he or she might select a new car or an item of clothing from an L. L. Bean catalogue. Make the nation home and its inhabitants kin and a different image of democratic citizenship emerges. Citizens will still be voters. But they will also call upon themselves and one another to do what needs to be done to maintain, improve, and enhance everyone's lives.

The youngsters in the Schoolhome are undergoing an apprenticeship in this new concept of citizenship already. While the little ones take field trips into the community, older students participate in community activities. The girl who a short while ago was playing Kate does volunteer work each Friday afternoon in a shelter for battered women. The girl from Cambodia serves as an interpreter at a local community center. A boy whose family was homeless for several months last year is helping to build housing for the poor. And, like one of Jessica Siegel's journalism students who wrote an article for the Seward Park High School paper about Chinatown's gangs, students who work on the *Schoolhome Journal* take turns writing on some community issue of special concern to them. Utilizing historical analysis, statistics, and quotations, just as Lun Cheung did, they too write pieces that are partly autobiographical.

Behind the vision of the citizen as a consumer stands a definition of democracy as nothing but a mechanism for choosing governments. Inscribe the domestic tranquillity clause on our hearts as well as our minds, give the four words "to insure domestic tranquillity" a positive rendering, and a much richer version of democracy and citizenship emerges.

Rousseau is the philosopher who thought of citizens as active participants in the democratic process. Arguing that men are free only insofar as they are their own legislators—I use the term "men" advisedly here, for he did not believe that women could govern themselves—he cast them in the role of rational decisionmakers. In a democracy dedicated to insuring domestic tranquillity citizenship entails more than this. The public spirit that Rousseau said must guide the decisions of true citizens will in our case not only guide those of both sexes but also oversee their actions and direct their impulses. That this spirit will have a decidedly domestic bent means that the cerebral form of citizenship recommended by Rousseau will be supplemented by daily doses of activity done with the public good in mind. In addition, when the civic is seen as the domestic, new endeavors become associated with democratic participation.

Once the borders of the domestic realm are made to coincide with our national boundaries, a citizen of the United States who seeks out tests of character will not have to take to woods, river, sea, or outer space. Sufficiently rigorous themselves, the challenges of the private home are compounded in our public one. For those attracted to an element of precipitousness, as William James was, there are work to be done in emergency rooms and on rescue squads, treatment to be given AIDS patients, and young people to be turned away from drugs and violence. For those bent on demonstrating Thoreau's resourcefulness there are housing to be built for the homeless, new forms of transportation to be devised, new architectural designs for living to be planned, and clean sources of energy to be found. For those sharing Hawkeye's love of nature and suspicion of human encroachment on it there are a complex natural environment to be protected and the problem of overpopulation to be solved. For those with Ishmael's yearning for the sea there are pollution to be stopped and species, including whales, to be saved. For those with Huck's compassion for the less fortunate there are migrant workers to be helped, political refugees to be befriended, and victims of domestic violence and abuse to be protected.

II

> I tell thee, thou foolish philanthropist, that I grudge the dollar, the dime, the cent I give to such men as do not belong to me and to whom I do not belong.
>
> Ralph Waldo Emerson, "Self-Reliance"

When in the late 1980s I proposed at a meeting of political theorists and philosophers that the domestic tranquillity clause be recovered and reread, a commentator on my paper told the audience and me how eager he had been as a young man to leave his home and family and how necessary to his development as a mature human being his escape had been. Having just attended a conference on moral education where the same material was greeted warmly, I was surprised by his hostility toward things domestic. Only dimly aware at that point of the repression of domesticity in American culture and not yet cognizant of the myriad forms resistance can take, I was quite bewildered when he proceeded to cite the American literary canon in support of his subjective feelings. In the event, however, his remarks prompted me to read our nineteenth-century classics with new eyes. They also helped me understand how closely a celebration of the individual is bound up in our cultural heritage with an antipathy toward home.

Walden is the one book on our list of American classics that might have been subtitled "A Diary of Domesticity." Yet, for all its details of household economy, its account of the attention Thoreau paid his rows of beans, its descriptions of house building, furniture, visitors, it offers up a derivative of home. Putting Emerson's transcendental philosophy into practice in the Concord woods, Thoreau launched an experiment in which human intimacy and interdependency were excluded from his reconstructed domicile.

Invoking that memorable image of a transparent eyeball, in *Nature* Emerson celebrated the separation from others that Thoreau enacted:

> In the woods, we return to reason and faith. There I feel that nothing can befall me in life—no disgrace, no calamity (leaving me my eyes), which nature cannot repair. Standing on the bare ground—my head bathed by the blithe air and uplifted into infinite space—all mean egotism vanishes. I become a transparent eyeball; I am nothing; I see all; the currents of the Universal Being circulate through me; I am part or parcel of God. The name of the nearest friend sounds then foreign and accidental: to be brothers, to be acquaintances, master or servant, is then a trifle and a disturbance.

Emerson also idealized disconnection from others when he said in his essay "Self-Reliance":

> Why should we assume the faults of our friend, or wife, or father, or child, because they sit around our hearth, or are said to have the same blood? All men have my blood and I all men's. Not for that will I adopt their petulance or folly, even to the extent of being ashamed of it. But your isolation must not be mechanical, but spiritual, that is, must be elevation. At times the whole world seems to be in conspiracy to importune you with emphatic trifles. Friend, client, child, sickness, fear, want, charity, all knock at once at thy closet door and say—"Come out unto us." But keep thy state; come not into their confusion. The power men possess to annoy me I give them by a weak curiosity. No man can come near me but through my act.

In the name of self-reliance Thoreau created a home where he could form a close connection to nature while forswearing intimate relationships with men, women, and children. What price philosophy! One who does not assume the faults of friend, wife, father, or child—not to mention mother or husband—even to the extent of being ashamed, will also not assume their triumphs, sorrows, joys even to the extent of being proud, happy, elated. If "mean egoism" thereby vanishes, so do kindness and care.

Thoreau is not the only unencumbered self to people the dreams that constitute our literary tradition. Rip, Huck, Hawkeye, and Ishmael all manage to shed relationships as easily as they slip out of their clothes. If Thoreau entered the woods leaving no one worth mentioning behind, Ishmael signed on the *Pequod* tied only to Queequeg, whom he had just met. Huck fled a vile Pap and a Widow Douglas who had unsuccessfully tried to impose on him her middle-class morality. Hawkeye had somehow lost mother, father, and sister. And Rip: well, he had such a violent, brawling wife and such no-account children that they were no loss.

Just as Emerson's ideal of a transparent eyeball cuts the heart out of flesh-and-blood human beings leaving us radically reduced versions of ourselves, a literary canon whose dreams are determined by the repression of domesticity diminishes American life. Celebrating separation from others as Emerson's imagery exalts the separation of mind from body, our literary heritage equates freedom with the absence of responsibility and represents ties to others as obstacles to self-fulfillment. One of the thousands of items that critics of education like Hirsch want every American to know is "brother's keeper, Am I my." In the simple life that Thoreau lived at Walden Pond and that the other authors on my list imagined for their protagonists, a man has no brothers or sisters.

Thus spoke the lifelong abolitionist Thoreau in the name of freedom and self-reliance:

> I sometimes wonder that we can be so frivolous, I may almost say, as to attend to the gross but somewhat foreign form of servitude called Negro Slavery, there are so many keen and subtle masters that enslave both north and south. It is hard to have a southern overseer; it is worse to have a northern one; but worst of all when you are the slavedriver of yourself.

Lest it be thought that he was being facetious, here is Emerson's creed:

Expect me not to show cause why I seek or why I exclude company. Then again, do not tell me, as a good man did today, of my obligation to put all poor men in good situations. Are they *my* poor? I tell thee, thou foolish philanthropist, that I grudge the dollar, the dime, the cent I give to such men as do not belong to me and to whom I do not belong.

Just as schoolmates are seen as family members when school is viewed as a moral equivalent of home, the citizens of our nation become kin when the domestic tranquillity clause is reclaimed. And with kinship come feelings that Emerson portrayed as inimical to self-reliance. Remember the child in the Casa dei Bambini who patted the little boy's napkin once he tucked it in? the youngsters who consulted with the young girl and stood by her until she began to feel better about her composition? As pride in someone else's accomplishment and concern for another's self-confidence flowed from the family affections in that small surrogate home, so they can in the large one that is our nation.

Will revitalizing the domestic tranquillity clause mean that the poor are, after all, *my* poor? that the preteen would-be rapist belongs to *you*? that *I* belong to those runaways on the streets who are involved with drugs and prostitution? that *I* shot the dutiful mother or that she was shot with *your* gun? that the young kids who have nowhere to go after school are *mine*? that the worst oil tanker accident in history is *your* responsibility and the latest government scandal *my* concern? To blame every problem on oneself and wallow in the resultant guilt is as self-indulgent as Emerson's alternative of maintaining one's spiritual purity by dismissing the woes of others from one's mind, and equally self-defeating. To make every problem literally one's own guarantees paralysis of thought and action.

Under a reread domestic tranquillity clause the poor would not be my poor or yours. They would be *our family's* poor and as such America could not ignore them. The children with nowhere to go would not be biologically mine and it would not be incumbent on me to open the doors of my private home to them. They would be part of *our larger family* and provisions would therefore have to be made for them. The violence in the schools, the playgrounds, the streets would not be my doing. It would be the doing of some of *our kinfolk* and untold others of them would be harmed by it. Thus, the problem would have to be placed at the top of our public agenda alongside the many other items pertaining to the pollution and destruction of the environment.

Perhaps at some past time an Emersonian isolation spelled spiritual elevation. It may be that the renunciation of the world demanded by his philosophy and glorified in our literary tradition once signified maturity. In our interdependent society, however, the isolation he recommended and our classics celebrate is not a realistic option. In this intranquil society it is not an acceptable moral ideal. Ignoring the lessons to be learned from Victor's case, this philosophy of personal isolation denigrates the relationships and sentiments that domesticate a human infant—that transform him or her into a member of human culture in the first place—and that also make each one of us a unique person. Clothing the flight from domesticity in a mantle of spirituality that hides the irresponsibility at its core, this doctrine of detachment replaces moral maturity with its own form of mean egoism.

Freud once said that in struggling to keep a repressed idea submerged a patient "can behave as though he were mentally deficient." Emerson seems to have been assuming that one can be a moral individual while systematically turning one's back on others. Opposed to conformity and imitation, approving wholeheartedly of sincerity and authenticity, he constructed a false dilemma: either be connected with others to the extent that you imitate them or be your own person and stand alone. In actuality, part of what it is to be one's own person is to take the needs and the points of view of others into account without losing sight of oneself.

Living in the twentieth instead of the nineteenth century, Emerson might have acknowledged his mistake. *Lest Inno-*

cent Blood Be Shed, by Philip Hallie, is the amazing story of "how goodness happened" in Le Chambon during World War II. It happened there because the people of that French village cared so much about the victims of Nazism that they did not merely feel their pain. They gave them shelter. When in 1942, nine thousand French police remained indifferent to the rounding up of twenty-eight thousand Jews in an arena in Paris from whence they were shipped to concentration camps, the inhabitants of Le Chambon were making their plans. While the citizens of neighboring villages were acting out Emerson's creed that one should not respond to knocks at one's closet door, Magda Trocmé had already said to a German Jew who had knocked at her front door, "Naturally, come in, and come in."

Does a sense of connection or kinship with others lead to conformity? In the France of the German Occupation Magda Trocmé, her pastor husband, André, their co-worker Edouard Theis, and the other Chambonnais were the nonconformists.

I have often wondered if the simple fact that the words "individualism" and "individuality" are so alike is what keeps us from differentiating the ideas lying behind them. Like Emerson, John Stuart Mill placed nonconformity at the center of his philosophy. "As it is useful that while mankind are imperfect there should be different opinions, so it is that there should be different experiments of living; that free scope should be given to varieties of character, short of injury to others; and that the worth of different modes of life should be proved practically, when anyone thinks fit to try them," he said in *On Liberty.* But the individuality he argued so eloquently for in 1859 did not entail disconnection. The social order he envisioned was like Le Chambon's where, according to Hallie, a person was "conscious of himself as a being who *of course* pays regard to others." If Mill had been able to read the future he might have written, "A person who *of course* says, 'Naturally, come in and come in.'"

Needless to say, the three Cs of care, concern, and connection carry with them no guarantees of individuality. Children often mouth the words and unthinkingly copy the actions of their parents. A wife who hates to hurt her husband may suppress thoughts he does not approve of and curb actions on which he might frown. Yet an ethics of care does not preclude diversity. Just think of the range of personalities in a single family. Think of Alcott's portrayal, based on the girlhood of herself and her sisters, of the quite different strengths and weaknesses, talents and foibles of Meg, Jo, Beth, and Amy. The web of love that bound the March girls together did not impose on them an artificial uniformity. Making it possible for them to tell one another their radically different "castles in the air," it taught each one tolerance for experiments in living she could not or would not have dreamed of wanting for herself.

A certain irony attaches to the fear that to write domestic tranquillity large is to stamp out individuality. One might call it another instance of projection. "The majority, being satisfied with the ways of mankind as they now are (for it is they who make them what they are), cannot comprehend why those ways should not be good enough for everybody," said Mill when writing about mid-nineteenth-century England. Not only does the description fit ourselves. The very schoolhouse that keeps love at arm's length breeds conformity.

Institutionalizing Emerson's philosophy of radical individualism but giving it a mundane dimension that he would not have liked, our schoolhouses inure children to disconnection. Labeling speaking to friends misbehavior and defining helping others as the cardinal sin of cheating, they treat our young as separated and isolated beings—small Thoreaus, really. Begrudging their charges the freedom of movement that Thoreau took for granted and that educational thinkers from Plato to Montessori and Dewey have said is necessary if children's "real" natures are to be discerned, schools today typically deny the value of individuality. In a recent study of relationships between mothers and teachers, the sociologist Sari Biklen recorded a woman's complaint about a conference with her child's teacher: "She really didn't know the kids individually at all. She talked about the whole group." A teacher, in turn, complained about a conference with a mother: "It's boring to talk about some kid's math for a whole hour." Substituting abstract norms—reading levels, IQs, standardized test scores—for concrete knowledge deriving from direct observation of active learners, the schoolhouse would, if it could, reduce a class of twenty-five or thirty unique individuals to a common denominator. Interpreting difference as a falling away from the norms, it treats variety as a problem to be overcome and individuality as a disease to be cured.

But might the Schoolhome, in the name of unity, not impose its own kind of conformity on our children? For the sake of simple justice it is imperative that the lives, times, and works of women and nonwhite men be incorporated into its curriculum. But inclusion does not have to mean acceptance in the sense of adoption. The inhabitants of the Schoolhome can appreciate Huck's flight from domesticity without emulating it; empathize with Meg, Jo, Beth, and Amy but plan to live and work in the public world as well as the private home. Inclusion is not a recipe for sameness, either. As the inhabitants of Martha's Vineyard were different from one another yet united through their knowledge of sign language, those of the Schoolhome can be united by their shared knowledge of one another while cherishing each person's individuality.

III

Not only is it, as we have just explained, *variable* and *specific*, but it is also exceedingly *mobile*.

Sigmund Freud, *Repression*

The resistances to remembering and reinterpreting the domestic tranquillity clause are many. Besides the argument from individuality there is the objection stemming from the sorry state of our private homes. Is it not hopelessly sentimental to look to home and family for models of the nation itself?

It does not have to be. In proposing that domestic tranquillity be inscribed on the whole society I do not glorify actual homes, past or present. Few of them may have ever approached the ideal of peace, love, and quiet life that Petruchio foresees for himself and a tamed Kate, and all too many have fallen far short. I do not suggest, either, that there once was a golden age of domestic tranquillity in America's private homes to which we can now return.

There is an enormous gap between ideal and reality, but this does not invalidate the project of reclamation. Mine is a vision of what our private and our public or civic worlds *should* be, not what either one ever was. I offer it in the belief that fears that the harsh realities of today's or yesterday's private home will pollute our public spaces are misplaced. The larger society is already a sphere of violence. Instead of assuming that the failings of the private home negate the value of domesticating society, why not ask if private violence would flourish so abundantly in a domesticated society? Why not speculate that the private home would not be such a dangerous haven if it were situated in a safe and loving world? Why not determine what needs to be done to make sure that the private home reaps the benefits of a tranquil public or civic realm?

Another objection derives from the sorry status of women when the ideology of domesticity prevails. Did not an earlier version of this mind set serve to oppress one half the population? If the nation is viewed as home, will not women be considered second-class citizens once again?

Quite the contrary. There is no reason why domestic tranquillity on a national scale should impose additional suffering on women unless one believes that only women are capable of doing the physical and intellectual work required to make our nation a safe, warm, secure place. Granted, if you assume that females have an inborn talent for housekeeping or that males have no capacity for intimacy and love, it follows that this form of domestic tranquillity will have to rely for its manual and emotional labor exclusively on girls and women.

But to accept either position is to embrace a biological determinism that flies in the face of the facts. Granted, psychologists have been discovering that girls and women in our culture tend to be more nurturant than boys and men and to develop stronger bonds of intimacy. But there are too many nurturant males in the world for the difference to be a consequence of biology.

Retaining the institutions of private home and family but rejecting as anachronistic a sex-based division of labor and embracing instead the goal of sex equality, my reclamation of the domestic tranquillity clause makes domestic tasks and responsibilities in the private home *everyone's* business. Assigning to *both* sexes the job of infusing the public world with a domestic spirit and atmosphere, it treats the asymmetry that now exists as a challenge to American culture and an opportunity for the Schoolhome—not as an invalidation of the project.

There is also the question of whether large-scale caring is possible. Citing the examples of politicians who claim to care in order to attract votes, supermarkets that display "we care" signs in order to lure customers, and corporations that say they care in order to gain investors, the philosopher Lorraine Code has asked: "Can an amorphous group care about everyone indiscriminately?"

That we may subvert care by giving it slogan status and emptying it of content is a definite danger. But the fact that declarations of care often serve as substitutes for the real thing does not mean that it is impossible for a group, a society, a nation to be governed by the three Cs. When just a few years ago I tripped over a curbstone and found myself sitting on the sidewalk nursing what turned out to be a broken hand and a broken nose, fifteen to twenty well-dressed people carefully picked their ways past me as they walked from their commuter train to their parked cars. Luckily, someone finally came along who asked if I needed help. So far as I was able to determine, like the citizens of Le Chambon, albeit in response to far less dire circumstances, this man simply was a person who paid regard to others. If he is predisposed to be caring, surely others can be too. And if enough of us learn to be, perhaps we will no longer be merely an amorphous group.

I realize that since mine was a face-to-face encounter, the question of whether caring can be impersonal remains. We know, however, that TV and film can bring strangers into our living rooms and establish stronger bonds of sympathy with some of them than with actual acquaintances. Moreover, the more I have thought about my encounter, the more convinced I am that it became a face-to-face one because that man had a predisposition to care. No doubt he acted in a caring way toward me because he saw my plight. But he saw it—whereas the other passersby apparently did not—because he was caring.

Warning that "impersonal carers seek to colonize their targets, oblivious to the possibility that those 'targets' might experience the proffered caring as insulting and invasive," Code wondered if people in positions of power can care without colonizing and if those in less powerful positions can accept care without being co-opted. Paternalism and colonialism are two distortions to which a reinterpreted domestic tranquillity clause is subject. But our nation does not face a choice between evils: either an unconcerned rugged individualism or an oppressive form of caring. The people of Le Chambon rescued the Jews, they did not colonize or patronize them. After asking me if I needed help, that stranger consulted me about what to do, he did not presume to act in my stead. Code is right that judicious, unpatronizing caring requires knowledge of the particular circumstances of those being cared for. But one has to be predisposed to care in the first place in order to seek out that knowledge.

To many the argument from democracy is even more pressing than that from the built-in limits of care. Does not the framers' concept of the nation as home endanger our very form of government? Is not the domestic metaphor an open invitation to totalitarianism?

This is not an idle concern. Before political theorists affirmed that men are born free and equal and that the political rule of one person over another is legitimate only if a social contract has been entered into, the family served as a metaphor for political order. The order it legitimated was absolute monarchy.

Sir Robert Filmer, whose claim to fame is that his philosophy was torn to shreds by John Locke in *Two Treatises of Government*, modeled political authority on the father-son relationship. "Slavery is so vile and miserable an Estate of Man, and so directly opposite to the generous Temper and Courage of our Nation," Locke wrote almost exactly one hundred years before that fateful Convention in Philadelphia, "that 'tis hardly to be conceived, that an *Englishman*, much less a *Gentleman*, should plead for't." But plead for the political subjection of the many to the one Filmer did. Claiming to derive a monarch's right to rule from God by way of Adam, Sir Robert equated political with paternal rule and treated the latter as absolute and unlimited.

The issue between social contract theorists like Locke and patriarchal ones like Filmer was whether political authority and subjection were natural. The contract theorists said no: in the state of nature men are both free and equal. In contrast, thinkers like Filmer claimed that men are born into subjection to their parents, and therefore cannot be free. Moving deftly from father rule to royal authority, Filmer made the case for the divine right of kings that Locke later put to rest.

In Filmer's hands the family metaphor justified the subjection of everyone. But the reasoning of those who say that because one application of that metaphor legitimated authoritarian rule all other applications also do is not valid. Focusing on a human relationship that at least in its early stages has inequality built right into it, Filmer ignored the aspects of family and home that the Constitution's language connotes. Peace, love, and the quiet life; interdependence and the three Cs of care, concern, and connection: since these played no part in his concept of family, how can they be blamed for his antidemocratic theory of government? Ignoring the father-son relationship while focusing on the positive aspects of domesticity, my proposal to consider the nation as home stands in stark contrast to Filmer's. His project was a prime instance of domesticity repressed. Mine represents its recovery.

Filmer's is not the only antidemocratic use of the family metaphor in the history of political thought. Believing that from the standpoint of the larger society private home and family are divisive institutions, Plato removed them from the lives of the rulers of the ideal state he described in the *Republic*. For the good of the whole these men and women were to live communally and to consider themselves one big family.

Plato scorned democracy. So far as he was concerned, those capable of ruling the state were a small proportion of the population. But he derived this conclusion from his firm belief that the masses do not have sufficient intelligence to govern well, not from the family model.

Applying to the whole nation the vision of a public family that Plato held up only for his guardian class, my proposal presupposes the democracy he despised. Valuing the freedom that is missing from his philosophy, it also assumes that the United States has been and should continue to be an open society. There is no denying that the family metaphor has been invoked by antidemocratic thinkers. Yet if we avoid every concept that has been put to bad use or used in bad theories, our capacity to think and to solve society's problems will be sadly diminished. At this historical juncture it is not the remembrance and affirmation of the nation as a home that pose a danger to democracy. Our peril lies in the repression of domesticity.

A related and equally urgent argument is the one from independence. Does not political independence require personal autonomy? To be an autonomous individual is it not necessary to avoid entangling relationships, including—perhaps especially—those that flourish at home?

This reasoning mistakes self-sufficiency for self-government. "Not one of us is self-sufficient, but needs many things," said Socrates in the *Republic* as he and his companions thought away existing institutions and in their imaginations witnessed the birth of a city. "As they need many things, people make use of one another for various purposes." Thus he built interdependence into the Just State's social structure even as he made the capacity for self-governance the feature that separated the rulers from the rest. Born with enough reason to be able to acquire knowledge of "The Good" and educated to that end, the rulers will know what ought to be done and will have sufficient control over their passions to do what they know is right.

Since it is rule by and for the people, democracy requires of its populace a degree of individual self-government. It does not require self-sufficiency. How paradoxical that we learn this lesson from Plato! Yet Socrates was right. Dependency is an inescapable fact of human life. Even Thoreau borrowed an ax, bought rice in a store, and built his house on property owned by Emerson. As for Thoreau's descendants, we could not be wholly self-sufficient if we tried.

Choosing to ignore our dependency on the people who bore, raised, and taught us—as well as on those who now grow and process our food, cook our meals, make our beds, clean our houses, tend our files, sweep our offices, design our cars, build our roads, draw up our wills, prescribe our medicines; the list could go endlessly on—we hold onto an illusory ideal of a nation composed of unconnected people. Equating dependency with its most malignant forms—slavery, servitude, exploitation, self-abnegation, not to mention dictatorship—we fail to explore benign versions.

The conflation of self-government and self-sufficiency is a luxury that a nation plagued by domestic intranquillity can ill afford. Creating the illusions that connectedness is antithetical to independence and that care and concern for others conflict with the genuine self-determination required of a good citizen, it prevents us from forging the kinship bonds that domestic tranquillity requires. Yet does not "true" self-government itself presuppose disconnection?

Convinced that one who takes into account the needs and

desires of another will mistake some private interest for the general good, Rousseau maintained that "every citizen should speak his own opinion entirely from himself." To insure this he proposed that men remain incommunicado while deliberating on public matters. Imagining that reliance on others is a blot on democracy, political and educational thinkers today uphold an ideal of self-sufficiency vis-à-vis governing even when they relinquish it in relation to living. But just as absolute self-sufficiency is an impossible dream, so is absolute self-government. To be "sufficiently informed," as Rousseau's citizens were meant to be and as we ourselves strive to be, one must lean on others for fact and theory, opinion and hypothesis, for there is no way that an ordinary human can know enough about every issue being decided. Indeed, if there were such a mortal, he or she would still have acquired most of that knowledge, as well as the skills to find and interpret it, at home and in school from teachers and texts.

The view that self-government entails disconnection wrongly equates it with unilateral action. Constructing a false dilemma—make up your own mind entirely by yourself or have it made up for you by someone else—theories of personal autonomy systematically obscure the fact that it is often in conversation with others that one learns one's own mind. They hide entirely that to decide on a course of action without consulting those whose lives will be affected is most often paternalistic. We do not know if anyone was hurt by Ishmael's decision to go to sea. All too many of the women and children who are abandoned in our own time by similarly self-governing men end up living in poverty, however. And even when men who dislocate and relocate their families do not relegate them to lives of destitution, in the name of their own self-government they nevertheless determine the fates of others. Even when they take what they believe are the best interests of their friends and relations into account when coming to decisions, they merely substitute paternalistic for purely unilateral action.

To raise money to send to an ailing father who was ministering to Civil War soldiers, Jo March had her long hair lopped off without telling anyone in advance. Hurting nobody but herself and herself only in her vanity, her unilateralism can hardly be faulted. But in *Middlemarch* an act of generosity that was also decided upon unilaterally had quite a different outcome. When payment was not forthcoming on the note Caleb Garth countersigned without consulting his wife, it was wife and daughter who paid the consequences. Interestingly enough Hawkeye, a self-governing independent man if there ever was one, did not always keep his own counsel. He consulted with Chingachgook about their best course of action in the woods, and the two often decided together what was to be done. And before proceeding Hawkeye sometimes even consulted the people he was guiding through the wilderness.

"What does dependence mean to you?" Carol Gilligan and her associates asked adolescent girls. Presenting dependence in a favorable light, the girls said that it is a matter of someone being there to help you, to talk to you, to listen to you. They added that it does not stand opposed to independence. One schoolgirl remarked: "I would say we depend on each other in a way that we are both independent, and I would say we are very independent but as far as our friendship goes, we are dependent on each other because we know that both of us realize that whenever we need something, the other person will always be there."

As we know all too well, Rousseau's fear that private interest might sway the citizens of a democracy from seeking the common good was well founded. Yet to seal people off from one another, to seek the solution to undue influence in disconnection, is to compound the problem. Surely it is the detaching of those private interests from the public good and of the citizens from one another that creates the problem in the first place. How else to explain why public servants pocket public monies, why private corporations pollute the public's environment and profit at its expense, why politicians sacrifice the public's interest to their personal ambitions, why wealthy citizens seek loopholes in tax laws and seem to prefer tax reductions for themselves to increased services for society? How else to explain why it is taken for granted that this is rational, albeit sometimes unlawful, behavior?

Not only, Freud said, is repression "*variable* and *specific*, but it is also exceedingly *mobile.*" One more argument to contend with is the free speech objection. Is not the concept of domesticity inimical to the free speech and free expression that characterize democracy? Does it not stand opposed to genuine disagreement and difference of opinion?

There can be no doubt that speech will change when the domestic tranquillity clause is taken seriously. Its images will become less violent, its terms for women less damning, its racial and ethnic epithets less derogatory. But shifts in usage do not spell abridgment. In fact, when self-government requires my knowing your needs, wishes, hopes, desires and your knowing mine, when it embraces joint decisionmaking and not just unilateral action, free speech is all the more essential to it. Mill defended freedom of opinion on the grounds that we cannot otherwise discover the truth. When the truths we must discover include the ways others see themselves and the world, the importance of that liberty is increased.

But can we rely on people to speak their minds when an atmosphere of affection has to be maintained? After all is said and done, do not the peace, love, and quiet life sought by Petruchio carry with them "awful rule and right supremacy"? Invoking the images of roaring lions, an angry boar, and neighing steeds in Act I when he determines to marry Kate, in the last scene of *Taming of the Shrew* Petruchio assures his friends, and his servant who had earlier likened Kate to a wildcat, that whereas he would wager twenty crowns on the obedience of his hawk or hound, he would venture twenty times as much on his wife's. And well he might. For to curb "her mad and headstrong humour," he has used the brainwasher's techniques of deprivation of sleep and food. He has also forced her to reject the testimony of her own eyes and affirm only what suits his whim.

What does Kate's taming bode, Petruchio is asked at the

end of the play. "What not, that's sweet and happy," is his answer. Contemporary research suggests that his behavior toward Kate may well render the hoped for domestic tranquillity illusory. Just as the American Revolution taught the British that arbitrary rule and absolute supremacy contain the seeds of insurrection, studies of family violence are now teaching that the incidence of physical abuse in the private home is much higher where the husband acts as the head of the household than where the spouses view themselves as equals. We also know now that domestic violence begets more of the same. Interpreters of Shakespeare have suggested that in Kate's final speech she is mocking Petruchio. They have neglected to add that if they are right, she may well discover her husband's abusive training methods spilling into their everyday life.

There is no reason to deny that the ends of peace, love, and happiness may require the gentling of characters like Kate, although not Petruchio's taming techniques. But in humans, if not in roaring lions and angry boars, making gentle does not have to entail making obedient and docile, nor should it. Conflicting with the most basic principle of democracy, the docile obedience to her husband's authority that Petruchio anticipates from Kate mimics the very political relationship the founding fathers left behind when they separated from England. Shays's Rebellion may have moved them to strengthen the Union, but it did not undermine their faith in the self-government for themselves—if not for their wives and their slaves—that Kate renounces in marriage. Indeed, upon hearing about Daniel Shays, Jefferson allowed that "a little rebellion now and then is a good thing, and as necessary in the political world as storms in the physical."

Still, one wonders if the connections woven by love and the three Cs are not so tenuous that differences of opinion are liable to damage them. To prevent feelings from being hurt and to preserve the peace, does not criticism have to be suppressed? Can controversial issues even be confronted by a people who see their nation as home and themselves as kin?

The issues of how to quell the violence, dampen the sadism,

stop the pollution are themselves controversial. If to face them we must renounce the goal of domestic peace, heaven help us all. Disagreement does not conflict with domestic tranquillity. Bullying and violence do. If we do not start seeing ourselves as kin and acting as such, how can we ever arrive at adequate solutions to the problems besetting our culture? Yes, we need the free flow of information, some of which is now jammed into company file cabinets and government archives. But solutions cannot possibly be reached if there is not also a shared desire for peace, love, and the quiet life—in short, "what not, that's sweet and happy"—in the nation itself.

IV

> Okonkwo was deeply grieved. And it was not just a personal grief. He mourned for the clan, which he saw breaking up and falling apart, and he mourned for the warlike men of Umuofia, who had so unaccountably become soft like women.
>
> Chinua Achebe, *Things Fall Apart*

Of that small domesticated society, Chautauqua, James wrote:

> This order is too tame, this culture too second-rate . . . What excites and interests the looker-on at life, what the romances and the statues celebrate and the grim civic monuments remind us of, is the everlasting battle of the powers of light with those of darkness; with heroism, reduced to its bare chance, yet ever and anon snatching victory from the jaws of death.

I was astonished when I first read these words. How could Henry James's brother have considered the martial virtues the bedrock of a first-rate culture, I wondered. William knew that theories and definitions that make creative genius dependent on machismo contradict the facts. What he ironically called the "happy week at the famous Assembly grounds on the borders of Chautauqua Lake" was the very stuff on which Jane

Austen's inspiration thrived. George Eliot could also have found sufficient drama in that middle-class society. And although Henry may have shared William's aversion to Chautauqua, his art did not meet the latter's macho requirements either.

Once I recalled Basil Ransom's panegyric to the masculine character, I began to understand why William found Chautauqua so distasteful. After I read Freud it also became clear to me why the domestic tranquillity clause has never been considered a part of our cultural heritage.

More than once in his essay on war and peace James the philosopher and psychologist associated the martial virtues with manliness. Yet James the novelist is the one who made explicit the links between hardihood and masculinity, softness and femininity that in his brother's philosophy were quietly assumed. William's martial type of character is Ransom's masculine character; the softness he scorned is Ransom's "damnable feminization!" Henry leaves no room for doubt that in William's eyes the martial virtues represent manliness. William in his turn does not allow us to interpret Ransom's fear of feminization as a simple case of literary license.

Ransom was afraid for his culture. Like his author's brother he worried that the loss of the masculine tone in the world would usher in the reign of mediocrity. Were we able to assure him that in a society where domestic tranquillity prevails the quality of high culture need not be strained, however, he would not be satisfied.

The examples of Austen and Eliot—not to mention John Keats, Anton Chekhov, Emily Dickinson—certify that high culture would be in no danger. Besides, even if genius did choose to cast its lot with those who suffer pain and anguish and live lives of high drama, we can rest assured that these commodities would be plentiful in a state governed by domestic tranquillity. To equate the gentling of society with a purge of danger, risk, tension, conflict is to overlook the patent fact that sickness, accident, and death, luck and contingency, conflicts of desire, loyalty, and obligation, and "acts" of nature such as hurricanes and earthquakes are inescapable elements of human existence. Yet if on one level Ransom is merely formulating one more resistance to the idea of the nation as home, he also allows us to glimpse the dread that attaches to a repudiation of the martial virtues.

According to Freud, the "motive and purpose" of repression is the avoidance of pain. When Okonkwo returned to his native land from a seven-year exile he discovered that the clan had undergone such profound change that it was barely recognizable. He was deeply grieved, Achebe tells us, because the clan was breaking up and falling apart and the warlike men of Umuofia had become "soft like women." Behind Ransom's scorn for a feminized world there also lurks a fear of feminization. Like Okonkwo's, this fear is not *of* women but of becoming *like* women—or, to be more precise, like what women are expected to be. Believing that the virtues they admire are masculine and that a decrease in masculinity is tantamount to an increase in femininity, he sees his nation and its male inhabitants at risk of becoming transsexuals.

Ransom can be forgiven his mistake. Scholars now know that what is considered masculine and feminine varies across cultures and over time and that, even within a culture, expectations and stereotypes differ according to race and social class. Still and all, it can safely be said that in both Achebe's and Henry James's fictional cultures, as in our actual one, the martial virtues equal manliness. It is also clear that in Ransom's eyes, as in those of Rafaela Best's boys, masculinity and femininity are the opposite poles of a single continuum. To the extent that the manly qualities appear to be crumbling, it would *seem* then to follow inexorably that on both the cultural and the personal levels masculinity is giving way to its opposite.

An Aristotelian analysis demonstrates that the inference is not valid, but what if it were? Why is the feminization that Ransom foresaw for his generation such a damnable fate? What is so bad about being like a woman?

A basic premise of our culture's story about gender is that individuals born male are expected, by virtue of the traits they possess, the actions they perform, and the roles they fill, to fall at the "masculine" end of the gender continuum. One moral of this tale is that to be a biological male and to fall at any distance from the corresponding pole is to be considered unnatural and to be made an object of derision if not actual harassment.

I do not have to repeat here the words about the other sex that immediately popped into the minds of the sixth-grade boys reported on by Derrick Jackson. What is so bad about being like a woman? It is painful to turn out to be what you have been taught to despise. How can you respect yourself? How can you maintain your self-esteem? It is dreadful to be classified as a member of a group your culture deems inferior. How can you acquire the privileges and perquisites you have been taught are rightfully yours? And as awful as this is on the individual level, it is worse on the cultural. The very idea of one's nation embracing the values associated with those who all along have been its second-rate citizens is bound to be repellent.

The framers' concept of the nation as home provokes pain, in other words, because of the "woman connection." Although both sexes have lived in private homes from the very beginning of American society and have reaped the benefits domestic environments yield, the idea of home—the very thought of domesticity—conjures up women. That sturdy principle of guilt by association makes reclaiming the domestic tranquillity clause unbearable. For since the thought of women provokes fear and anxiety, the recollection of women's culturally assigned tasks, functions, skills, and responsibilities does too.

The association with the "other" sex is sufficient to explain why the domestic tranquillity clause of the Constitution has been forgotten and why its remembrance will be so difficult. I cannot help suspecting, however, that there is more to the story. One major project of Western culture—perhaps *the* major project—has been to separate man from the animals. Some philosophers, including Plato, have said that man is distinct by virtue of his rationality. Some, like Marx, have said that he is distinct because he is a toolmaker. Christian theologians have said that he is distinct because he is formed in God's image. The reason differs according to the thinker but the motive is always the same: "separate from" means "superior to."

When man is distinguished from the animals and placed above them, it is seldom made explicit just who is included in the category "man," perhaps because Western culture is so ambivalent about woman's place in the Great Chain of Being. It stands to reason that as man's mate she too is distinct from the animals—a resident of culture not nature. Yet logic insists that as man's opposite, she has to belong to nature and be one of the brutes. This, of course, is precisely where those sixth-grade boys located the opposite sex. "However rude, dirty, conceited or crazy the boys are," Jackson commented, "the girls at least gave them credit for having a mind. The boys had the girls' bodies charted like a road atlas."

Sherry Ortner, the anthropologist who described so well the civilizing function of the domestic context of a society, also made the point that women are viewed as closer to nature than men because of their domestic roles. This proximity to nature and the greater distance from culture it implies is, she argued, the reason why women are judged inferior to men. Whether it is the whole reason I do not know. I am not even sure if women are devalued because they are perceived as being close to nature or if they are located there because they are devalued. There is no doubt, however, that in reducing girls to body parts, those schoolboys placed the other sex alongside the untamed animals that reminded Petruchio of the undomesticated Kate. There is not a shade of a doubt, either, that Western civilization has prided itself on its separation from nature's creatures.

According to Freud, neuroses are caused by a sexual trauma in the early years—for instance, a witnessing of "the primal scene"—or rather by a memory thereof, not by the event itself. By analogy, in *Totem and Taboo* he speculated that in some far distant time the brothers killed and devoured their father and that this "was the beginning of so many things—of social organization, of moral restrictions and of religion." By analogy, let me speculate that the source of domesticity repressed is to be found in the earliest years of human civilization; or rather, in Western culture's memory thereof. Let me speculate that according to the story our culture both tells and tries to forget, our collective infancy was marked by a different kind of primal scene. Instead of a killing of the father there was a wrenching, a pulling away from mother nature. In the terms of this narrative it is not just domesticity's association with women that makes it an unbearable idea. It is the proximity of both to nature. To remember domesticity is to remember what the West considers that most shameful of all facts— man's kinship with the plants and animals.

V

> The battle over curricula is also a conflict between different conceptions of social order and is therefore fundamentally moral.
>
> Basil Bernstein, *Class, Codes and Control*, 1975

Over at the Schoolhome, the little ones are watching a play about Native American culture written by a group of older children. It paints such a different picture of nature from that of the West that I am very glad that the whole school has been invited. For their play, the children have used books about Native Americans. Listen to Chona, a Papago woman:

> Sometimes, when I was in the desert digging roots, I would see the centipedes and the little red spiders talking together, planning how to make rain. Just after daybreak I would see a coyote darting past the house and I would know he had come to see me.
> I saw other things, too. I would see a spider on the central

post of the house, who stopped and looked at me, just ready to speak. And in the desert, when I saw a little gray horned toad just in front of my foot, it looked at me as though it understood something.

Once I was digging roots and I got very tired. I made a pile of earth with my digging stick, put my head on it and lay down. In front of me was a hole in the earth made by the rats, and there hung a gray spider, going up and down, up and down, on its long thread. I began to go to sleep and I said to it, "Won't you fall?" Then the spider sang to me.

One evening a little bird came and sat above the door and began calling. I did not understand. But at night, when I was asleep, the bird came again and then, in my dreams, I could understand. He said, "You think I am only a little bird, but it is I who make the night go and the morning come with my singing."

Those youngsters impersonating centipedes and spiders, bird and gray horned toad are having a wonderful time and so are the children who are singing the song they composed for the gray spider. I am very impressed also by the ones in front who are signing the play for the hearing impaired students and teachers in the audience. But now an Omaha tribesman is speaking:

When I was a youth, the country was very beautiful. Along the rivers were belts of timberland, where grew cottonwood, maple, elm, ash, hickory, and walnut trees, and many other kinds. Also there were many kinds of vines and shrubs. And under these grew many good herbs and beautiful flowering plants.

In both the woodland and the prairies I could see the trails of many kinds of animals and could hear the cheerful songs of many kinds of birds. When I walked abroad, I could see many forms of life, beautiful living creatures which *Wakanda* had placed here.

The narrator has just stepped forward to explain that "Wakanda" means "the Great Spirit," and now the tribesman is speaking once more:

But now the face of all the land is changed and sad. The living creatures are gone. Sometimes I wake in the night, and I feel as though I should suffocate from the pressure of this awful feeling of loneliness.

In my very first week of college my classmates and I were asked to write an essay on a topic I still remember. Two Chinese gentlemen—philosophers, I realize now—were standing on a bridge looking at the fish in the water below. Their discussion, unintelligible to one who had never in her life been privy to such an abstract interchange, had to do with whether one could know if the fish had minds. After an hour of anguish during which I barely wrote a word, I joined my newfound friends to review the ordeal we had just undergone. To a woman, those few who seemed to have fathomed what kind of essay to compose said they had written about the fish asking each other if they thought the men had minds.

It was not accidental that those philosophers were standing on a bridge in China. Over the centuries Western philosophers and theologians have devoted their considerable talents to arguing that nature and all its creatures except human beings are mindless, therefore only we have a point of view worth considering. Denial of the fishes' standpoint is not a staple of every culture, but it is a major ingredient of the heritage our elders want to transmit to our nation's young. Even as the curriculum education's critics wish to restore schools children to be spectators of this great spectacle of life, it teaches them to stand outside nature and look at it from afar.

Since a disinterested distance is the very stance toward nature favored by science, is it not the proper one for education to instill? The new scholarship that has caused our elders to think they see a toad jumping in broad daylight has demonstrated that modern science's distance and disinterest mask Western man's desire for mastery and control. Representing science as male and nature as female, our poets and natural philosophers speak of wresting nature's secrets from her—if necessary putting her on the rack and torturing her. One need not be a Greenpeace activist to know that, environmentally speaking, the world has entered an age in which an aggressive relationship with nature courts disaster. One does not require a crystal ball to realize that educating this nation's young even for "pure" spectatorship endangers the earth.

"We have inherited a large house," Martin Luther King once said, "a great 'world house' in which we . . . must learn somehow to live with each other in peace." Going well beyond the founding fathers' vision in calling the whole world home, King wanted humans of all races, religions, ethnicities to live together as kin. Recognizing the dangers implicit in a nation-based interpretation of domestic tranquillity—when our nation is viewed as home, how tempting it will be to treat the people of other countries as "the Other"!—the Schoolhome hopes to teach its students to make King's larger perspective their own. It knows, however, that while it is incumbent on it to do what it can to mend and strengthen human bonds across nations, that great world house King said we inherited also needs tending.

The original drama performed at the Schoolhome makes visible the alienation from nature that most of us cannot even see in ourselves. Of course there is not just one single alternative to detached spectatorship. Like the members of a Cape Cod bird walk, one can acquire the kind of familiarity with nature that Americans usually reserve for friends and acquaintances. Like Henry David Thoreau, one can think of oneself as living in it. Like many environmental activists today, one can work to guard it from human destruction. Or one can seek to subdue and conquer it.

Strangely enough, the fact that in the American schoolhouse a single attitude toward nature has been granted favored status is not acknowledged. The privileged position is never defended. Can it be that the match between the stance and our cultural image of a "pure" scientist justifies the hold it has over the American curriculum?

In the first place, the stereotype does not do justice to the full range of scientific practice. Barbara McClintock, for one, described her own methodology in quite different terms:

> No two plants are exactly alike. They're all different, and as a consequence, you have to know that difference . . . I start with the seedling, and I don't want to leave it. I don't feel I really know the story if I don't watch the plant all the way along. So I know every plant in the field. I know them intimately, and I find it a great pleasure to know them.

Remarking to her biographer, Evelyn Fox Keller, that the more she worked with chromosomes the bigger and bigger they got, McClintock said,

> when I was really working with them I wasn't outside, I was down there. I was part of the system. I was right down there with them, and everything got big. I even was able to see the internal parts of the chromosomes—actually everything was there. It surprised me because I actually felt as if I were right down there and these were my friends.

The personal knowledge of her subject matter that Mc-Clintock possesses, the intimate relationship in which she stands to her corn, the merging of self and objects of study are also central features of the scientific practice of Anna Brito. The philosopher June Goodfield monitored Brito's thought and work for five years, during most of which Brito headed a cancer research laboratory in New York City. In a letter to Goodfield, Brito wrote:

> We T- and B-lymphocytes travel most of the time in journeys of blood and lymph, and we rest from time to time: in the spleen, the lymph nodes, and Peyer's patches. We don't mix much in an obvious way, but naturally we talk to each other infinitely more than people who look at us realize. In times of great distress—such as when some of us are killed by antilymphocyte serum—the fact that normally we interact becomes more apparent. And when some of us, T-cells, are killed a great increase in the number of pairs of B-cells and of B- and T-cells is observed.

In conversation she said, "Most importantly, of course, you must identify with what you're doing. You must identify totally. If you really want to understand about a tumor, you've got to *be* a tumor."

But even if the stereotype of the scientist were valid, the question arises of why in the education of children the scientist's point of view toward nature should prevail. It is not good enough to answer that this standpoint is an integral part of Western culture. Our heritage has partaken of militarism from the beginning. Religious intolerance has been one of its staples too. Should we instill these along with the scientist's detached perspective?

The British sociologist Basil Bernstein was right when he said that the battle over curricula is a conflict between different conceptions of social order. We like to think of our cultural heritage as something handed to us on a platter, all salted and cured and ready to serve up to the next generation. The imagery relieves us of moral and social responsibility, but the truth is that every society must pick and choose just what elements of its past—what knowledge, traditions, values, worldviews—constitute the capital it wants to transmit to the next generation. Some may wonder if the choices made by past generations are not good enough for us. As the world changes, either a culture's choices change or the education it extends to its young will begin to be dysfunctional.

What stance toward nature should the Schoolhome teach? I do not believe that there is such a thing as *the* correct approach. It seems to me that anybody who has enough faith in the future to dream of designing education for the next generation must by virtue of that very ambition reject James's warlike mentality. The less aggressive but equally callous attitudes toward nature that our elders learned in school also seem unacceptable. But the moral imperatives of environmental nurturing and protection leave open a wide range of options. The children who are working in the Schoolhome's garden are as excited about the growing vegetables that they themselves have planted as the children in Rome were at the sight of a rose in bloom. Their teachers are keenly aware, however, that one of the many challenges the Schoolhome faces is to teach its children to extend the purview of the three Cs to the earth itself and at the same time explore with them alternative ways of thinking about and acting toward nature.

The Schoolhome has its work cut out for it. This moral equivalent of home is determined to make *all* our children feel at home in it. Knowing that in today's world domesticity has got to become everyone's business, it plans to transmit the *full* sweep of our heritage to the next generation—the knowledge, skills, attitudes, values, mind sets associated with both sides of Woolf's bridge. It also means to make domesticity *everyone's* business. Believing that in this violent society of ours those will be blest whose blood and judgment are well commeddled, it intends to replace the kind of training in spectatorship that Rodriguez received with an education for *living.* Understanding that although our children may see the world differently they live in the same world, it is committed to providing them with an education for living *together.*

As if these goals were not enough, the Schoolhome realizes that its very existence depends on its working through with children the cultural resistances to domesticity. Because it perceives the links between these and Western culture's attitudes toward both women and nature, it does not dare treat the one problem while ignoring the others. Besides, it knows better than to allow the next generation to adopt a hostile or even a neutral stance toward nature, just as it is far too wise to let the gender wars of the past be perpetuated.

Another task the Schoolhome faces—perhaps the most important of all—is to teach its students a new form of citizenship: the insuring of domestic tranquillity in society at large. Keenly aware that the idea of school as a moral equivalent of home requires a remapping of the logical geography of education as well as a revisioning of the public world across the bridge, the Schoolhome can do its part to bring into alignment the values of home, school, and world by deriving its overarching aim from a rewritten domestic tranquillity clause.

Educating its children to insure domestic tranquillity in their private homes is also on the list. Without fail, discussions of American education mention the goals of schooling as teaching our young to be good citizens and economically self-sufficient individuals. The critics also cite school's function of transmitting the cultural heritage. Teaching the next generation to *live in private homes and families* is not on anyone's mind. How can it be when home and world are located at opposite ends of our conceptual map and the windows of school face out on the world?

The Schoolhome knows better than to believe that it can singlehandedly turn a culture that represses domesticity while embracing a philosophy of radical disconnection into one that thinks of the nation as home and its citizens as kin. It is neither so arrogant nor so prone to self-deception as to suppose that it can work through the resistances all by itself. Yet there is no reason why it cannot work in concert with our other institutions to prime the process of collective remembering. At the very least, the act of replacing the exclusionary impulse that has prompted so many educational recommendations in the last decade with something like the Vineyard's response to deafness will make all of us far more receptive to the task of reclaiming the domestic tranquillity clause.

Taking the relativity of the domestic seriously, however, the Schoolhome wants to share with its inhabitants a vision not just of the nation but of the whole world as home. For the sake of clarity, perhaps I should say the whole world of nations *and* that world called planet Earth. Over on the promontory, a group of teachers and students are standing in a huddle. As the Schoolhome prepares to celebrate the completion of the walkway that connects it to the world on the far side of Woolf's bridge, they are talking about concentric circles. They are picturing the Schoolhome as the innermost point in a set of concentric circles, each one of which is a moral equivalent of home.

The Here and Now

It is time to leave our spectator's spot on the bridge and walk back into the world. Having seen with our own eyes the changed social realities, and having figured out what corresponding changes in American education will suffice, we need to ask ourselves what can be done here and now. *If* the world changes—*if* it is suddenly governed by domestic tranquillity—the Schoolhome will be the institution of choice. But I labor under no delusion that this nation will be transformed overnight. I know that we will not wake up tomorrow in a state of domestic tranquillity. The question is, Must we wait until the world is turned around for the Schoolhome on the promontory to become a reality, or can we begin the process of transforming American education right away?

We can begin now, provided we think of the transformation of the schoolhouse as a gradual process rather than an all-or-nothing affair and do not set our sights too high. Instead of trying to change the whole American school system in one fell swoop—or even the entire system of a city or township—we can concentrate on a single school. After all, Montessori built her Casa dei Bambini in the only too real world inhabited by Rome's poor. The Charles River Creative Arts Program that provided its participants with a moral equivalent of home exists in the United States we know. The Martin Luther King federally funded child care center was not a figment of Valerie Suransky's imagination. The Atrium School in Watertown, Massachusetts, which I recently visited, is not an invention of the alumna who wrote to her former teachers: "Every night I dream the same dream. It only lasts a second, but I always picture Atrium as one big hug. A huge crowd of people all hugging one another."

The first thing I noticed when I entered the third-grade classroom at the Atrium School was the silence: twenty-five girls and boys and not a single sound. Then I spied four small girls sitting in a row on a sofa, each reading her own book. Near them, two boys were curled up in an easy chair, one poring over Madeleine L'Engle's *A Wrinkle in Time* and the other engrossed in a thick paperback whose small print signaled its large vocabulary. The genre of the month was fantasy fiction, the school's founder informed me as she led me to a corner of the room where four more children, each one glued to a book, had stowed themselves away in the loft of a playhouse. "This is the time when the slow readers get private help from the teacher and the others read on their own," Virginia Kahn whispered. "Later today the children will discuss their books with one another." "Do they really want to talk about books?" I asked. "Oh yes," she said. "And they love to make recommendations to their friends." This is the woman who once told a group of parents, "Friendships are the other curriculum at school. Early friendships are like love relationships."

Last month's genre had been biography, I was told, with the high point of the unit a Biography Breakfast to which parents were invited. Each child came dressed as a character in one of the books he or she had read and prepared to answer questions about the book. By then, the children had already discussed different genres and story structures with their teacher. "Whose book has a good lead-in?" the teacher might ask. A volunteer would then read one aloud.

While one half of that third grade was reading fantasies, the other half was sitting at desks and tables writing in those black and white, hard-covered copy books that you and I also used when we were young. "Dear Mike," the teacher's entry in one bearing the boy's name began:

Hi! Thanks for explaining what a rune is. Can the person using a rune make anything they want happen? Can they make good *and* bad things happen? Which of the three L'Engle books has been your favorite? Why? You are a *great* reader!

What has been your favorite reading genre this year? Why? What has been your favorite book you have read this year? Why? I love hearing you talk about the books you have read because you can summarize and explain them so well. It has been great for the other kids in our class to hear what you have to say about what you are reading and to get book recommendations from you. You are great!

Write soon and tell me about your book!

Love, Jessie

Before my eyes, twelve Mikes and Lucys were composing replies to their teacher about the plots of their fantasy books, the main characters, the genre they liked best.

On the bulletin board of the first-grade room I visited next there were photographs, including baby pictures, of one of the children. "Tania is the VIP of the Week," my guide told me. "She and her family brought in the snapshots and whatever information about her they wished—her favorite color, the sport she likes best, and so on." This much is done in many preschools, I was assured, but in the Atrium School's first grade every child is given a writing assignment—Tania and Her Pets, Tania and Her Friends, Tania's Summer Vacation. The teacher then interviews Tania and everyone has a chance to ask questions. By Friday, the children will have written their Tania stories, collected them in a looseleaf notebook, and presented their testimonial to the VIP herself. "You can't imagine what this means to the children. When they are eighteen they will be able to look at these books and remember their childhood. The parents are thrilled by the booklet too."

According to Descartes, the cause of anything must have at least as much reality as the effect. In education the smallest details—seemingly insignificant events—can have immense consequences. When I taught fifth and sixth graders the children in my class wanted to put on a play for the younger grades based on *Winnie the Pooh*. "Fine," I said. But when it came to casting, a girl who was far too shy, withdrawn, awkward, and inarticulate to play anybody asked if she could be Pooh. I was fully convinced that the play would be doomed if she were given the main role. Yet no one else volunteered and in good conscience I did not feel that I could deny her request. The scene the children decided to perform was the one in which Pooh eats too much honey and gets stuck in Rabbit's hole. Need I say that the child who would have been my last choice to play Pooh was a sensation? Everyone who saw the play laughed and cheered and wanted more. As an unknown actor on Broadway becomes a star overnight, my ten-year-old recluse, who before her debut had communicated her needs by grunting and had never looked me or her classmates in the eye, became a different person.

At the Atrium School a "grandmother" and a young boy are reading together. At the Chelsea, Massachusetts, Early Learning Center reported on by the *Washington Post* columnist Mary McGrory, white paper hearts on the wall record the children's acts of care, concern, and connection: "Josephine hugged Isaiah when he fell down." At the Czech school in England that Vera Gissing attended, group singing was a popular activity. At the Montlake Community Day School in Seattle where one of Ludtke's girls was a student, the third-grade teacher spoke to her class about an argument that had taken place during recess: "It might look macho. It might look chic, but we know better . . . You have choices to make. So grab for happiness. You're smart. Be wise. I love you and worry about you all the time. I want you to make good choices."

Small actions can have big effects. Inexpensive measures can have momentous results. But the process of transforming American education does not have to begin with a whole school. Individual classrooms can be moral equivalents of home even if the schools in which they are situated are not, for the American classroom is a relatively private place, its door closed to outsiders, its upkeep in the hands of its inhabitants, its ethos a function of the relationships and activities that constitute daily life within its walls. Acting on custom, a teacher in this "safe and sealed-off domain," as Tracy Kidder called it, can set about to tighten nuts and bolts and prepare the product under manufacture for the next station on the assembly line. Believing in the efficacy of the profit motive and in the values embodied in life on the other side of Woolf's bridge, he or she can instead create a micro-marketplace in which learning is a by-product of making money. Or, remembering the domestic vacuum in so many children's lives, she and he can create a small haven in a hostile world where education, affection, safety, and trust go hand in hand and the three Cs flourish. "These kids live in stark reality," that Seattle teacher said. "For most of them school is a sanctuary."

Who knows! If enough classrooms change, an entire school may be transformed. The idea of the Schoolhome includes major shifts in the way we think about—the way we define— teaching, learning, curriculum, and the aims of education, as well as about life in classrooms. Is it possible in that safe and sealed-off domain to bring new voices and perspectives into the course of study so that everyone will feel at home; to place at the center of the curriculum activities that integrate minds and bodies, heads and hearts, thought and action, reason and emotion; to make domesticity everyone's business?

With the cooperation of principals and supervisors and the support of parents, even such enormous changes as these can emerge from small beginnings. I am optimistic, in part because at Seward Park High School in Manhattan Jessica Siegel found the time for students in the required American literature course to listen to Martin Luther King's "I Have a Dream" speech. If she was able to do this, others may already have brought in *Betsey Brown* or *A Raisin in the Sun*. I am also optimistic because the Boston secondary school teacher I happened to sit beside at a play when I was writing this Epilogue explained at intermission that she was reading *A Raisin in the Sun* because it is now on her school syllabus. A week after this encounter I attended a conference of the National S.E.E.D. Project on Inclusive Curriculum. The teachers there were not only bringing new voices into their classrooms, they were leading seminars on the subject in their schools. Examples like these make me think that our nation's inclusionary juices are starting to flow. That Siegel gave the members of her journalism class an experience something akin to the integrative one that stands at the center of the Schoolhome's curriculum, and that other journalism teachers—and drama teachers—have surely done this too, in turn gives me hope that coalitions dedicated to the integration of head, hand, and heart will soon begin to form.

What specific policy advice follows from the idea of school as a moral equivalent of home in which all children feel at home and learn to live in the world together? Perhaps just this: think small, think locally, think experimentally, and never forget the domestic vacuum in children's lives today. Keep in mind, too, the changed and changing composition of the population and the violence everywhere. And always remember that there is no single form that a Schoolhome must take, no foolproof recipe to be followed. The brief descriptions I have given of Montessori's schools in Italy, the Charles River Creative Arts Program, and the Atrium School show that what is needed in American education today is also possible. The scenes I have presented from that Schoolhome on the promontory are meant to suggest a new realm of possibilities.

By midmorning in that particular Schoolhome, domestic work and related study are in most cases replaced by the more central pursuits, each of which generates its own rhythms of work and play, living and learning. Lunch—a time for lively conversation about what the various groups have been doing—comes as a welcome break between the morning and afternoon segments of the curriculum. The free hour in which clubs meet and music and dance groups practice is also a period everyone loves, the major problem being how to schedule meetings so that the budding historians, debaters, auto mechanics, computer programmers can participate fully in the activities of the cultural clubs and in artistic endeavors too. Another especially happy time comes toward the end of the day when Huck, Betsey, Meg, Jo, Beth, Amy, and the others take the spotlight. Some of the most meaningful and profound conversations in the Schoolhome take place then. For some reason this is also the time when a music teacher is most likely to stroll by playing an accordion or guitar and students are apt to gather round for a "spontaneous" sing.

"We sang 'Zebra Dun,'" I told a classmate who had been unable to attend our elementary school reunion. "Do you remember 'Zebra Dun'?" his wife asked him. "Remember 'Zebra Dun.' Of course he does!" I exclaimed, and he nodded his agreement. Who is Zebra Dun? A horse, but that is not the point. As music has charms to soothe a savage breast, group singing can strengthen metaphorical bonds of kinship. When the songs are drawn from the many cultures whose people have come to the United States, as they were in my school, and celebrate a variety of ways of living on both sides of Woolf's bridge, music can make all our children feel that this land really is theirs.

I like to think that forty years hence the boys and girls from the Schoolhome on the promontory will return for a reunion feeling very much as my classmates and I did and as Gissing and her singing schoolmates also did. Gissing reported:

> The forty middle-aged passengers were talking away happily, without a trace of awkwardness, shyness or reserve. To any onlooker the scene would have appeared that of a large close-knit family, or of intimate friends. No one could have guessed that the last time we had all been together we had been no more than children, and that many had travelled great distances, some half-way across the globe, just to meet up again.

I like to think that in half this time, the small changes that are made right here and now will add up to the transformation of the American schoolhouse into the American Schoolhome.

Bibliography

A Nation at Risk. Washington: U.S. Department of Education, 1983.

Achebe, Chinua. *Things Fall Apart*. Greenwich, Conn.: Fawcett Publications, 1959.

Adler, Mortimer. *The Paideia Proposal*. New York: Macmillan, 1982.

Alcott, Louisa May. *Little Women*. Boston: Little, Brown, 1936.

Aristotle. *Nicomachean Ethics*, trans. H. Rackham. In Richard Brandt, ed., *Value and Obligation*. New York: Harcourt, Brace and World, 1961.

"Ask Beth." *Boston Globe Magazine*, March 19, 1989.

"Average Pay for Women Is Reportedly Two-Thirds That of Men." *Boston Globe*, April 26, 1990.

Banks, Linda Ann. Letter to the Editor. *Boston Globe*, June 14, 1989.

Belenky, Mary Field, Blythe McVicker Clinchy, Nancy Rule Goldberger, and Jill Mattuck Tarule. *Women's Ways of Knowing*. New York: Basic Books, 1986.

Bernstein, Basil. *Class, Codes and Control*. Vol. 3. London: Routledge and Kegan Paul, 1975.

Best, Rafaela. *We've All Got Scars*. Bloomington: Indiana University Press, 1983.

Biklen, Sari Knopp. "Mothers' Gaze from Teachers' Eyes: Relationships between Middle-Class White Mothers and Female Elementary Schoolteachers." Paper delivered at the symposium "Reconceiving Curriculum: Teachers as Mothers/Mothers as Teachers," American Educational Research Association Annual Meeting, Boston, April 1990.

Bloom, Allan. *The Closing of the American Mind*. New York: Simon and Schuster, 1987.

Boyer, Ernest. *College*. New York: Harper and Row, 1987.

——— *High School*. New York: Harper and Row, 1983.

Breines, Wini, and Linda Gordon. "The New Scholarship on Family Violence." *Signs* 8, no. 3 (1983): 490–531.

Bronfenbrenner, Urie. *Two Worlds of Childhood*. New York: Russell Sage Foundation, 1970.

Bryant, Nelson. "The Sorcery of War." *New York Times Magazine*, June 3, 1984.

Canfield, Dorothy. *The Brimming Cup*. New York: Penguin Books, 1987.

Clark, Lorenne. "The Rights of Women: The Theory and Practice of the Ideology of Male Supremacy." In William R. Shea and John King-

Farlow, eds., *Contemporary Issues in Political Philosophy*, pp. 49–65. New York: Science History Publications, 1976.

Clark, Margaret. *The Great Divide.* Canberra: Curriculum Development Centre, 1989.

Code, Lorraine. "Who Cares? The Poverty of Objectivism for Moral Epistemology." Paper delivered at the Conference on Interdisciplinary Approaches to Knowledge and Gender, Calgary, June 1991.

Conway, Jill Ker. *The Road from Coorain.* New York: Alfred A. Knopf, 1990.

Cooper, James Fenimore. *The Deerslayer.* Laurel, N.Y.: Lightyear Press, 1984.

Crewdson, John. *By Silence Betrayed.* Boston: Little, Brown, 1988.

Dewey, John. *Experience and Education.* New York: Collier Books, 1963.

—— *The School and Society.* Chicago: University of Chicago Press, 1956.

Eck, Diana L. "Responses to Pluralism: World Views in an Interdependent World." Working Paper Series, no. 4. Cambridge: Project on Interdependence, Radcliffe College.

Eliot, George. *Middlemarch.* Boston: Houghton Mifflin, 1956.

Emerson, Ralph Waldo. *Nature.* In Brooks Atkinson, ed., *The Complete Essays and Other Writings of Ralph Waldo Emerson.* New York: Random House, 1950.

—— "Self-Reliance." In Brooks Atkinson, ed., *The Complete Essays and Other Writings of Ralph Waldo Emerson.* New York: Random House, 1950.

English, Bella. "No Support, But Nice Tan." *Boston Globe,* May 15, 1989.

Fiedler, Leslie. *An End to Innocence.* Boston: Beacon Press, 1948.

—— *Love and Death in the American Novel.* New York: Criterion Books, 1960.

Fine, Michelle, and Nancie Zane. "Bein' Wrapped Too Tight: When Low-Income Women Drop Out of High School." In L. Weis, E. Farrar, and H. Petrie, eds., *Dropouts from School.* Albany: SUNY Press, 1989.

Finkelhor, David. *A Sourcebook on Child Sexual Abuse.* Beverly Hills: Sage Publications, 1986.

Fisher, Dorothy Canfield. *The Montessori Mother.* New York: Henry Holt, 1912.

Fisk, Erma. *Parrots' Wood.* New York: Norton, 1985.

Freedman, Samuel. *Small Victories.* New York: Harper and Row, 1990.

Freud, Sigmund. *A General Introduction to Psychoanalysis.* New York: Garden City Publishing Company, 1943.

—— "Repression." In *Collected Papers,* vol. 4. New York: Basic Books, 1959.

————— *Totem and Taboo.* New York: Norton, 1950.

Gamson, Zelda F., and Associates. *Liberating Education.* San Francisco: Jossey-Bass, 1984.

Gelles, Richard J., and Claire Pedrick Cornell. *Intimate Violence in Families.* Beverly Hills: Sage Publications, 1985.

Gilligan, Carol. *In a Different Voice.* Cambridge: Harvard University Press, 1982.

————— "Remapping the Moral Domain: New Images of Self in Relationship." In Carol Gilligan, Janie Victoria Ward, and Jill McLean Taylor, eds., *Mapping the Moral Domain.* Cambridge: Harvard University Center for the Study of Gender, Education and Human Development, 1988.

Gissing, Vera. *Pearls of Childhood.* New York: St. Martin's Press, 1989.

Goodfield, June. *An Imagined World.* New York: Harper and Row, 1981.

Goodlad, John. *A Place Called School.* New York: McGraw-Hill, 1984.

Goodman, Ellen. "An ABC for Better Child Care." *Boston Globe,* March 22, 1988.

Gordon, Linda. *Heroes of Their Own Lives.* New York: Viking, 1988.

Groce, Nora Ellen. *Everyone Here Spoke Sign Language.* Cambridge: Harvard University Press, 1985.

Hacker, Andrew. "Trans-National America." *New York Review of Books* 37, no. 18 (November 22, 1990): 19–24.

Hall, Roberta M., and Bernice R. Sandler. *The Classroom Climate: A Chilly One for Women?* Washington, D.C.: Project on the Status of Women, 1982.

Hallie, Philip. *Lest Innocent Blood Be Shed.* New York: Harper and Row, 1979.

Hansberry, Lorraine. *A Raisin in the Sun.* Rev. ed. New York: Samuel French, Inc., 1988.

Hayden, Dolores. *Redesigning the American Dream.* New York: Norton, 1984.

Hirsch, E. D., Jr. *Cultural Literacy.* Boston: Houghton Mifflin, 1987.

Hirsch, E. D., Jr., Joseph F. Kett, and James Trefil. *The Dictionary of Cultural Literacy.* Boston: Houghton Mifflin, 1988.

Hobbes, Thomas. *Leviathan.* Indianapolis: Bobbs-Merrill, 1958.

Irving, Washington. "Rip Van Winkle." In *The Sketch Book of Geoffrey Crayon, Gent.* London: Dent, 1963.

Jackson, Derrick Z. "Black Studies: Why Harvard Should Blush." *Boston Globe,* November 18, 1990.

————— "The Seeds of Violence." *Boston Globe,* June 2, 1989.

Jacobs, Sally, and Kevin Cullen. "Gang Rivalry on the Rise in Boston." *Boston Globe,* March 26, 1989.

————— "School's Assignment: Keep the Turf Wars Outside." *Boston Globe,* March 26, 1989.

James, Henry. *The Bostonians.* Hammondsworth, Middlesex, England: Penguin Books, 1966.

James, William. "A Moral Equivalent of War." In Richard A. Wasserstrom, ed., *War and Morality.* Belmont, Calif.: Wadsworth, 1970.

—— "On a Certain Blindness in Human Beings." In *Talks to Teachers.*

—— *Talks to Teachers.* New York: Norton, 1958.

—— "What Makes a Life Significant?" In *Talks to Teachers.*

Jefferson, Thomas. Letter to Martha Jefferson. In Merrill D. Peterson, ed., *The Portable Thomas Jefferson,* pp. 366–367. New York: Penguin, 1977.

—— Letter to Thomas Jefferson Randolph. In Peterson, ed., *The Portable Thomas Jefferson,* pp. 511–514.

—— *Notes on the State of Virginia.* In Peterson, ed., *The Portable Thomas Jefferson.*

Keller, Evelyn Fox. *A Feeling for the Organism.* San Francisco: Freeman, 1983.

—— *Reflections on Gender and Science.* New Haven: Yale University Press, 1985.

Kidder, Tracy. *Among Schoolchildren.* Boston: Houghton Mifflin, 1989.

Kilpatrick, William Heard. *The Montessori System Examined.* Boston: Houghton Mifflin, 1914.

Kolodny, Annette. *The Lay of the Land.* Chapel Hill: University of North Carolina Press, 1975.

Kozol, Jonathan. *Rachel and Her Children.* New York: Crown, 1988.

Kramer, Rita. *Maria Montessori.* Chicago: University of Chicago Press, 1976.

Laird, Susan. "Women and Gender in John Dewey's Philosophy of Education." *Educational Theory* 38, no. 1 (1988): 111–129.

Landers, Ann. "A Few Survival Tips for Working Parents." *Boston Globe,* February 26, 1990.

Lane, Harlan. *The Wild Boy of Aveyron.* Cambridge: Harvard University Press, 1979.

Langone, J. *Violence.* Boston: Little, Brown, 1984.

Lightfoot, Sara Lawrence. *The Good High School.* New York: Basic Books, 1983.

Locke, John. *Two Treatises of Government.* New York: New American Library, 1965.

Ludtke, Melissa. "Through the Eyes of Children." *Time,* August 8, 1988, pp. 32–57.

Machung, Ann. "Talking Career, Thinking Job: Gender Difference in Career and Family Expectations of Berkeley Seniors." *Feminist Studies* 15, no. 1 (1989): 35–58.

Macpherson, C. B. *The Life and Times of Liberal Democracy.* Oxford: Oxford University Press, 1977.

Mann, Patricia S. "City College as a Postmodern Public Sphere." *Social Text*, no. 25/26 (1990): 81–102.

Martin, Jane Roland. *Reclaiming a Conversation*. New Haven: Yale University Press, 1985.

——— "Science in a Different Style." *American Philosophical Quarterly* 25, no. 2 (1988): 129–140.

——— "To Insure Domestic Tranquillity: Liberal Education and the Moral Life." Working Paper Series, no. 8. Cambridge: Project on Interdependence, Radcliffe College.

——— "Two Dogmas of Curriculum." *Synthese* 51, no. 1 (1982): 5–20.

——— "What Should We Do with a Hidden Curriculum When We Find One?" *Curriculum Inquiry* 6, no. 2 (1976): 135–151.

Marx, Leo. *The Machine in the Garden*. New York: Oxford University Press, 1964.

Mayhew, Katherine Camp, and Anna Camp Edwards. *The Dewey School*. New York: D. Appleton-Century, 1936.

McGrory, Mary. "A Healing in Chelsea." *Boston Globe*, May 9, 1991.

Melville, Herman. *Moby-Dick*. New York: Random House, 1930.

Mill, John Stuart. *On Liberty*. Indianapolis: Bobbs-Merrill, 1956.

Mintz, Steven, and Susan Kellogg. *Domestic Revolutions*. New York: Free Press, 1988.

Montessori, Maria. *The Absorbent Mind*. New York: Dell, 1984.

——— *Education for Peace*. Chicago: Henry Regnery, 1972.

——— *The Montessori Method*. New York: Schocken Books, 1964.

Mydans, Seth. "A Shot at the Action for Hispanic Citizens." *New York Times*, June 10, 1990.

Nabokov, Peter, ed. *Native American Testimony*. New York: Thomas Y. Crowell, 1968.

Naples, Robert. Letter to the Editor. *Boston Globe*, May 26, 1989.

NCTV News 11 (3–5), April–June 1990.

Nelson, Bryant. "The Sorcery of War." *New York Times Magazine*, June 3, 1984.

Okin, Susan Moller. *Justice, Gender, and the Family*. New York: Basic Books, 1989.

——— *Women in Western Political Thought*. Princeton: Princeton University Press, 1979.

Ortner, Sherry B. "Is Female to Male as Nature Is to Culture?" In Michelle Zimbalist Rosaldo and Louise Lamphere, eds., *Women, Culture and Society*, pp. 67–87. Stanford: Stanford University Press, 1974.

Ozick, Cynthia. "The Muse, Postmodern and Homeless." *New York Times Book Review*, January 18, 1987.

Pestalozzi, Johann Heinrich. *Leonard and Gertrude*. Boston: D. C. Heath, 1885.

Peters, R. S. *Ethics and Education.* Glenview, Ill.: Scott, Foresman, 1967.
——— "What Is an Educational Process?" In R. S. Peters, ed., *The Concept of Education.* New York: Humanities Press, 1967.
Plato. *The Republic,* trans. G. M. A. Grube. Indianapolis: Hackett, 1974.
Powell, Arthur, Eleanor Farrar, and David Cohen. *The Shopping Mall High School.* Boston: Houghton Mifflin, 1985.
Ravich, Diane, and Chester E. Finn, Jr. *What Do Our 17-Year-Olds Know?* New York: Harper and Row, 1987.
Reid, Alexander, and Renee Graham. "Mother Wants Son, 11, to Remain behind Bars." *Boston Globe,* April 28, 1989.
Ribadeneira, Diego. "Weapons Are Ominous Part of a School Day in Boston." *Boston Globe,* November 18, 1990.
Ribadeneira, Diego, and Peggy Hernandez. "Boston Schools Steer Hispanics down a Path to Failure." *Boston Globe,* June 10, 1990.
Richmond, George. *The Micro-Society School.* New York: Harper and Row, 1973.
Rodriguez, Richard. *Hunger of Memory.* Boston: David R. Godine, 1982.
Rollins, Judith. *Between Women.* Philadelphia: Temple University Press, 1985.
Rousseau, Jean Jacques. *The Social Contract.* New York: Hafner Publishing Company, 1947.
Schmid, R. E. "Unmarried Couples Increase, Top 2.3 Million." *Boston Globe,* May 13, 1988.
Shakespeare, William. *Hamlet.* In *The Complete Works of Shakespeare.* Chicago: Scott, Foresman, 1951.
Sizer, Theodore R. *Horace's Compromise.* Boston: Houghton Mifflin, 1984.
Spender, Dale. "Talking in Class." In Dale Spender and Elizabeth Sarah, eds., *Learning to Lose,* pp. 148–154. London: Women's Press, 1980.
Stacey, Judith. "Sexism by a Subtler Name? Postindustrial Conditions and Postfeminist Consciousness in the Silicon Valley." *Socialist Review* 17, no. 6 (1987): 8–28.
Starkey, Marian L. *A Little Rebellion.* New York: Knopf, 1955.
Suransky, Valerie Polakow. *The Erosion of Childhood.* Chicago: University of Chicago Press, 1982.
Teeter, Anita. Letter to the Editor. *Boston Globe,* May 6, 1991.
Tenenbaum, Samuel. *William Heard Kilpatrick: Trail Blazer in Education.* New York: Harper and Row, 1951.
Thoreau, Henry David. *Walden; or Life in the Woods.* New York: Anchor Press, 1973.
Twain, Mark. *Huckleberry Finn.* New York: Airmont Books, 1962.
Ulrich, Laurel Thatcher. *Good Wives.* New York: Oxford University Press, 1983.

Underhill, Ruth M. *Papago Woman*. New York: Holt, Rinehart and Winston, 1979.

Weinstein, Allen. "Massachusetts Uprising Affected the U.S. Constitution." *Boston Globe*, February 2, 1989.

Welter, Barbara. "The Cult of True Womanhood: 1820–1860." In Michael Gordon, ed., *The American Family in Social-Historical Perspective*, 2nd ed. New York: St. Martin's Press, 1978.

White, Jessie. *Montessori Schools: As Seen in the Early Summer of 1913*. London: Oxford University Press, 1914.

Wittgenstein, Ludwig. *Philosophical Investigations*, trans. G. E. M. Anscombe. New York: Macmillan, 1953.

Woolf, Virginia. *Three Guineas*. New York: Harcourt Brace Jovanovich, 1938.

Zinn, Howard. *A People's History of the United States*. New York: Harper and Row, 1980.

Notes

Notes are keyed by page number. Full citations of works listed here appear in the Bibliography.

Prologue: The View from the Bridge

  1 Virginia Woolf, *Three Guineas*, pp. 16, 62, 18, 75.

  2 Ibid., p. 66.

2–3 "Ask Beth," *Boston Globe Magazine*, March 19, 1989.

  3 Melissa Ludtke, "Through the Eyes of Children," p. 45.

1. Home and School

  5 Tracy Kidder, *Among Schoolchildren*, pp. 23, 211.

  5 Samuel Freedman, *Small Victories*, p. 15.

6–7 Steven Mintz and Susan Kellogg, *Domestic Revolutions*; R. E. Schmid, "Unmarried Couples Increase, Top 2.3 Million"; Judith Stacey, "Sexism by a Subtler Name?"

  9 Maria Montessori, *The Montessori Method*, p. 60.

10 Ibid., p. 52.

10 Dorothy Canfield Fisher, *The Montessori Mother*, pp. 31, 33.

12 *The Montessori Method*, pp. 62, 68–69.

13 Maria Montessori, *Education for Peace*, p. 101; cf. Montessori, *The Absorbent Mind*, ch. 7.

13 *The Montessori Method*, p. 348.

13 Fisher, p. 34.

14 Ibid., p. 31.

14 *The Montessori Method*, p. 348.

14 Fisher, p. 17.

14 Montessori, *Education for Peace*, p. 33.

14–15 *The Montessori Method*, p. 87, author's emphasis.

15 McClintock quoted in Evelyn Fox Keller, *A Feeling for the Organism*, p. 69.

15 *The Montessori Method*, pp. 87, author's emphasis, 346–347.

16 Ibid., p. 347.

16 Fisher, p. 25.

16 Jessie White, *Montessori Schools*, p. 155.

19 William James, *Talks to Teachers*, pp. 73, 83.

19 *The Montessori Method*, pp. 156, 157, 158.

20 Ibid., pp. 158, 158–159, 161, 159.

20 Montessori, *Education for Peace*, pp. 67, 105, xiii.

21 Montessori, *The Absorbent Mind*, p. 267.

21 William James, "A Moral Equivalent of War," p. 11.

21–22 Montessori, *Education for Peace*, p. 20.

22 *The Montessori Method*, pp. 95, 101, 69.

23 James, "A Moral Equivalent of War," p. 7.

23 William James, "What Makes a Life Significant?" p. 174.

24 Melissa Ludtke, "Through the Eyes of Children," p. 43.

24 Linda Ann Banks, Letter to the Editor, *Boston Globe*.

24 Sally Jacobs and Kevin Culler, "Gang Rivalry on the Rise in Boston."

25 *The Montessori Method*, p. 52.

25 Jonathan Kozol, *Rachel and Her Children*, p. 28.

26 Ibid., pp. 44, 64, 31.

27 Sherry B. Ortner, "Is Female to Male as Nature Is to Culture?" pp. 77–78, 79–80.

28 *The Montessori Method*, pp. 41, 42.

29 Ibid., pp. 150, 152, 153, 66.

30 Jane Roland Martin, "Two Dogmas of Curriculum."

32 "Ask Beth," *Boston Globe Magazine*, March 19, 1989.

33 Ludtke, p. 48.

33 Alexander Reid and Renee Graham, "Mother Wants Son, 11, to Remain Behind Bars."

35. For more on Victor see Harlan Lane's fascinating study, *The Wild Boy of Aveyron*.

35 *The Montessori Method*, p. 373.

36 Valerie Polakow Suransky, *The Erosion of Childhood*, p. 135.

39 Fisher, pp. 14, 46.

39–40 Suransky, p. 142.

40–41 Anita Teeter, Letter to the Editor, *Boston Globe*.

41 George Richmond, *The Micro-Society School*.

44 Robert Naples, Letter to the Editor, *Boston Globe*.

44 *NCTV News* 11, no. 3–5 (April–June 1990): 8–9.

45 John Dewey, *The School and Society*, p. 7.

46 Rafaela Best, *We've All Got Scars*, pp. 80, 5.

47 Ibid., p. 80.

2. Culture and Curriculum

49 Vera Gissing, *Pearls of Childhood*, p. 174.

50 Seth Mydans, "A Shot at the Action for Hispanic Citizens"; Diego Ribadneira and Peggy Hernandez, "Boston Schools Steer Hispanics Down a Path to Failure"; Andrew Hacker, "Trans-National America," p. 19.

51 Nora Ellen Groce, *Everyone Here Spoke Sign Language*, pp. 1–2, 4.

51–52 Ibid., 108.

53 Lorenne Clark, "The Rights of Women: The Theory and Practice of the Ideology of Male Supremacy."

54 Jill Ker Conway, *The Road from Coorain*, p. 171.

55 Michelle Fine and Nancie Zane, "Bein' Wrapped Too Tight: When Low-Income Women Drop Out of High School," p. 33.

55 Derrick Z. Jackson, "Black Studies: Why Harvard Should Blush."

55 Quoted in Groce, p. 53.

56 Woolf, *Three Guineas*, p. 18.

58 E. D. Hirsch, Jr., *Cultural Literacy*.

58 Arthur Powell, Eleanor Farrar, and David Cohen, *The Shopping Mall High School*.

58 Cynthia Ozick, "The Muse, Postmodern and Homeless."

59 John Goodlad, *A Place Called School*, p. 208.

59 Among the most widely read reports and criticisms are: *A Nation at Risk*; Mortimer J. Adler, *The Paideia Proposal*; Ernest Boyer, *High School*; Goodlad, *A Place Called School*; Hirsch, *Cultural Literacy*; Diane Ravich and Chester E. Finn, Jr., *What Do Our 17-Year-Olds Know?*; Theodore R. Sizer, *Horace's Compromise*. Cf. critics of higher education such as Allan Bloom, *The Closing of the American Mind*; Ernest Boyer, *College*.

60 Chinua Achebe, *Things Fall Apart*, ch. 11.

62 Zelda F. Gamson and Associates, *Liberating Education*, p. 86.

63 Achebe, p. 186.

64 Bloom, p. 346.

65–66 Hirsch, p. 21.

66 Ibid., pp. 21, 29.

67 Henry James, *The Bostonians*, p. 290.

72 Rafaela Best, *We've All Got Scars*, pp. 24, 22.

72 Derrick Z. Jackson, "The Seeds of Violence."

72 Margaret Clark, *The Great Divide*, p. 25.

73 Ibid., pp. 25, 39, 40.

74 R. S. Peters, *Ethics and Education*, p. 3.
77 Achebe, pp. 155–156.
78 Fine and Zane, pp. 33, 34.
80 Plato, *Republic*, 378d.
82 Ludwig Wittgenstein, *Philosophical Investigations*, pars. 66, 67.

3. Learning to Live

85 Diego Ribadeneira, "Weapons Are Ominous Part of a School Day in Boston."
87–88 George Eliot, *Middlemarch*, p. 52.
88 Ibid., pp. 43, 146.
89 Richard Rodriguez, *Hunger of Memory*, p. 71.
89 *Middlemarch*, pp. 46, 150, 207.
89 Rodriguez, p. 176.
90 The list of big questions is Allan Bloom's, *The Closing of the American Mind*, p. 227.
91 Linda Ann Banks, Letter to the Editor, *Boston Globe*.
92 William James, "On a Certain Blindness in Human Beings," p. 150.
98 Sally Jacobs and Kevin Cullen, "Schools' Assignment: Keep the Turf Wars Outside"; Ribadeneira, "Weapons Are Ominous Part of a School Day in Boston."
98–99 Thomas Hobbes, *Leviathan*, p. 107.
99 Ibid., p. 108.
99 Ribadeneira.
99 Hobbes, p. 107.
99 Susan Moller Okin, *Justice, Gender, and the Family*, pp. 10ff.
100 Stan Grossfeld, "Women Suffer on the Homefront"; Wini Breines and Linda Gordon, "The New Scholarship on Family Violence"; J. Langone, *Violence*; John Crewdson, *By Silence Betrayed*. Cf. Linda Gordon, *Heroes of Their Own Lives*; Richard J. Gelles and Claire Pedrick, *Intimate Violence in Families*; David Finkelhor, *A Sourcebook on Child Sexual Abuse*.
100 Dolores Hayden, *Redesigning the American Dream*, p. 221.
101 Virginia Woolf, *Three Guineas*, p. 72.
101–102 Roberta M. Hall and Bernice R. Sandler, *The Classroom Climate: A Chilly One for Women?*, pp. 1, 3, 7, 10, 11.
102 Clark, *The Great Divide*, pp. 22, 23, 24, 23.

102–103   Dale Spender, "Talking in Class," p. 150.

103   Clark, pp. 25, 42.

104   For more on what to do with a hidden curriculum see Jane Roland Martin, "What Should We Do with a Hidden Curriculum When We Find One?"

104   Clark, pp. 27–28.

104   Plato, *Republic*, 462b.

104   The survey was conducted by Averil E. McClelland, Director, Project on the Study of Gender and Education, Kent State University.

105   Clark, p. 45.

106   "William's Doll" reprinted by permission from the book *Free To Be . . . You and Me*, copyright © 1974 Free to Be Foundation, Inc. Music and lyrics by Mary Rodgers and Sheldon Harnick, copyright © 1972 Ms. Foundation for Women, Inc., based on the book *William's Doll* by Charlotte Zolotow, copyright © 1972 Harper and Row Publishers, Inc.

107   Best, p. 98.

108   Ibid., p. 89.

108   Aristotle, *Nichomachean Ethics*, pp. 71–72, 73.

109   Barbara Welter, "The Cult of True Womanood: 1820–1860."

116   Plato, 456d.

117   For more on gender sensitivity see Jane Roland Martin, *Reclaiming a Conversation*.

4. Domesticity Repressed

121   John Goodlad, *A Place Called School*, p. 70.

121   Sara Lawrence Lightfoot, *The Good High School*, p. 199.

122   Sigmund Freud, "Repression," p. 86.

122   Freud, *A General Introduction to Psychoanalysis*, pp. 250, 249.

122–123   Ibid., p. 253.

124   Rita Kramer, *Maria Montessori*.

124   William Heard Kilpatrick, *The Montessori System Examined*, pp. 61, 4, 30.

125   Ibid., p. 11.

125   Freud, *A General Introduction to Psychoanalysis*, p. 256.

125   Kilpatrick, pp. 63, 62–63.

125   Freud, *A General Introduction to Psychoanalysis*, p. 258.

125   Samuel Tenenbaum, *William Heard Kilpatrick*, p. 75.

125 Kilpatrick, pp. 66, 67.

126 Freud, "Repression," p. 88.

127 Katherine Camp Mayhew and Anna Camp Edwards, *The Dewey School*, pp. 406, 43. For a discussion of the domestic curriculum of the Laboratory School see Susan Laird, "Women and Gender in John Dewey's Philosophy of Education."

127 Goodlad, p. 88.

128 William James, *Talks to Teachers*, pp. 51–52, 51.

129 Louisa May Alcott, *Little Women*, p. 88.

129 Freud, *A General Introduction to Psychoanalysis*, p. 255.

130 James, *Talks to Teachers*, pp. 46, 49.

131 John Dewey, *Experience and Education*, p. 61.

133 Bryant Nelson, "The Sorcery of War."

133 William James, "What Makes a Life Significant?" pp. 174, 173.

135 Freud, *A General Introduction to Psychoanalysis*, p. 256.

135 R. S. Peters, "What Is an Educational Process?"

137–138 Dorothy Canfield, *The Brimming Cup*, pp. 25–26.

141 Thomas Jefferson, *Notes on the State of Virginia*, pp. 101, 102, 103.

142 Jefferson, Letter to Thomas Jefferson Randolph, p. 511.

142 Jefferson, *Notes on the State of Virginia*, p. 217.

142 But see Leslie Fiedler, *Love and Death in the American Novel*, p. xx; cf. Leo Marx, *The Machine in the Garden*; Annette Kolodny, *The Lay of the Land*.

142 Jefferson, Letter to Martha Jefferson, p. 366.

142–143 Ibid., p. 367.

143 Washington Irving, *Rip Van Winkle*, pp. 31, 29.

143 Mark Twain, *Huckleberry Finn*, pp. 11, 28.

144 Ibid., p. 318.

144 Henry David Thoreau, *Walden; or Life in the Woods*, pp. 16, 8–9, 28, 44–45.

144–145 James Fenimore Cooper, *The Deerslayer*, pp. 33, 408–409, 405.

145 Fiedler, *Love and Death in the American Novel*, p. xx; cf. Fiedler, *An End to Innocence*.

146 Herman Melville, *Moby-Dick*, p. 775.

146 Kolodny, p. 115.

147 Irving, p. 30.

147 *Moby-Dick*, p. 1.

147 Fiedler, *An End to Innocence*, p. 148.

148 Bella English, "No Support, But Nice Tan."

148 Irving, pp. 27, 31, 29.

149 Ibid., p. 42.

150 Freud, "Repression," p. 93.

150 Ann Machung, "Talking Career, Thinking Job: Gender Differences in Career and Family Expectations of Berkeley Seniors," p. 53.

151 Judith Stacey, "Sexism by a Subtler Name?"; Ellen Goodman, "An ABC for Better Child Care"; "Average Pay for Women is Reportedly Two-Thirds That of Men."

151 Laurel Thatcher Ulrich, *Good Wives.*

152 Ann Landers, "A Few Survival Tips for Working Parents."

153 Ibid.

155 Melissa Ludtke, "Through the Eyes of Children," p. 53.

155 For an account of the history of domestic service in the United States and the role played by black women see Judith Rollins, *Between Women.*

155 Du Bois is quoted in Rollins, p. 51.

156 Mary Field Belenky, Blyth McVicker Clinchy, Nancy Rule Goldberger, and Jill Mattuck Tarule, *Women's Ways of Knowing.*

156 Erma Fisk, *Parrots' Wood.*

159 Freud, "Repression," p. 96.

160 Freud, *A General Introduction to Psychoanalysis,* p. 313.

5. Home and World

162 Marian L. Starkey, *A Little Rebellion.* Cf. Howard Zinn, *A People's History of the United States;* Allen Weinstein, "Massachusetts Uprising Affected the U.S. Constitution."

166 Plato, *Republic,* 372d.

170 Urie Bronfenbrenner, *Two Worlds of Childhood,* pp. 9, 8, 9.

172 For a discussion of this model of citizenship see C. B. Macpherson, *The Life and Times of Liberal Democracy.*

173 Jean Jacques Rousseau, *The Social Contract.*

174 Jane Roland Martin, "To Insure Domestic Tranquillity: Liberal Education and the Moral Life."

175 Ralph Waldo Emerson, *Nature,* p. 6.

175 Emerson, "Self-Reliance," pp. 159–160.

176 E. D. Hirsch, Jr., Joseph F. Kett, and James Trefil, *The Dictionary of Cultural Literacy.*

176 Henry David Thoreau, *Walden; or Life in the Woods,* pp. 10–11.

177 Emerson, "Self-Reliance," p. 149.

178 Sigmund Freud, *A General Introduction to Psychoanalysis*, p. 258.
179 Philip Hallie, *Lest Innocent Blood Be Shed*, p. 120.
179 John Stuart Mill, *On Liberty*, p. 68.
179 Hallie, p. 284.
179 Mill, p. 69.
180–181 Sari Knopp Biklen, "Mothers' Gaze from Teachers' Eyes: Relationships between Middle-Class White Mothers and Female Elementary Schoolteachers," pp. 14, 11.
183 Lorraine Code, "Who Cares? The Poverty of Objectivism for Moral Epistemology," p. 2.
184 Ibid.
185 John Locke, *Two Treatises of Government*, p. 175.
186 Plato, 369b.
188 Rousseau, p. 27.
189 Carol Gilligan, "Remapping the Moral Domain: New Images of Self in Relationship," p. 16.
190 Freud, "Repression," p. 89.
191 Jefferson quoted in Starkey, p. 4.
192 William James, "What Makes a Life Significant?" pp. 173–174, 172.
194 Freud, "Repression," p. 92.
194 Achebe, *Things Fall Apart*, p. 168.
196 Derrick Z. Jackson, "The Seeds of Violence."
197 Freud, *Totem and Taboo*, p. 142.
197–198 Ruth M. Underhill, *Papago Woman*, pp. 50, 52, 67, 83.
198 Peter Nabakov, ed., *Native American Testimony*, pp. 231–232.
199 Ibid., p. 232.
200 King quoted in Diana L. Eck, "Responses to Pluralism: Worldviews in an Interdependent World," p. 20.
201 Evelyn Fox Keller, *A Feeling for the Organism*, pp. 198, 117.
201 June Goodfield, *An Imagined World*, p. 62.
202 Ibid., p. 226. For further discussion of Brito's and McClintock's methodology see Evelyn Fox Keller, *Reflections on Gender and Science*, ch. 9; Jane Roland Martin, "Science in a Different Style."
202 Basil Bernstein, *Class, Codes, and Control*, vol. 3, p. 81.

Epilogue: The Here and Now

208 Mary McGrory, "A Healing in Chelsea."
208 Melissa Ludtke, "Through the Eyes of Children," p. 36.
209 Ibid.
211 Vera Gissing, *Pearls of Childhood*, p. 9.

Acknowledgments

I wish to thank the John Simon Guggenheim Foundation for the great gift of time without which this book could not possibly have been written; Radcliffe College for an office of my own during my term as a Guggenheim Fellow; Margaret Bearlin, Jere Confrey, Carol Gilligan, Susan Laird, Peggy McLaughlin, and Howard Zinn for directing me to readings of particular importance to this project; Grazia Marzot for discussing with me the meaning of "casa"; Carolyn Swift for giving me vital statistics on violence and for invaluable criticism of the essay that served as the basis of Chapter 5; Katie Cannon, Blythe Clinchy, Nancy Fraser, Eugenia Kaledin, Nona Lyons, Frances Maher, Jeanne Paradise, Susan Reverby, Phyllis Silverman, Nancy Rosenblum, and Jill Tarule for helpful comments on successive versions of that same essay; Ann Diller, Susan Franzosa, Barbara Houston, Susan Laird, Beatrice Nelson, Jennifer Radden, and Janet Farrell Smith for commenting on early drafts of Chapters 1, 4, and 5 and for collectively coining the term "domephobia"; audiences at the University of Maine in Orono and Baruch College in New York and members of the seminar "The Educational Legacy of Romanticism" at the University of Calgary for raising important issues about my rereading of Montessori; audiences at the Conference on Ethics in Today's World at the University of Illinois in Champaign-Urbana, the Conference on Post-Structuralism and Law at Northeastern University, the 1987 meeting of the Association for Moral Education, the 1988 meeting of the Conference for the Study of Political Thought, and the 1988 meeting of the National Conference of Education for Women's Development for asking the hard questions about my reclamation of the domestic tranquillity clause; Tatsuro Sakamoto for helpful comments on an early draft of the whole manuscript; Susan Laird and Ann Diller for detailed suggestions on two later drafts; Jane Williams for comments on an early and a late draft and a recommendation that turned the book around; and Angela von der Lippe and Camille Smith for superb editorial advice. I also am deeply indebted to Carol Gilligan for continued encouragement and sound advice at every turn; Jane Williams for unfailing moral support; and Michael Martin for listening to my ideas, helping me untie philosophical knots, reading everything, and being there.

Index